ENGLISH
900
BOOK THREE

鄭　憲　鎭　共譯
李　東　浩

prepared by

ENGLISH LANGUAGE SERVICES, INC.

ENGLISH 900 의 三位一体	
완전합본	ENGLISH 900 원문
	주　해　서
	연습, 자습용 WORKBOOK

桂 苑 出 版 社

ENGLISH 900의 三位一体

900원문 ┼ 주해서 ┼ Workbook

ENGLISH 900을 배우고저하는 사람을 위하여 파격적인 제작원가로 봉사하며 이 한권의 책으로 완전히 마스터 할 수 있도록 합본하였다.

ENGLISH 900
(영어회화교본)

미국무성 산하 English Language Series 엮음
The Macmillan Co, 발행

全六卷	
	English 900 Book 1 ┼ 주해서 ┼ Workbook
	English 900 Book 2 ┼ 주해서 ┼ Workbook
	English 900 Book 3 ┼ 주해서 ┼ Workbook
	English 900 Book 4 ┼ 주해서 ┼ Workbook
	English 900 Book 5 ┼ 주해서 ┼ Workbook
	English 900 Book 6 ┼ 주해서 ┼ Workbook

ENGLISH 900 주해서
(영어회화교본)

1. English 900 원문을 완역.
2. 충실하고 정확한 번역.
3. 문법책을 겸한 충분하고 자세한 문법설명.
4. 간단 명확하고 친절한 diagram식 설명.
5. 새로 나온 낱말과 숙어 풀이.

ENGLISH 900의 Workbook
연습용·자습용·복습용

ENGLISH 900의 원문에서 읽힌 회화를 좀더 습관화 하고 생활화 할 수 있도록 조직적이고 과학적으로 문제를 다루워 놓았으므로 이를 풀이해 본다면 회화에 좋은 반려자가 되리라 믿어 의심치 않는다.

이는 한국 초유의 문제 배열로 ENGLISH 900 1 권부터 6 권 까지 전 권에 함께 엮어 누구나 쉽게 연습, 자습, 복습 할 수 있도록 하였다.

완전합본

머 리 말

English 900는 영어를 세계적으로 보급하기 위해서 미국 정부의 위촉을 받아 English Language Services Inc.가 교재의 연구개발을 담당하고, The Mc Millan Co.가 발행을, 그리고 Collier-McMillan이 보급을 맡은 영어회화 교재입니다.

English 900는 영어를 외국어로 하는 사람들이 기초부터 중급에 이르기까지 공부할 수 있도록 엮은 교재로서 전부 6권으로 되어 있읍니다. English 900란 제목은 총 6권의 text에 나오는 기본문형의 수가 900개란 데서 연유한 것으로서 900개의 기본문형에는 영어의 기본적인 문장구조와 어휘가 모두 들어 있읍니다. 900개의 기본문형은 각 과의 첫머리에 15개씩 수록되어 있고, 또한 한개의 기본문형마다 대개 4개의 변형문이 수록되어 있으므로 문장의 개수는 전부 3,600개라 할수 있을 것입니다.

매과의 구성요소를 살펴 보면 15개의 기본문형이 나오고, 뒷페이지에 Intonation 연습, 이어 기본문형으로 연습해보게 되어 있는 Questions and Answers나 Verb Study, 그 다음에는 활용연습을 위한 Substitution Drills, 그 다음에는 독해력 향상을 위한 Reading, 마지막으로 앞에서 익힌 대화를 실제로 응용해 볼 수 있는 Conversation으로 되어 있읍니다. 특히 매 과에 Exercise가 붙어 있어서, 그것 마저 스스로 해 보면 영어적 습관이 입술에 붙게되지 않을까 생각됩니다.

원래는 각과와 병용할 수 있는 Workbook도 각각 마련되어 있으나 우리나라에서는 Workbook이 있다는 사실조차 모를 뿐 아니라 Workbook의 구입도 쉽지 않으므로 본 해설서에는 독자를 위해서 매권 권말에 Workbook을 특히 같이 달아 놓았읍니다. English 900의 Workbook은 교실에서의 학습내용을 기초로 하여 학생들의 실력을 테스트하는 한편, 미처 익히지 못한 중요사항을 복습하기 위한 것입니다.

English 900는 예문 하나 하나가 모두 일상 회화체의 문장으로서 영어가 모국어가 아닌 외국인을 상대로 한 책이기 때문에 내용이 비교적 쉽고 노력만 하면 누구나 영어 회화를 할 수 있겠금 펴낸 책입니다. 게다가 이 주해서만 가지면 문법 책을 따로 볼 필요 없이 정확한 회화를 배울 수 있으리라 확신합니다.

English 900는 Edwin T. Cornelius, Jr.와 Joyce R. Manes의 지도로 제작된 것임을 밝혀 둡니다.

Intonation (抑揚)에 관하여

다른 사람에게 다음 두 문장을 읽게 하고 두 문장이 어떻게 다른가를 비교하여 보면

    그 분이 오셨어요. (서술문)

    그 분이 오셨어요? (의문문)

모음이나 자음에는 아무 차이도 없으나 음성의 고저에는 차이가 있다는 것을 알수 있다. 이와 같이 말할 때의 음조를 Intonation이라 한다. 언어학자들은 이 억양을 선이나, 숫자, 또는 음악의 악곡표시 같은 것으로 나타내지만 본서는 어디까지나 900의 해설서이므로 900에서 취급하고 있는 방법, 즉 선에 의해서 설명하고자 한다.

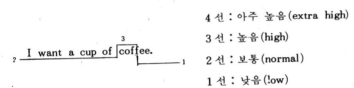

4선 : 아주 높음 (extra high)

3선 : 높음 (high)

2선 : 보통 (normal)

1선 : 낮음 (low)

위의 맨밑의 선 1은 가장 낮은 소리, 2는 보통 소리, 3은 높은 소리를 나타낸다.

높이는 부분이 문장끝에 온 단음절의 낱말이면 소리를 점차로 낮추어 선을 곡선으로 나타낸다.

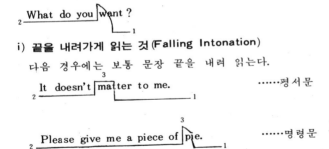

i) 끝을 내려가게 읽는 것 (Falling Intonation)

다음 경우에는 보통 문장 끝을 내려 읽는다.

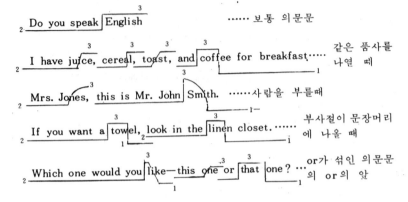

What beautiful trees those are! ······감탄문

What would you like to eat? ······의문사로 시작되는 의문문

ii) 끝을 올려서 읽는 것 (Rising Intonation)

다음 경우에는 보통 문장 끝을 올려 읽는다.

Do you speak English ······보통 의문문

I have juice, cereal, toast, and coffee for breakfast······ 같은 품사를 나열 할 때

Mrs. Jones, this is Mr. John Smith. ······사람을 부를때

If you want a towel, look in the linen closet. ······ 부사절이 문장머리에 나올 때

Which one would you like—this one or that one? ··· or가 섞인 의문문의 or의 앞

iii) 특수한 예

부가 의문문의 경우에는 Intonation이 Rising이냐 Falling이냐에 따라 뜻이 달라진다.

He likes ice-cream, doesn't he? ······상대방의 동의를 구할 때

He likes ice-cream, doesn't he? ······의문의 뜻이 강할 때

특히 4선은 감탄문의 경우 있을 수 있으나 보통의 경우에는 쓰이는 일이 드물다.

액센트에 관하여

두 음절 이상의 단어에 있어서 영어에서는 습관적으로 한 음절은 강하게, 다른 한 음절은 약하게 발음하는 것이 보통이다. 이 때 강하게 발음되는 음절을 **액센트가 있는 음절**(accented syllable) 이라고 한다.

액센트의 위치를 표시하는 방법에는 다음의 세 가지가 있다.

(a) 액센트가 있는 음절 앞에 표식을 한다. 〔보기〕 **dictionary**

(b) 액센트가 있는 음절의 모음 위에 표식을 한다. 〔보기〕 **díctionary**

(c) 액센트가 있는 음절 뒤에 표식을 한다. 〔보기〕 **dic′tionary**

이상 세 가지 중에서 만국표음기호로 발음을 표시할 때에는 (a)의 형식을 쓰고, 철자(綴字)에다 직접 액센트의 표식을 할때에는 (c)의 형식을 사용하는 것이 보통이지만, (b)의 형식이 아주 확실하고 잘못 볼 염려가 없으므로 우리나라 사전에서는 거의 이 형식을 채택하고 있다.

때로는, 특히 다음절(多音節)인 단어에서는 리듬 관계로 두 개 이상의 액센트를 붙이는 수가 있다. 이 때 두 액센트가 똑 같이 강하면 둘다 (′) 표로 표시하고, 강약의 차가 있을 때에는 강한 쪽의 액센트는 (′)로 표시하고, 약한 쪽은 (`)로 표시한다.

〔보기〕 **thirteent**〔θə́:tí:n〕 **afternoon**〔á:ftənú:n〕 **cigarette**〔sìgərét〕 **independent**〔ìndipéndənt〕 (독립한) **characteristic**〔kæ̀riktərístik〕 (특징있는)

액센트의 형

영어의 액센트의 형에는 다음과 같이 여러 가지 종류가 있다.

(1) **이음절어**(二音節語)

a) — ⌣

〔보기〕 **father**〔fá:ðə〕 **mother**〔mʌ́ðə〕

visit〔vízit〕 **pretty**〔príti〕

limit〔límit〕 (제한하다)

b) ⌣ ∸

[보기] away [əwéi] about [əbáut]

address [ədrés] prepare [pripéə]

permit [pəmít]

c) ⌣ ⌒

[보기] thirteen [θə́:tí:n] fourteen [fɔ́:tí:n] *etc.*

이 형태에 속하는 것이 다른 단어 뒤에 올 때에는 리듬관계로 a) 또는 b)
의 형태로 되는 수가 있다.

예를 들면

She is júst thirtéen.   (ʹ) ⌣ ⌒

She is thirteen yéars of age.   ⌒ ⌣ (ʹ)

(2) **삼음절어**(三音節語)

a) ⌒ ⌣ ⌣

[보기] honesty [ɔ́nisti] (정직)

beautiful [bjú:tiful]

Englishman [íŋgliʃmən]

b) ⌣ ⌒ ⌣

[보기] tomato [təmá:tou]

potato [pətái̯tou]

banana [bəná:nə]

attention [əténʃ(e)n] (주의)

c) ⌒ ⌣ ⌒

[보기] cigarette [sìgərét] (담배)

chandelier [ʃæ̀ndilíə] (샨데리아)

engineer [èndʒiníə] (기사[技師])

(3) **다음절어**(多音節語)

음절의 수가 많아짐에 따라 액센트의 형도 복잡해지는데, 중요한 것은 주요
한 액센트의 위치를 정확하게 배우고 필요한 때는 리듬에 따라 제 2 의 액센트
를 붙여야 한다는 것이다.

PREFACE

ENGLIST 900®, a course for students of English as a second language, contains material from beginning through intermediate levels of study. The whole series consists of textbooks, workbooks, and tape recordings, with a teacher's handbook.

ENGLISH 900® is one of the basic instructional courses in the Collier-Macmillan English Program. Included in the Program is a series of graded readers in which six are keyed to the vocabulary and structure of each study unit in the basic texts of ENGLISH 900®.

The series takes its name from the 900 base sentences presented in the six textbooks. The sentences cover the basic structures and a basic vocabulary of the English language. They are introduced at the rate of fifteen in each study unit, or a hundred and fifty in each book, and are numbered consecutively from Base Sentence 1 in the first unit of Book One through Base Sentence 900 in the last unit of Book Six. These structures provide "building blocks" for all of the material studied in the series, e.g., there are approximately four variation sentences for each base sentence. As a part of his mastery of English, therefore, the student practices and learns approximately 3,600 variation sentences in addition to the basic 900 patterns.

There are ten study units in each textbook in the series. Each study unit contains a group of fifteen base sentences related to a meaningful situation. In Book One of the series, the typical study unit begins with the presentation of the fifteen *Base Sentences* together with *Intonation* patterns. *Questions and Answers* follow and give the student practice in pairing and matching the base sentences into conversational form. *Substitution Drills* introduce the variation sentences, using vocabulary and grammatical substitution techniques. These early sections of the unit provide the pronunciation practice and drill material needed for the mastery of language forms. The *Conversation* section consists of short dialogues giving the student the opportunity to practice the new lesson material in informal conversation in the classroom. *Exercises* in each unit can be used as oral and written drills for all of the materials introduced in the unit.

Units in the succeeding books in the series (Books Two to Six) contain Base Sentences, Intonation practice, Substitution Drills, Conversation, and Exercises, and, in addition, certain new features. Beginning with Book Two, a *Reading Practice* section is added to each unit, and, beginning with Book Three, a *Verb Study* section. Books Four, Five, and Six include *Participation Drills* for classroom use, and Books Five and Six present *Grammar Study* materials and *review exercises*.

Each textbook includes a *Key* to the exercises and a *Word Index* which lists in alphabetical order every word introduced in the book, and cites the sentence and unit number in which the new word first occurred. There are special *Review Units* in Books One through Four.

A companion Workbook is available for each of the six textbooks, and a series of 180 pre-recorded tapes has been prepared for language laboratory use. ENGLISH 900® Workbooks are unique in that they have been programmed for use by the student as home study material to reinforce classroom work. The Workbooks "test" the student on the textbook materials, and review the important points in each unit that he may not have mastered in class.

For classes that meet for three to five hours a week, each textbook in the series provides material for approximately three months of study. Suggestions for teaching the course, as well as detailed descriptions of all of the materials in ENGLISH 900®, have been given in the Teacher's Manual which accompanies the series.

A wide range of material has been created for the Collier-Macmillan English Program by the Materials Development Staff of English Language Services, Inc., under the co-direction of Edwin T. Cornelius, Jr. and Willard D. Sheeler. ENGLISH 900® was prepared under the direction of Edwin T. Cornelius, Jr., with Joyce R. Manes as Project Editor.

CONTENTS

The numbers of the Base Sentences in each unit follow the unit titles.

UNIT 1 DESCRIBING OBJECTS

301   What color is your book?

302   My book has a dark blue cover.

303   How much does that typewriter weigh?

304   It's not too heavy, but I don't know the exact weight.

305   This round table weighs about forty-five pounds.

306   What size suitcase do you own?

307   One of my suitcases is small, and the other one is medium size.

308   I like the shape of that table.

309   How long is Jones Boulevard?

310   That street is only two miles long.

311   Will you please measure this window to see how wide it is?

312   This window is just as wide as that one.

313   The walls are three inches thick.

314   This material feels soft.

315   This pencil is longer than that one.

UNIT *1* DESCRIBING OBJECTS

301. 당신의 책은 무슨 색깔입니까?
302. 내 책의 표지는 짙은 푸른 색입니다.
303. 저 타이프라이터는 무게가 얼마입니까?
304. 지나치게 무겁진 않지만, 정확한 무게는 모릅니다.
305. 이 원형 테이블은 무게가 약 45파운드 쯤 됩니다.
306. 당신은 어떤 크기의 여행용 가방을 가지고 있읍니까?
307. 내 여행용 가방 중 하나는 작고 다른 하나는 중간 크기의 것입니다.

308. 나는 저 테이블의 모양을 좋아합니다.
309. 죠운즈 가로(街路)는 길이가 얼마입니까?
310. 그 길은 거리가 단지 2마일 입니다.
311. 이 창문의 폭이 얼마인지 재 주시겠읍니까?
312. 이 창문은 저 창문과 폭이 꼭 같습니다.
313. 그 벽의 두께는 3인치입니다.
314. 이 물건은 촉감이 부드럽읍니다.
315. 이 연필은 저것 보다 더 깁니다.

✻ 새로 나온 단어와 어귀 ✻

color 「색깔」 **dark** 「짙은, 어두운」 **cover** 「표지」 **weigh** 「무게가…이다」 **too** 「아주, 너무나」 **heavy** 「무거운」 **exact** 「정확한」 **weight** 「무게」 **round** 「둥근」 **pound** 「파운드, 453그램」 **size** 「크기」 **suitcase** 「소형 여행용 가방」 **own** 「소유하다, 가지다」 **medium** 「중간의」 **shape** 「모양」 **boulevard** 「가로 (가로수가 있는 넓은 길)」 **measure** 「재다」 **wide** 「넓은」 **thick** 「두꺼운」 **material** 「물질의, 재료」 **feel** 「느끼다」 **soft** 「부드러운」 **typewriter** 「타자기」

▒▒▒ 문 법 ▒▒▒

301. **What color is your book?**

　　　　Your book is *blue.*

　What color is your book?
　　　↑_____

　　What color는 blue의 의문형이다. 이와같이 what을 명사 앞에 써서 「어떤 ~?」의 뜻이 된다.

　　　What book do you read?
　　　(어떤 책을 읽읍니까?)
　　　What flower do you like best?
　　　(어떤 꽃을 가장 좋아합니까?)
　　　What color is your pencil?
　　　(당신의 연필은 어떤 색 입니까?)
　　　What color is your hair?
　　　(당신의 머리칼은 어떤 색 입니까?)
　　　What color are your shoes?
　　　(당신의 신발은 어떤 색 입니까?)

302. **a dark blue cover :**

　　a *dark* blue 「짙은 청색」　　　a *light* blue 「연한 청색」
　　a *bright* red 「선명한 빨강」

303. **How much does that typewriter weigh?** : weigh는 「명사」 weight는 「동사」

　　　That typewriter weighs *twenty pounds.*

　How much does that typewriter weigh?
　　　↑

　　How much does that table weigh?
　　(그 식탁은 무게가 얼마입니까?)
　　How much does that dog weigh?
　　(그 개는 무게가 얼마입니까?)
　　How much that elephant weigh?
　　(그 코끼리는 무게가 얼마입니까?)

306. **What size suitcase do you own?** : What size~는 301번의 What color~, nat book~, What flower~ 와 같은 원리이다.

　　What size notebook~?　　(어떤 크기의 공책~?)
　　What size house~?　　　(어떤 크기의 집~?)
　　What size apartment~?　(어떤 크기의 아파트~?)
　　What size diamond~?　　(어떤 크기의 다이아몬드~?)

307. **One of my suitcases is~ and the other one~** : 두 개 중에서 막연히 말해서 하나를 one이라 칭하고 나머지 하나를 the other라 칭한다.
　　I have two brothers. *One* lives in Pusan and *the other* lives in Seoul.
　　(나에게 형님이 둘 있는데, 한 분은 부산에 또 한 분은 서울에 살고 계 시다)

One of my suitcases is large, and *the other* one is medium.

(내 여행용 가방중의 하나는 대형이고, 또 다른 하나는 중형이다)

309. How long is Jones Boulevard? : How long～? 은 303번의 How much 와 같은 원리이다.

Jones Boulevard is *two miles long.*

How long is Jones Boulevard?

how에 long, wide, high, tall 등을 붙여 앞에 내놓으면 의문문이 되는 동시,
「길이, 넓이, 높이, (키의) 높이」 등을 묻는 말이 된다.

How long is Jones Boulevard? (죠운즈 가로는 길이가 얼마입니까?)

How wide is Jones Boulevard? (죠운즈 가로는 넓이가 얼마입니까?)

How tall are you? (당신은 키가 얼마입니까?)

How high is the mountain? (저 산은 높이가 얼마입니까?)

How deep is the pond? (저 연못은 깊이가 얼마입니까?)

310. That street is only two miles long : long, wide, thick, high, tall, deep
등 앞에 숫자를 써서 「길이, 넓이, 두께, 높이, (키의) 높이, 깊이」 등을 나타낸
다. Jones Boulevard is *seventy feet wide.*

(죠운즈 가로는 넓이가 70피이트 입니다)

The walls are *three inches thick.* (저 벽은 두께가 3인치입니다)

The tree is *thirty feet high.* (저 나무는 높이가 30피이트입니다)

311. ~to see how wide it is? : to see～「~을 알아 보기 위해서」 와
how wide it is (그것이 넓이가 얼마인지」의 결합형.

Will you pleasure measure this window to see *how narrow it is*?

(이 창문이 얼마나 좁은지 재 주시겠읍니까?)

Will you please measure this window to see *how high it is*?

(이 창문이 높이가 얼마인지 재 주시겠읍니까?)

312. ~is just as wide as that one : as～as는 정도가 동일함을 나타낸다.

~as long as~   *~as wide as~*   *~as thick as~*

~as high as~   *~as tall as~*

He is *as* tall *as* his father. (그는 아버지와 키가 같다)

314. This material feels soft : *feel soft* 「감촉이 부드럽다」 *feel hard* 「감
촉이 딱딱하다」 *feel rough* 「감촉이 거칠디」

INTONATION

301　What color is your book?

302　My book has a dark blue cover.

303　How much does that typewriter weigh?

304　It's not too heavy, but I don't know the exact weight.

305　This round table weighs about forty-five pounds.

306　What size suitcase do you own?

307　One of my suitcases is small, and the other one is medium size.

308　I like the shape of that table.

309　How long is Jones Boulevard?

310　That street is only two miles long.

311　Will you please measure this window to see how wide it is?

312　This window is just as wide as that one.

313　The walls are three inches thick.

314　This material feels soft.

315　This pencil is longer than that one.

VERB STUDY

1. **weigh**
   a. How much does that typewriter weigh?
   b. This table weighs about forty-five pounds.
   c. Did you weigh the suitcase?
   d. Yes, I weighed the suitcase this morning.

2. **like**
   a. I like the shape of that table.
   b. Do you like the shape of that window?
   c. I liked the movie very much.
   d. He likes the medium size suitcase.

3. **measure**
   a. Will you please measure this window?
   b. I've already measured that window.
   c. I'm measuring the window right now.
   d. Did he measure the table to see how long it is?

4. **feel**
   a. This material feels soft.
   b. I feel fine today.
   c. I didn't feel well yesterday.
   d. He felt the material to see how soft it was.

5. **own**
   a. What size suitcase do you own?
   b. I own a small suitcase and a medium size one.
   c. He owns that automobile.
   d. Last year he owned a good automobile.

6. **have**
   a. My book has a dark blue cover.
   b. I have two suitcases.
   c. Last year I had a good typewriter.
   d. Does he have a dark blue book?

7. **be**
   a. What color is your book?
   b. The walls are three inches thick.
   c. I'm a doctor.
   d. He was in New York yesterday.
   e. Isn't John your brother?

VERB STUDY

1. weigh (무게를 재다, 무게가 ~이다)
   a. 저 타이프라이터는 무게가 얼마입니까?
   b. 이 테이블은 무게가 약 45 파운드입니다.
   c. 그 여행용 가방의 무게를 달았읍니까?
   d. 네, 오늘 아침 그 여행용 가방의 무게를 달았읍니다.

2. like (좋아하다)
   a. 나는 저 테이블의 모양을 좋아합니다.
   b. 당신은 저 창문의 모양을 좋아합니까?
   c. 나는 그 영화를 매우 좋아 했읍니다.
   d. 그는 중간 크기의 여행용 가방을 좋아합니다.

3. measure (치수를 재다)
   a. 창문을 재어 주시겠읍니까?
   b. 나는 저 창문을 이미 쟀었읍니다.
   c. 나는 지금 그 창문을 재고 있읍니다.
   d. 그는 그 테이블의 길이가 얼마인지 알아보기 위해서 쟀었읍니까?

4. feel (느끼다, 촉감이 ~하다)
   a. 이 물건은 촉감이 부드럽다.
   b. 오늘은 상쾌한 기분입니다.
   c. 어제는 기분이 좋지 않았읍니다.
   d. 그는 그 물건이 얼마나 부드러운지 알아보기 위해서 만져 봤읍니다.

5. own (소유하다)
   a. 어떤 크기의 여행용 가방을 당신은 가지고 있읍니까?
   b. 나는 작은 것 하나와 중간 크기의 것 하나를 가지고 있읍니다.
   c. 그는 저 자동차를 가지고 있읍니다.
   d. 작년에 그는 멋있는 자동차 한대를 가졌읍니다.

6. have (가지다)
   a. 내 책의 표지는 짙은 푸른색 입니다.
   b. 나는 두 개의 여행용 가방을 가지고 있읍니다.
   c. 작년에 나는 좋은 타이프라이터 한대를 가지고 있었읍니다.
   d. 그는 짙은 푸른색 표지의 책을 한권 가지고 있읍니까?

7. be (~이다, 있다)
   a. 당신의 책은 무슨 색깔입니까?
   b. 그 벽의 두께는 3 인치 입니다.
   c. 나는 의사입니다.
   d. 그는 어제 뉴욕에 있었읍니다.
   e. 존은 당신의 형이 아닙니까?

✻ 새로 나온 단어와 어귀 ✻

window「창문」　　**movie**「영화」　**right now**「지금 당장」.　**automobile**「자동차」
doctor「의사」　　**brother**「형」

SUBSTITUTION DRILLS

1. What color is your | book | ? Do you remember?
    | pencil |
    | typewriter |
    | camera |

2. My book has a | dark blue | cover. Have you seen it?
    | light blue |
    | bright red |
    | red and blue |

3. How much does that | typewriter | weigh? Can you tell me?
    | table |
    | dog |
    | elephant |

4. It's | not too heavy | , but I don't know the exact weight.
    | not awfully heavy |
    | very light |
    | pretty light |
    | fairly heavy |

5. This | round | table weighs about forty-five pounds.
    | square |
    | long |
    | narrow |
    | small |

6. What size | suitcase | do you own?
    | notebook |
    | house |
    | apartment |
    | diamond |

7. One of my suitcases is | small | , and the other one is medium.
    | large |
    | little |
    | big |

8. I like the | shape / size / color / weight | of that table. Do you like it?

9. How | long / wide / narrow / big | is Jones Boulevard? Do you know?

10. That street is only | two miles long / two blocks long / 300 yards long / two miles in length / 900 feet long | . What's the name of the street?

11. Will you please measure this window to see how | wide / narrow / high / big / small | it is?

12. This window is just as | wide / narrow / high / big / small / high and wide | as that one.

13. The walls are | three inches / two feet / one yard / 3 in. / 2 ft. / 1 yd. | thick. How high are the walls?

14. This material feels

| soft |
| hard |
| wet |
| dry |
| hard and dry |
| soft and wet |

. How does that material feel?

15. This pencil is

| longer |
| shorter |
| bigger |
| smaller |
| heavier |
| lighter |

than that one.

16. This book weighs

| two pounds |
| twenty ounces |
| 2 lbs. |
| 25 oz. |

. What's the weight of that book?

17. This window is

| two feet |
| twenty-six inches |
| 2′ |
| 26″ |

wide. What's the width of that window?

18.

| What size |
| How big |

is your apartment?

19. Do you

| have |
| own |
| want |

a large suitcase?

20. Your suitcase

| is |
| looks |
| feels |

very heavy.

SUBSTITUTION DRILLS

1.
책은
연필은
타이프 라이터는
카메라는

2.
짙은 푸른색의
연한 푸른색의
선명한 빨간색의
적청색의

3.
타이프 라이터는
테이블은
개는
코끼리는

4.
너무 무겁지 않(습니다마는)
아주 무겁지는 않(〃)
아주 가볍(〃)
꽤 가볍(〃)
상당히 무겁(〃)

5.
원형의
정방형의
긴
좁은
작은

6.
가방을
공책을
집을
아파트를
다이아몬드를

7.
작은
큰
적은
큰

8.
모양
크기
색깔
무게

9.
넓이가(얼마입니까?)
폭이 (〃)
좁기가(〃)
크기가(〃)

10.
2마일의 거리
2블록의 거리
300야아드 길이
2마일 길이
900피이트 길이

11.
폭이(얼마입니까?)
좁기(〃)
높이(〃)
크기(〃)
작기(〃)

12.
폭이(~와 같읍니다)
좁기가(〃)
높이가(〃)
크기가(〃)
작기가(〃)
높이와 폭이(〃)

13.
3인치
2피이트
1야아드
3인치
2피이트
1야아드

14.
부드러운
단단한
축축한
메마른
단단하고 메마른
부드럽고 축축한

15.
더 긴
더 짧은
더 큰
더 조그만
더 무거운
더 가벼운

16.
2파운드
20온스
2파운드
25온스

17.
2피이트
26인치
2피이트
26인치

18.
크기가 어떻니까
얼마나 큽니까

19.
가지고 있읍니까
소유하고 있읍니까
원합니까

20.
(무겁)습니다.
(무거워)보입니다
(무겁게)느껴집니다.

READING PRACTICE

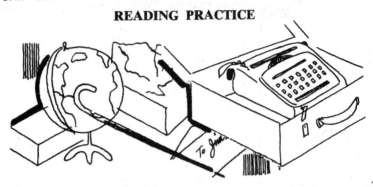

Describing Objects

Yesterday was Jim's birthday. He got a lot of presents from his friends and family. All the gifts were wrapped in colored paper. Some of the packages were large, but others were very small. Some were heavy, and others were light. One square package was blue; there was a book in it. Another one was long and narrow; it had an umbrella in it. Jim's sister gave him a big, round package. He thought it was a ball, but it was not. When he removed the yellow paper that covered it, he saw that it was a globe of the world.

After that his brother gave Jim another gift. It was a big box wrapped in green paper. Jim opened it and found another box covered with red paper. He removed the paper and saw a third box; this one was blue in color.

Everyone laughed as Jim opened the boxes. There were six of them! In the last one he found a small white envelope. There was a piece of paper in the envelope which said: "Go to the big bedroom. Look in the closet near the high window. You will see three suitcases: a black one, a brown one and a gray one. Your birthday present is in one of these."

Jim went in the large bedroom. He went to the closet and began opening the suitcases. He had to open all of them before he saw his brother's present. He was very happy. It was just what Jim wanted—a portable typewriter.

Questions

1. What was in the square blue package?
2. What did Jim's sister give him?
3. What was in the long, narrow box?
4. Describe the gift from Jim's brother.
5. Was Jim happy with the gift from his brother? Why?

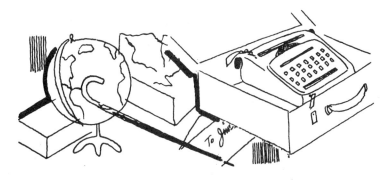

READING PRACTICE
〔물건에 대한 설명〕

　어제는 짐의 생일이었읍니다. 그는 친구와 가족으로부터 많은 선물을 받았읍
니다. 모든 선물은 천연색 포장지로 싸여져 있었읍니다. 포장물 중의 몇개는 크
고 다른 몇개는 아주 작은 것 이었읍니다. 어떤 것은 무거웠고, 또 어떤 것은
가벼웠읍니다. 네모지게 포장된 것 하나는 푸른색 이었는데, 그 속에는 책이 들
어 있었읍니다. 또 하나는 길고 좁다란 것 이었는데, 그 속에는 우산이 들어있었
읍니다. 짐의 누이는 그에게 크고 둥근 포장물을 주었읍니다. 짐은 그것이 공
인줄 알았는데 공은 아니었읍니다. 그것을 싸고 있는　란 포장지를 풀어 보
니 그것은 지구본 이였읍니다.
　그후 짐의 형은 짐에게 다른 선물을 주었읍니다. 그것은 초록색 포장지로 싸
인 커다란 상자였읍니다. 짐은 그것을 풀어보니 빨간 포장지로 싸인 또 하나의
상자를 발견했읍니다.
　그가 포장지를 벗기니 세번째 상자가 보였읍니다. 이것은 파란 것 이었읍니다.
짐이 상자들을 열었을 때 모두들 웃었읍니다. 상자는 여섯 개나 되었읍니다.
마지막 상자에서 짐은 조그마한 하얀봉투 하나를 발견했읍니다. 봉투 속에는 종
이가 한장 들어있었고 거기에는 "큰 침실로 가 봐라. 높은 창문 가까이의 벽장
을 들여다 보아라. 까만색, 갈색, 회색의 세개의 여행용 가방이 있는데 너의 생
일 선물은 이 셋 중 하나에 들어있다"라고 씌어 있었읍니다.
　짐은 그 큰 침실로 갔읍니다. 짐은 벽장으로 가서 가방들을 열어보기 시작했
읍니다. 짐은 가방들을 다 열어보고 나서야 형의 선물을 찾아낼 수 있었읍니다.
짐은 매우 기뻤읍니다. 그것은 바로 짐이 원하던 것 즉 휴대용 타이프라이터 였
읍니다.

━━━━━━━━━ ✳ 새로 나온 단어와 어귀 ✳ ━━━━━━━━━

a lot of「많은」　**present**「선물」　**friend**「친구」　**family**「가족」　**gift**「선물」
wrap「싸다」　**colored**「색깔이 있는」　**package**「소포; 포장물」　**square**「4 각의」
narrow「좁은」　**yellow**「노란」　**box**「상자」　**bedroom**「침실」　**portable**「손에
들고 다니는, 휴대용」

CONVERSATION

Judy comes home late with a surprise for her husband, Fred.

FRED: Judy! Where have you been? It's after six o'clock.

JUDY: Wait until I tell you, Fred! I've been downtown and I saw just what I wanted.

FRED: I know. A green dress to match the green shoes you bought last week.

JUDY: No. Not a green dress or a red one or a yellow one. It isn't anything for me. It's for our house.

FRED: Our house? What is it?

JUDY: You'll never guess. It's a new sofa. A yellow one.

FRED: We already have a sofa, Judy. A very good one.

JUDY: I never liked it. It's brown and our other furniture is light blue. It doesn't match. The yellow one will look good with our other things.

FRED: Very well. Tell me about it.

JUDY: First of all, it's exactly the right size for the wall near the window. The sofa we have now is too short.

FRED: Is it wide or narrow?

JUDY: It's as wide as our old sofa, but it looks narrower because it's longer.

FRED: Fine. Then I'll have a very good place to sleep after dinner.

CONVERSATION

〈쥬디는 남편 프레디를 놀래줄 소식을 갖고 늦게 집에 돌아온다〉

Fred : 쥬디! 어디 갔었소? 여섯시가 넘었는데.

Judy : 말 할때 까지 기다리세요, 프레드! 시내에 나갔다가 바로 내가 원했던 것을 보았어요.

Fred : 알겠오, 지난주 샀던 당신의 초록색 구두에 어울리는 초록색 드레스 말이로군.

Judy : 아네요, 초록색 드레스도 아니고, 빨간 드레스도, 노란 드레스도 아네요. 나를 위한 것이 아니예요. 우리집을 위한 거예요.

Fred : 우리 집을 위한 것이라니? 그게 무어요?

Judy : 당신은 모를 거예요. 최신형 소파예요. 노란 색갈 이예요.

Fred : 쥬디, 소파는 있지 않소, 아주 훌륭한 것이 말이요.

Judy : 난 그게 싫었어요. 그건 색깔이 갈색이구 우리집 가구는 연한 청색이라 어울리지 않아요. 노란 것 이어야 우리집 가구에 잘 어울릴 거예요.

Fred : 좋소, 말 해 보아요.

Judy : 무엇보다도 그 소파는 창문 가까이의 벽 길이에 꼭 맞는단 말예요. 지금 우리가 갖고 있는 소파는 너무 짧잖아요.

Fred : 그 소파는 폭이 넓은 거요, 좁은 거요?

Judy : 폭은 우리가 이미 갖고 있는 소파만큼 돼요, 그렇지만 길이가 더 기니까 좁다랗게 보여요.

Fred : 좋소, 그럼 저녁 식사후에 기분좋게 잠잘 곳이 생기겠군.

✳ 새로나온 단어와 어귀 ✳

after 「뒤에, 후에」 until 「~할 때 까지」 have been 「갔다 오다」 downtown 「시내에」 saw=see 「보다」의 과거. just 「바로」 want 「원하다」 green 「초록의」 shoes 「신발」 match 「조화되다」 the green shoes you bought 「당신이 산 녹색 신발」 last week 「지난주」 for 「~을 위한」 never 「결코 ~않다」 guess 「추측하다, 짐작하다」 furniture 「가구」 sofa 「안락침대」 old 「낡은, 예전의」 place 「장소」 look good 「좋아보이다」 sleep 「잠자다」

EXERCISES

1. Complete the following sentences with the correct word.

    Example: My automobile is *longer* than yours. (*longer, length, medium, small*)

    a. This typewriter weighs _____. (*light, heavy, 25 lbs., 10 inches*)

    b. The typewriter is _____ than this pencil. (*light, heavy, lighter, heavier*)

    c. This pencil is _____ than the typewriter. (*light, heavy, lighter, heavier*)

    d. Jones Boulevard measures _____ in width. (*36 lbs., heavy, 36 oz., 36 feet*)

    e. It is _____ than Lane Street. (*wide, wider, width, weight*)

    f. I don't know the exact _____ of the window. (*wide, wider, width, high*)

    g. This window is _____ than that one. (*narrow, narrower, height, width*)

    h. This wall is just as _____ as that one. (*thick, thickness, width, height*)

2. Complete the sentences with the correct word from the list below:

    weight   size   color   shape   length
    height   width   material

    a. The _____ of this book is blue.
    b. The _____ of this table is round.
    c. The _____ of this suitcase is 20 lbs.
    d. The _____ of the street is 2 miles.
    e. This suitcase is a small _____.
    f. This window is high. Its _____ is three feet.
    g. This is a wide street. Its _____ is 36 feet.
    h. This _____ feels soft.

3. Complete the sentences below with the appropriate words from the list:

large	wide	long	light	hard
narrow	thick	soft	small	dry
thin	heavy	wet	short	

Example: Elephants are big. They are not *small.*

a. This suitcase is awfully heavy. It is not ———.

b. This table is pretty small. It is not ———.

c. This material feels fairly soft. It is not ———.

d. Jones Boulevard is very wide. It is not ———.

e. The window was wet. It was not ———.

f. These walls are two feet thick. They are not ———.

g. This street is very long. It is not ———.

h. This is a thin book. It is not ———.

i. This is a narrow window. It is not ———.

j. This is a light briefcase. It is not ———.

k. This is a hard bed. It is not ———.

l. This street is dry. It is not ———.

m. This table is short. It is not ———.

4. Complete the questions with one of the expressions from the list below:

how wide	how long	what is the weight
how thick	what color	what is the thickness
what sizes	what shape	what is the width
how much heavier	what is the length	how tall

Example: What is the width of that window? It is 3 feet wide.

a. ——— of that pencil? It weighs 2 oz.

b. ——— is that window? It is 41 inches in width.

c. ——— is that street? It is two miles in length.

d. _____ is that wall? It is three feet thick.

e. _____ of that street? It is 36 feet wide.

f. _____ is this book than that one? They are the same weight.

g. _____ is your book? It is red and blue.

h. _____ are your suitcases? One is small and the other is medium.

i. _____ is that table? It is round.

j. _____ of that material? It is three yards long.

k. _____ is John? His height is exactly six feet.

5. **Use the right verb form:**

      weighing   weigh   weighs   am   is   are
            measure   measures   measuring

a. How many pounds do you _____?

b. I don't know how many pounds I _____.

c. John _____ one hundred and fifty pounds.

d. You _____ your suitcase to see what size it is.

e. My mother _____ the windows to see how wide they are.

f. I _____ heavier than my sister.

g. These windows _____ wider than those.

h. Dogs _____ smaller than elephants.

i. How much does that typewriter _____?

j. They are _____ the windows now to see how high they are.

k. I am _____ my suitcase to see what its weight is.

l. The boulevard _____ only three miles long.

m. That man is _____ the boulevard now to see what its width is.

n. That street _____ longer than this one.

o. Will you _____ the length of this material for me, please?

WORD LIST

apartment
as . . . as
awfully
big, bigger, biggest
bright
camera
color
cover
dark
diamond
elephant
fairly
foot, feet
hard
heavy, heavier, heaviest

high
inch
large
length
light, lighter, lightest
long, longer, longest
material
medium
mile
narrow
only ·
ounce
pound
round
shape

short, shorter, shortest
size
small, smaller, smallest
soft
square
suitcase
thick
too
typewriter
weight
wet
wide
width
yard

Verb Forms

p. = past; p. part. = past participle
feel, felt (*p. and p. part.*)
measure, measured (*p. and p. part.*)
own, owned (*p. and p. part.*)
weigh, weighed (*p. and p. part.*)

Expression

how much

Weights and Measures

26″ = twenty-six inches
26 in. = twenty-six inches
2′ = two feet
2 ft. = two feet
1 yd. = one yard
25 oz. = twenty-five ounces
2 lb. = two pounds

Supplementary Word List

(Conversation and Reading Practice)

ball
bedroom
box
closet
colored
covered
downtown
dress

furniture
gifts
globe
laughed
match
package
portable
presents

removed
shoes
sofa
surprise
umbrella
why
wrapped

UNIT 2 ASKING PEOPLE TO DO THINGS

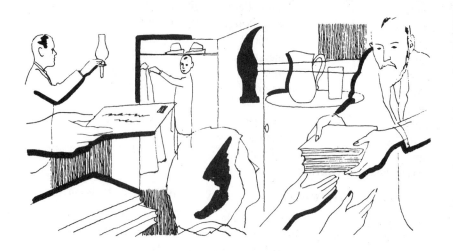

316   Would you please tell Mr. Cooper that I'm here?
317   Take these books home with you tonight.
318   Please bring me those magazines.
319   Would you help me lift this heavy box?
320   Please ask John to turn on the lights.
321   Put your books down on the table.
322   Get me a hammer from the kitchen, will you?
323   Hang up my coat in the closet, will you please?
324   Please don't bother me now. I'm very busy.
325   Would you mind mailing this letter for me?
326   If you have time, will you call me tomorrow?
327   Please pick up those cups and saucers.
328   Will you do me a favor?
329   Please count the chairs in that room.
330   Please pour this milk into that glass.

UNIT 2 ASKING PEOPLE TO DO THINGS

316. 쿠우퍼 씨에게 내가 여기 있다고 말좀 해 주시겠읍니까?

317. 오늘 밤 이 책들을 집에 가져 가십시오.

318. 저 잡지들을 내게 좀 가져다주십시오.

319. 이 무거운 상자를 드는데 좀 도와 주시겠읍니까?

320. 존에게 불 좀 켜 달라고 해 주세요.

321. 당신의 책들을 테이블 위에 내려놓으세요.

322. 부엌에서 망치 좀 갖다 주시겠어요?

323. 벽장에 내 코우트 좀 걸어 주시겠어요?

324. 나를 제발 성가시게 굴지 마세요. 난 매우 바쁩니다.

325. 이 편지 좀 내 대신 부쳐 주시겠어요?

326. 시간 있으시면, 내일 저에게 전화 좀 해 주시겠어요?

327. 저 차 잔과 차잔 받침들 좀 집어 주세요.

328. 제 청을 들어 주시겠읍니까?

329. 방에 있는 의자를 좀 세어보세요.

330. 저 유리 잔에 이 우유 좀 부어 주십시오.

---

* 새로 나온 단어와 어귀 *

take「가지고 가다」 that I'm here「내가 여기 있다는 것」 bring「가지고 오다」 lift「들어올리다」 ask~to…「~에게 …하라고 요청하다」 put「놓다」 put down「내려 놓다」 get~…「~에게 …을 가져다 주다」 hammer「망치」 kitchen「부엌」 hang up「걸다」 closet「장농, 벽장」 bother「괴롭히다」 would you mind~「~해 주시겠읍니까?」 mail「우송하다」 pick up「집어올리다」 saucer「컵 받침」 count「세다」 pour「붓다」 do~ a favor「~에게 친절을 베풀다」

::::: 분 ::::::::::: 법 :::::

316. Would you please tell Mr. Cooper that I'm here ? : 명령문에 please 를 쓰면 보다 접잖은 부탁이 된다는 것은 이미 말한 바 있다. 그러나 would 〔will〕 you please~ ? 와는 의문문은 그보다 더 정중한 표현이다.   이것은 의문문의 형태를 빌린 부탁이다.

　　Help me. (나를 도우라)

　　Please, help me. (나를 도와 주시오)

　　Would you please help me ? (나를 좀 도와 주시겠읍니까 ?)

이에 대한 답은 I'd be glad to. 나 I'd love to. With pleasure. 라고 대답한다. 격식을 차리지 않는 말로는 Sure(Surely)가 있다.

~tell Mr. Cooper that I'm here. 는 tell Mr. Cooper(쿠퍼씨에게 말하다) 와 that I'm here(내가 여기 있다는 것)의 결합형이다.

　　Would you please tell him that I'm here ?

　　　(그에게 내가 여기 있다는 것을 말씀 좀 드려 주시겠읍니까 ?)

　　Would you please advise him that I'm here ?

　　　(그에게 내가 여기 있다는 것을 좀 알려 주시겠읍니까 ?)

　　Would you please let him know that I'm here ?

　　　(그에게 내가 여기 있다는 것을 좀 알려 주시겠읍니까 ?)

319. Would you help me lift this heavy box ? : help me lift~「내가 ~을 드는 것을 돕다」. 영국 영어에서는 help me to lift라 하고 미국 영어에서는 help me lift라고만 쓴다.

　　Would you *help me carry* this heavy box ?

　　　(내가 이 무거운 상자를 운반하는 것을 도와 주시겠읍니까 ?)

　　Would you *help me move* this heavy box ?

　　　(내가 이 무거운 상자를 움직이는 것을 도와 주시겠읍니까 ?)

　　Would you *help me wrap* this heavy box ?

　　　(내가 이 무거운 상자를 싸는 것을 도와 주시겠읍니까 ?)

320. Please ask John to turn on the lights : ask~to…「~에게 …을 해 달 라고 청하다」

　　Please *ask* John *to turn* on the lights.

　　　(죤에게 전등을 켜 달라고 청하시오)

　　Please *ask* John *to turn off* the lights.

　　　(죤에게 전등을 꺼 달라고 청하시오)

　　Please *ask* John *to help* you.

　　　(죤에게 너를 도와 달라고 청하시오)

321. Put your books down on the table. : put자체는「놓다」의 뜻이지만, put down이라고 쓰여지면「내려 놓다」의 뜻이 된다. 이와 같이 두개의 낱말이

합쳐서 한 동작의 개념을 나타내기도 한다.

turn on 「(불을) 켜다」 　　　　　*turn off* 「(불을) 끄다」

hang up 「걸다」　　　　　　　　*pick up* 「집어 들다」

put back 「(제자리로)되돌려 놓다」

322. Get me a hammer~ : get me~ 「나에게 ~을 가져다 달라」의 뜻.

Get me *a nail* from the Kitchen.

(부엌에서 못 하나 가져다 주시오」

Get me *a ruler* from the kitchen.

(부엌에서 자를 가져다 주시오)

325. Would you mind mailing this letter~ ? : Would you mind~ing~ ? 는 Would you please~ ? 보다 더 공손히 부탁을 하는 표현이다. 특히 이 표현에 대해서 부탁을 들어줄 생각이면 No, Not at all, with pleasure, of course not등으로 답해야 한다. 이것은 mind자체의 뜻이 「싫다, 꺼리다」의 뜻인 까닭이다.

Would you mind wrapping this package?

(이 소포를 싸주시겠읍니까?)

Would you mind calling Mr. Cooper?

(쿠퍼 씨에게 전화 좀 걸어 주시겠읍니까?)

Would you mind opening the door for me?

(제 대신에 문 좀 열어 주시겠읍니까?)

326. If you have time~ 「시간이 있으시다면」의 뜻.

If you have time, will you come to see me tomorrow?

(시간이 있으시다면 내일 절 만나러 와 주시겠읍니까?)

If you are able to, will you mail a letter for me tomorrow?

(가능하시다면, 내일 저에게 편지주시겠읍니까?)

If you think of it, will you call me tomorrow?

(생각나시면 저에게 내일 전화주시겠읍니까?)

328. Will you do me a favor? : do me a favor 「나에게 친절을 행하다 → 나의 청을 들어주다」

INTONATION

316   Would you please tell Mr. Cooper that I'm here?

317   Take these books home with you tonight.

318   Please bring me those magazines.

319   Would you help me lift this heavy box?

320   Please ask John to turn on the lights.

321   Put your books down on the table.

322   Get me a hammer from the kitchen, will you?

323   Hang up my coat in the closet, will you please?

324   Please don't bother me now. I'm very busy.

325   Would you mind mailing this letter for me?

326   If you have time, will you call me tomorrow?

327   Please pick up those cups and saucers.

328   Will you do me a favor?

329   Please count the chairs in that room.

330   Please pour this milk into that glass.

VERB STUDY

1. **tell, ask**
   a. Please tell Mr. Cooper that I'm here.
   b. I've already told him.
   c. Please ask John to help me.
   d. I've already asked John to help you.

2. **take, bring, get**
   a. Take these books home with you tonight.
   b. I took those books home with me last night.
   c. Please bring me those magazines.
   d. He brought me two magazines.
   e. Get me a hammer from the kitchen, will you?
   f. He got me a hammer from the kitchen.

3. **turn on, turn off**
   a. Please ask John to turn on the lights.
   b. John already turned on the lights.
   c. Please ask John to turn off the lights.
   d. John already turned off the lights.

4. **pick up, put down, hang up**
   a. Please pick up those cups and saucers.
   b. He already picked up those cups and saucers.
   c. Please put your books down.
   d. I've already put my books down.
   e. Hang up my coat, will you please?
   f. He hung up my coat in the closet.

5. **bother, help**
   a. Please don't bother me now.
   b. Is he bothering you?
   c. Would you help me?
   d. He helped me lift the heavy box.

6. **count**
   a. Please count the chairs in that room.
   b. I've already counted the chairs in that room.

7. **pour**
   a. Please pour this milk into that glass.
   b. I've already poured the milk into the glass.

8. **call**
   a. If you have time, will you call me tomorrow?
   b. He called me last night.

VERB STUDY

1. **tell, ask** (말하다, 청하다)
   a. 내가 여기 있다고 쿠우퍼 씨에게 말해 주세요.
   b. 나는 그에게 이미 말했읍니다.
   c. 존에게 나를 도와 달라고 부탁해 주세요.
   d. 나는 존에게 당신을 도우라고 이미 말했읍니다.

2. **take, bring, get** (가지다, 가져오다, 얻다.)
   a. 이 책들을 오늘 밤 집에 가져 가시오.
   b. 나는 어젯 밤 저 책들을 집에 가져 갔읍니다.
   c. 저 잡지를 저에게 갖다 주십시오.
   d. 그는 내게 두권의 잡지를 가져 왔읍니다.
   e. 부엌에서 망치 좀 갖다 주시겠읍니까?
   f. 그는 부엌에서 망치를 내게 갖다 주었읍니다.

3. **turn on, turn off** (〈불을〉 켜다, 끄다)
   a. 존에게 불 좀 켜달라고 해 주세요.
   b. 존은 이미 불을 켰읍니다.
   c. 존에게 불 좀 꺼 달라고 해 주세요.
   d. 존은 이미 불을 껐읍니다.

4. **pick up, put down, hang up** (집다, 놓다, 걸다)
   a. 저 찻잔과 찻잔 받침들을 좀 집어 주십시오.
   b. 그는 이미 그 찻잔과 찻잔 받침들을 집었읍니다.
   c. 책들을 좀 내려 놓으십시오.
   d. 나는 이미 책들을 내려 놓았읍니다.
   e. 내 코우트 좀 걸어 주시겠읍니까?
   f. 그는 벽장에 내 코우트를 걸었읍니다.

5. **bother, help** (성가시게 굴다. 돕다)
   a. 나를 제발 성가시게 굴지 말아 주세요.
   b. 그가 당신을 귀찮게 하나요?
   c. 저 좀 도와 주시겠읍니까?
   d. 그는 내가 그 무거운 상자를 드는 것을 도왔읍니다.

6. **count** (세다)
   a. 저 방안의 의자들 좀 세어 주시오.
   b. 나는 그 방안의 의자들을 벌써 세었읍니다.

7. **pour** (붓다)
   a. 저 유리 잔에 이 우유를 부어 주십시오.
   b. 나는 이미 그 유리 잔에 우유를 부었읍니다.

8. **call** (전화 걸다)
   a. 시간이 있으시면 내일 제게 전화하시겠어요?
   b. 그는 지난 밤 내게 전화를 했읍니다.

✳ 새로 나온 단어와 어귀 ✳

take 「휴대하다, 가지고 가다」의 뜻으로 with you(me, her) 등을 동반한다. **bring**
「가져오다, 데려오다」 **get**=bring   **turn on** 「켜다」 **turn off** 「끄다」

SUBSTITUTION DRILLS

1. Would you please | tell him / advise him / let him know / remind him | that I'm here?

2. Take these books | home / to the meeting / to the library | with you tonight.

3. Please | bring / give / hand / throw | me those magazines. They're not very heavy.

4. Would you help me | lift / carry / move / wrap / weigh / measure | this heavy box?

5. Please ask John to | turn on the lights / turn off the lights / turn the lights on / turn the lights off | .

6. | Put your books down / Put down your books / Put your books / Leave your books / Place your books | on the table, will you please?

7. Get me | a hammer / a nail / a ruler / a yardstick | from the kitchen, will you?

8. | Hang up my coat / Hang my coat up / Put my coat / Leave my coat / Put my coat back | in the closet, will you?

9. Please don't | bother / interrupt / talk to / argue with | me now. I'm very busy.

10. Would you mind | mailing this letter / mailing this package / wrapping this package / calling Mr. Cooper | for me? I'm busy this afternoon.

11. If you have time, will you | call / visit / come to see / do a favor for / mail a letter for | me tomorrow?

12. Please pick up those | cups and saucers / plates and glasses / knives and forks / spoons | , will you?

13. Will | you / he / she / they | do me a favor? I'm very busy this afternoon.

14 Please count | the chairs / the desks / the pictures / the rugs | in that room. How many are there?

15. | Would you please pour / Will you please pour / Could you please pour / Would you mind pouring | this milk into that glass?

16. Would you please ask John to | hang my coat up / get me a hammer / take back these books / bring me those magazines | ?

17. | If you have time / If you are able to / If you think of it | , will you call me tomorrow?

SUBSTITUTION DRILLS

1. 그에게 말하다
   그에게 충고하다
   그에게 알게 하다
   그에게 생각나게 하다

2. 집으로
   회합에
   도서관에

3. 가져 오세요
   주세요
   건네 주세요
   던져 주세요

4. 들어 올려
   운반해
   옮겨
   포장해
   저울에 달아
   치수를 재어

5. 불을 켜 달라고
   불을 꺼 달라고
   불을 켜 달라고
   불을 꺼 달라고

6. 책좀 내려 놓아 주세요
   책좀 내려 놓아 주세요
   책좀 놓으세요
   책좀 내버려 두세요
   책좀 놓으세요

7. 망치를
   못을
   자를
   야아드 자를

8. 코우트 좀 걸어 주세요
   코우트 좀 걸어 주세요
   코우트 좀 놓아 두세요
   코우트 좀 내버려 두세요
   코우트 좀 도로 갖다 두세요

9. 성가시게 굴지 (마세요)
   방해하지 (〃)
   말걸지 (〃)
   ~와 논쟁하지 (〃)

10. 이 편지 좀 부쳐,
    이 소포 좀 부쳐,
    쿠우퍼 씨에게 전화 좀 걸어

11. (제게)전화 좀 해
    (저를)방문 해
    (저를)만나러 와
    (제)청을 들어
    편지 한 통 부쳐

12. 찻잔과 찻잔 받침을
    접시와 유리잔을
    칼과 포오크를
    스푼을

13. 너는
    그는
    그녀는
    그들은

14. 의자들을
    책상들을
    그림들을
    융단들을

15. 좀 부어 주시겠읍니까
    좀 부어 주시겠읍니까
    좀 부어 주시겠읍니까
    좀 부어 주시겠읍니까

16. 코우트 좀 걸어 달라고
    망치 좀 갖다 달라고
    이 책들을 도로 가져 가라고
    저 잡지들을 가져 오라고

17. 시간이 있으면
    가능하다면
    생각나면

READING PRACTICE

Asking People To Do Things

When Henry Allen came home from the office last Thursday night he saw a note from his wife on the kitchen table. "Henry," the note said, "my mother isn't well and I am going home to be with her for a few days. There are a few things that ought to be done while I'm away.

"First, take your blue coat to the dry cleaner's and leave your shirts at the laundry. At the same time, would you please stop at the shoe repairman's and get my brown shoes? And go to the supermarket and get some coffee, milk, and butter.

"When you get home, please telephone Mary Bickford and tell her I won't be able to go to her party tomorrow evening. Tell her why I can't come.

"There are three things that must be done before you go to work tomorrow morning: leave a note for the milkman asking for just one quart of milk, not two; put the garbage in the backyard; give the dog something to eat.

"If you have time on Saturday, cut the grass. Don't forget the grass in the backyard. The newspaper boy will come on Saturday afternoon. Be sure to give him money.

"I think that's all. I'll telephone this evening and let you know how Mother is.

Love,
Alice"

Henry looked out the window at the grass Alice wanted him to cut. His wife had asked him to do many things. He hoped her mother would be well very quickly.

Questions

1. What did Henry find on the kitchen table?
2. Where had Alice gone? Why?
3. What was the first thing Alice wanted Henry to do?
4. Why did Henry have to telephone Mary?
5. What did Alice ask Henry to do on Saturday if he had time?

READING PRACTICE
(사람들에게 하는 여러가지 부탁)

헨리 알렌이 지난 목요일 밤 사무실에서 집에 돌아 왔을 때, 식탁 위에서 아내가 쓴 쪽지를 보았읍니다. 쪽지에는 "헨리, 어머니가 편찮으셔서 몇일간은 어머니와 함께 있으려고, 집에 갑니다. 제가 없는 동안 당신이 해야 할 일이 몇가지 있어요.

"첫째, 드라이 크리닝 집에 당신의 푸른 코-우트를 갖다 주시고, 세탁소에 샤쓰를 갖다 맡기세요. 그리고 구두 수선집에 들러서 제 갈색 구두를 가져다 주시겠어요? 또한 수퍼 마아켓에 가서 커피, 밀크, 버터 좀 사다 놓으세요.

집에 들어 오시면, 메어리 빅포오드에게 전화를 해서 제가 내일 저녁 그녀의 파아티에 갈수 없다는 것을 전해 주세요. 못가는 이유도 말씀 해 주시고요.

당신이 내일 아침에 회사에 가기전에 해야 할 일이 세 가지 있어요. 우유 배달부에게 우유를 2 쿼어트가 아니고 1 쿼어트만 주문하는 쪽지를 써 놓으세요. 또 쓰레기는 뒷 뜰에 갖다 놓으시고, 개에게 먹이를 좀 주세요.

토요일에 시간 있으시면, 풀을 베세요. 뒷 뜰에 있는 풀을 잊지 마세요. 신문 배달 소년이 토요일 오후에 올텐데, 그 애에게 꼭 신문 대금을 주세요.

이게 모두예요, 오늘 저녁에 전화해서 어머니가 어떠신지 알려 드릴께요.

앨리스."

헨리는 창문으로 앨리스가 베어달 라고 한 풀을 내다 보았읍니다. 그의 아내는 그에게 할 일을 많이 부탁했읍니다. 그는 그녀의 어머니가 하루 빨리 완쾌하기를 빌었읍니다.

＊ 새로 나온 단어와 어귀 ＊

from the office「사무실에서」a note「쪽지, 메모」 a note from his wife「부인으로로 부터의 쪽지 → 부인이 남겨놓은 쪽지」 be well「건강하다」 be not well「편찮으시다」 to be with her「어머니와 같이 있으려고」 ought to be done「행해지지 않으면 안된다」 a few things that ought to be done「하지 않으면 안되는 서너 가지 일」 while I'm away「내가 떠나 있는 동안 → 나의 부재중」 dry cleaner's「드라이클리닝하는 집」 leave「맡기다」 shirt「샤쓰」 laundry「세탁소」 at the same time「동시에」 stop at「들르다」 shoe repairman's「구두 수선집」 super-market「수퍼 마아켙」 be able to~「~할수 있다」 won't be able to~「~할수 없을 것이다」 why I can't go「왜 내가 갈 수 없는지」 a not ~ asking for 「~을 청하는 쪽지」 quart 양(量) 의 단위. garbage「쓰레기」 backyard「뒷뜰」 something to eat「먹을 것」 be sure to~「반드시 ~하다」 give「주다」 that's all「그것이 전부다 → 이만 끝이다」 telephone「전화하다」 let you know 「당신에게 알리다」

CONVERSATION

1. Frank asks Tom to help him.

FRANK: Would you mind helping me for a minute, Tom?
TOM: I'd be glad to, Frank. What do you want me to do?
FRANK: Help me hang up this picture. Hold it straight while I put in the nail.
TOM: I'd be glad to.
FRANK: Hand me the hammer. Give me one of those nails, too, please.
TOM: Here you are.
FRANK: There. How does that look? Tell me if I have it straight.
TOM: Yes, it's straight, but it's upside down.

2. Ella prepares a birthday cake.

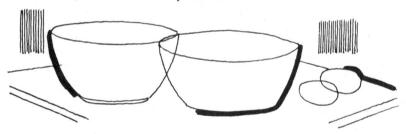

ELLA: Will you bring me two eggs from the refrigerator, Barbara?
BARBARA: Here are the eggs. Anything else I can do for you?
ELLA: Yes. Put the egg whites in one bowl and the yolks in another.
BARBARA: What are you making? A cake?
ELLA: That's right. Don't tell Harry. It's for his birthday. Keep it a secret.
BARBARA: I won't tell anyone.

CONVERSATION

1. 프랭크는 톰에게 자기를 도와 달라고 부탁을 한다.

Frank : 잠깐 나 좀 도와줄래? 톰?
Tom : 기꺼이 도울께. 프랭크, 어떻게 하면 되니?
Frank : 이 그림을 거는데 좀 도와 줘. 내가 못을 박고 있는동안 똑바로 잡고 있으라구.
Tom : 그럴께.
Frank : 망치 좀 이리 줘. 저 못도 하나 줘.
Tom : 여기 있어.
Frank : 자, 어떻게 보이니? 똑바로 붙였는지 말해 줘.
Tom : 응, 똑바로 됐어. 그런데 그림이 꺼꾸로 붙었군.

2. 엘라는 생일 케이크를 장만하고 있다.

Ella : 바버러, 냉장고에서 달걀 2 개만 갖다 주겠어요?
Barbara : 여기 달걀이 있어요. 또 뭐 도와 줄 일이 없어요?
Ella : 예, 사발 하나에는 달걀 흰자위를 담고 다른 사발에는 노른자위를 담으세요.
Barbara : 무엇을 만들고 있어요? 케이크 예요?
Ella : 맞아요, 해리에게 말 하지 말아요. 그의 생일을 위한 것이니까 비밀로 하세요.
Barbara : 아무한테도 말하지 않겠어요.

* 새로 나온 단어와 어귀 *

for a minute 「잠깐」 I'd be glad to [help you] 기꺼이 돕겠다. What do you want me to do 「내게 무엇을 하기를 원하는가?」 hold it straight 「그것을 똑바로 잡고 있으시오」 while~ 「~하는 동안」 put in 「박다」 nail 「못」 hand me ~=give me~ Here you are 「자, 여기 있어요」 무엇을 남에게 줄 때 하는 말. Tell me 「나에게 말해 주시오」 + if I have it straight 「그것을 내가 똑바로 갖고 있는지 아닌지를」 upside down 「거꾸로」 refrigerator 「냉장고」 egg 「달걀」 anything else 「다른 어느것」 egg white 「달걀 흰자위」 bowl 「사발」 yolk 「노른자위」 keep it a secret 「그것을 비밀로 하다」 secret 「비밀」

EXERCISES

1. Complete the following sentences with the appropriate words from the list below:

doing for	hang up	turn on	put down
wait for	pick up	turn off	taking back

   a. Please ask John to _____ the lights _____. It's dark in here.

   b. _____ your books _____ on the table, please.

   c. _____ my coat _____ in the closet, will you?

   d. Please don't _____ me. I'll be busy all afternoon.

   e. Would you mind _____ a favor _____ me?

   f. Would you please _____ those cups and saucers from the table?

   g. Would you mind _____ these books_____ to the library?

   h. Tell him to _____ the lights _____ when he goes to bed.

2. Change the following to questions using the expression "Would you please . . ." Follow the example.

   Example: I want you to turn on the lights.
   Would you please turn on the lights?

   a. I want you to get me a hammer.
   b. I want you to count the chairs in this room.
   c. I want you to pour this milk into that glass.
   d. I want you to help me lift this heavy box.
   e. I want you to take these books home.
   f. I want you to turn the lights off.
   g. I want you to bring me those magazines.

3. Complete the following sentences with the correct form of the word in parentheses.

   Examples: Please *bring* me the magazine. (*bring*)
   Would you mind *bringing* me the magazine? (*bring*)
   Ask John to *bring* me the magazine. (*bring*)

a. Would you please _____ me wrap this box? (*help*)

b. Would you mind _____ me wrap this box? (*help*)

c. Please don't _____ me wrap this box. (*help*)

d. Would you ask John to _____ me wrap this box? (*help*)

e. Would you please _____ this letter for me? (*mail*)

f. Would you mind _____ this letter for me? (*mail*)

g. Please don't _____ this letter for me. (*mail*)

h. Ask John to _____ this letter for me. (*mail*)

i. Would you please _____ your coat up? (*hang*)

j. Would you mind _____ your coat up? (*hang*)

k. Please don't _____ up your coat. (*hang*)

l. Would you ask John to _____ his coat up? (*hang*)

4. Change the following to negative sentences.

Examples: I am a doctor. *I'm not a doctor.*
Bring me a glass of milk. *Don't bring me a glass of milk.*

a. Wait for me at five o'clock.
b. She'll have time to do me a favor.
c. He got me a glass of milk yesterday.
d. Are you going to help me wrap this box?
e. Bring me a yardstick.
f. These nails weigh too much.
g. I turned off the radio.
h. I am very busy.
i. Pour me a cup of coffee.
j. He helped me lift the heavy box.
k. Count all the chairs in this room.
l. He is bothering me.
m. Is he talking to you?
n. Take these magazines back to the library.
o. Leave your books on the table.

WORD LIST

box	kitchen	package	saucer
closet	knife, knives	picture	spoon
fork	library	plate	that
hammer	light	rug	yardstick
into	nail	ruler	

Verb Forms

advise, advised (*p. and p. part.*)
argue, argued (*p. and p. part.*)
bother, bothered (*p. and p. part.*)
bring, brought (*p. and p. part.*)
carry, carried (*p. and p. part.*)
count, counted (*p. and p. part.*)
hand, handed (*p. and p. part.*)
hang up, hung up (*p. and p. part.*)
help, helped (*p. and p. part.*)
interrupt, interrupted (*p. and p. part.*)
let (someone) know, let (someone) know (*p. and p. part.*)
lift, lifted (*p. and p. part.*)
mail, mailed (*p. and p. part.*)
move, moved (*p. and p. part.*)
pick up, picked up (*p. and p. part.*)

place, placed (*p. and p. part.*)
pour, poured (*p. and p. part.*)

put, put (*p. and p. part.*)
put back, put back (*p. and p. part.*)
put down, put down (*p. and p. part.*)
remind, reminded (*p. and p. part.*)

take, took (*p.*), taken (*p. part.*)
take back, took back (*p.*), taken back (*p. part.*)

throw, threw (*p.*), thrown (*p. part.*)
turn off, turned off (*p. and p. part.*)
turn on, turned on (*p. and p. part.*)
wrap, wrapped (*p. and p. part.*)

Expressions

be able to
do a favor (for)

Supplementary Word List

(Conversation and Reading Practice)

backyard	garbage	milkman	straight
bowl	grass	note	supermarket
cut	hold	quart	upside down
dry cleaner	keep	refrigerator	why
eggs	laundry	secret	yolks
egg whites	love	shoe repairman	

UNIT 3 GETTING INFORMATION AND DIRECTIONS

331   Excuse me, sir. Can you give me some information?

332   Can you tell me where Peach Street is?

333   It's two blocks straight ahead.

334   Which direction is it to the theater?

335   Turn right at the next corner.

336   How far is it to the university?

337   It's a long way from here.

338   The school is just around the corner.

339   The restaurant is across the street from the hotel.

340   You can't miss it.

341   Do you happen to know Mr. Cooper's telephone number?

342   Could you tell me where the nearest telephone is?

343   Should I go this way, or that way?

344   Go that way for two blocks, then turn left.

345   I beg your pardon. Is this seat taken?

UNIT 3 GETTING
INFORMATION AND
DIRECTIONS

331. 실례합니다. 좀 여쭈어 봐도 괜
찮읍니까?

332. 피이치 가(街)가 어디 있는지
말해 주실 수 있읍니까?

333 앞으로 곧장 두 구역만 가면 됩
니다.

334. 극장은 어느 방향에 있읍니까?

335. 다음 길 모퉁이에서 오른쪽으로
돌아가십시요.

336. 대학까지는 거리가 얼마나 됩니
까?

337. 대학은 여기서 상당히 먼 거리
에 있읍니다.

338. 그 학교는 길 모퉁이를 돌면 바
로 있읍니다.

339. 그 음식점은 호텔 길 건너편
에 있읍니다.

340. 당신은 아주 쉽게 찾아 갈수
있읍니다.

341. 혹시 쿠우퍼 씨의 전화번호
를 알고 계십니까?

342. 가장 가까운 전화가 어디 있
는지 말해 주실 수 있읍니까?

343. 이 길로 가야 합니까? 아니
면 저 길로 가야 합니까?

344. 그 길로 두 구역만 가서 왼편
으로 도십시오.

345. 잠깐 실례합니다. 이 자리는
손님이 있읍니까?

✻ 새로 나온 단어와 어귀 ✻

sir 「선생, 귀하」상대방에 대한 존대의 호칭. information 「정보, 알림」 block
「(도시의)한 구역」 straight 「똑 바로, 직선으로」 ahead 「앞으로」 direction
「방향, 지시」 which direction~? 「어느 방향~?」 theater 「극장」 turn 「돌다」
right 「오른 쪽으로」 corner 「구석, 모퉁이」 at the next corner 「다음 모퉁이에
서」 far 「먼」 how far~? 「얼마나 먼~?」 university 「대학」 to the university 「대학까지」 around~ 「~을 돌아서」 around the corner 「모퉁이를 돌아서」
across 「건너서」 across the street 「길 건너편에」 miss 「놓치다, 찾지 못하
다」 happen to 「(우연히, 혹시) …하다, …에게 생기다」 telephone number 「전
화번호」 nearest near의 최상급으로 「가장 가까운」 should 「…해야 한다」 this
way 「이쪽으로」 that way 「저쪽으로」 then 「그리고 나서, 그때」 I beg your
pardon 「실례합니다」 seat 「좌석」 be taken 「취해지다, 자리를 잡다」

문 법

331. Excuse me, sir. : 남에게 무엇을 묻거나 부탁을 할 경우, 특히 모르는 사람의 경우 「실례합니다」의 뜻으로 Excuse me를 말하고 용건을 말하는 것이 좋다. sir는 상대방에 대한 호칭, 상대방의 신분이나 성별에 따라 다음 여러 가지가 있다.

Excuse me, *sir.* (선생이나 손 윗 사람의 경우)

Excuse me, *miss.* (처녀의 경우) Excuse me, *officer.* (경관, 장교등)

Excuse me, *Captain.* (선장, 대위등) Excuse me, *Colonel.* (대령)

332. Can you tell me where Peach Street is? : Can you tell me (저에게 말씀 해 주실 수 있읍니까) + Where Peach Street is(피이치 가(街)가 어디 있는지)

Excuse me. 다음에 Can you tell me the way to~? 라든가 Can you tell me where~? 혹은 Will you show me the way to~? 등의 말을 묻게 된다. 특히 tell은 「말로 가르쳐 주다」의 뜻이지만 show에는 「안내하다, 데리고 가다」의 뜻이 있다.

Can you tell me *where the airport is*?

(공항이 어디 있는지 말해 주실수 있읍니까?)

Can you tell me *the way to the university*?

(대학에 가는 길을 말해 주실수 있읍니까?)

Will you show me *the way to the bank*?

(그 은행으로 안내해 주시겠읍니까?)

333. It's two blocks straight ahead. : 길을 가르켜 주는 경우 시간위주로 It is ten minutes' walk.(10분 걸어가면 되는 거리) 혹은 It is one hour's ride. (1시간 차를 타고 가면 되는 거리) 라고 말하기도 하고 거리 위주로 It's two blocks ahead. (앞으로 두 구역만 가면 되는 거리) 혹은 It's three blocks away. (세 구역 떨어져 있는 거리) 라고 말하기도 한다.

334. Which direction is it to the theater? : 방향을 물을 경우 Which direction~,? 거리를 물을 경우 How far~?를 쓴다.

Which direction is it to the post office?

(우체국으로 가려면 어느 방향입니까?)

Which direction is it to the bank?

(은행으로 가려면 어느 방향입니까?)

How far is it to the theater?

(극장까지 얼마나 멉니까? → 거리가 얼마입니까?)

How far is it to the bank? (은행까지 거리가 얼마입니까?)

How far is it to the church?(교회까지 거리가 얼마입니까?)

335. Turn right~ :

    Turn *left*.   (왼쪽으로 돌라)

    Go *straight ahead*. (똑 바로 앞으로 가라)

    Go *to the right*.   (오른쪽으로 가라)

    Go *to the left*.   ·(왼쪽으로 가라)

337. It's a long way from here. : 「방향」을 물을 때나 거리를 물을 때나 it 를 주어로 물은 것 처럼 대답할 때에도 it를 주어로 대답한다. it에는 실질 적인 뜻은 없다.

    It's a short distance from here to the university.

      (여기에서 대학까지 짧은 거리이다)

    It's a short walk from here to the university.

      (여기서 대학까지 잠깐 걸으면 되는 거리이다)

338. The school is just around the corner. :

    in the middle of the block. (그 구역 중간 지점에)

    right *on the corner* (바로 모퉁이에)

    up there *on the left* (그쪽 왼편에)   on the second *floor* (이층에)

    down those stairs (층계 아래에)   *in the basement* (지하실에)

342. Could you tell me where the nearest telephone is? : 332번의 Can you tell me where~ ? 와 같은 표현으로서 단지 can이 could가 되어 있을 뿐 이다. 그러나 Could는 과거의 뜻이 아니고 can보다 더 「겸손함」을 나타 낸 다. 시제는 같은 현재이다.

    Could you tell me where the hospital is?

     (병원이 어디에 있는지 말해 주실 수 있읍니까?)

    Could you tell me where the ladies room is?

     (숙녀 화장실이 어디에 있는지 말해 주실 수 있읍니까?)

344. Go that way for two blocks. :

    that way 「그쪽으로」   for two blocks 「두 구역을」

    Go that way *for a block or two*. (한 두 구역쯤 그쪽으로 가시오)

    Go that way *for about two miles*. (약 2마일쯤 그쪽으로 가시오)

345. I beg your pardon. : 끝을 내려 말하면 Excuse me. 와 같이 「실례합니 다」의 뜻. 말끝을 올려 Beg (your) pardon? 이라고 하면 「죄송하지만 다 시 한번 말씀해 주십시오」의 뜻.

INTONATION

331 Excuse me, sir. Can you give me some information?

332 Can you tell me where Peach Street is?

333 It's two blocks straight ahead.

334 Which direction is it to the theater?

335 Turn right at the next corner.

336 How far is it to the university?

337 It's a long way from here.

338 The school is just around the corner.

339 The restaurant is across the street from the hotel.

340 You can't miss it.

341 Do you happen to know Mr. Cooper's telephone number?

342 Could you tell me where the nearest telephone is?

343 Should I go this way, or that way?

344 Go that way for two blocks, then turn left.

345 I beg your pardon. Is this seat taken?

VERB STUDY

1. excuse

    a. Excuse me, sir.
    b. The teacher excused me from class yesterday.
    c. The teacher excuses somebody from class every day.

2. give

    a. Can you give me some information?
    b. Mr. Cooper gave me a book.
    c. John gives me a newspaper every morning.

3. turn

    a. Turn right at the next corner.
    b. He turned right at the corner.
    c. Please turn the page.

4. miss

    a. You can't miss it.
    b. I didn't turn right, and I missed the street.
    c. I miss all my friends very much.
    d. He is in California now, and he misses his friends here in New York.

5. go

    a. Should I go this way, or that way?
    b. He goes this way, and I go that way.
    c. Yesterday I went to the restaurant at 6 p.m.
    d. I'm going to the restaurant tonight.

6. beg

    a. I beg your pardon.
    b. He begged my pardon.
    c. Every day he begs me to take several books home with me.

7. happen to

    a. Do you happen to know Mr. Cooper's telephone number?
    b. I just happened to know his telephone number.
    c. Yes, I know her. She happens to be my sister.
    d. Did you happen to listen to the radio last night?

VERB STUDY

1. **excuse** (면제하다, 용서하다, 방면하다)
   a. 실례합니다.
   b. 선생님은 어제 내가 수업에 빠지도록 해 주셨다.
   c. 선생님은 매일 누군가를 수업에 쉬게 해 주신다.

2. **give** (주다)
   a. 말 좀 해 주시겠읍니까?
   b. 쿠우퍼 씨는 내게 책을 한 권 주었읍니다.
   c. 죤은 매일 아침 나에게 신문을 줍니다.

3. **turn** (돌다)
   a. 다음 모퉁이에서 오른쪽으로 돌으시요.
   b. 그는 모퉁이에서 오른편으로 돌았읍니다.
   c. 페이지를 넘기십시요.

4. **miss** (만나지 못하다, 놓치다, 그리워 하다)
   a. 당신은 쉽게 찾아갈 수 있읍니다.
   b. 나는 오른편으로 돌지 않아서, 길을 찾지 못했읍니다.
   c. 나는 모든 친구들을 그리워 합니다.
   d. 그는 지금 캘리포니아에서 살고 있어서 이곳 뉴욕에 있는 그의 친구들을 그리워 하고 있읍니다.

5. **go** (가다)
   a. 이 길로 가야 합니까? 아니면, 저 길로 가야 합니까?
   b. 그는 이 길로 가고 나는 저 길로 갑니다.
   c. 어제 나는 오후 6시에 음식점에 갔읍니다.
   d. 나는 오늘밤 음식점에 가려합니다.

6. **beg** (빌다, 간청하다)
   a. 실례합니다.
   b. 그는 나에게 용서를 빌었읍니다.
   c. 그는 매일 나에게, 책을 집에 갖다 달라고 간청합니다.

7. **happen to** (우연히…하다)
   a. 혹시 당신은 쿠우퍼 씨의 전화 번호를 아십니까?
   b. 나는 마침 우연히 그의 전화 번호를 알고 있었읍니다.
   c. 예. 나는 그녀를 압니다. 그녀는 마침 내 누이 입니다.
   d. 혹시 당신은 지난 밤에 라디오를 들었읍니까?

---

* 새로 나온 단어와 어귀 *

excuse ~ from class 「~에게 수업을 쉬게 해 주다」 **turn the page** 「책의 페이지를 넘기다」 **beg me to** ~ 「나에게 ~해 달라고 간청하다」

SUBSTITUTION DRILLS

1. Excuse me, | sir / miss / Officer / Captain / Colonel | Can you give me some information?

2. Can you tell me where | Peach Street / the restaurant / the post office / the airport / the railroad station | is?

3. The post office is | two blocks straight ahead / two miles straight ahead / on the other side of the street | .

4. Which direction is it to | the theater / the post office / the university / the bank / the church | ? Do you know?

5. | Turn right / Turn left / Go straight ahead / Go to the right / Go to the left | at the next corner. You can't miss it.

6. How far is it to the university? | Can you tell me / Would you tell me / Could you tell me / Would you mind telling me | ?

7. It's a | long way / short distance / short walk / long drive | from here to the university.

8. The school is | just around the corner / in the middle of the block / right on the corner / up there on the left | . You can't miss it.

9. The restaurant is | across the street | from the hotel.
      | around the corner |
      | a mile |
      | a short walk |

10. Do you happen to know Mr. Cooper's | telephone number | ?
      | address |
      | profession |
      | age |
      | height and weight |
      | office address |

11. I don't happen to know | his | address.
      | her |
      | John's |

12. Could you tell me where the nearest | telephone | is?
      | hospital |
      | ladies' room |
      | men's room |

13. Where's the | post office | ? Should I go this way, or that way?
      | university |
      | bank |
      | airport |

14. Go that way for | two blocks | , then turn left.
      | a block or two |
      | about two miles |

15. I beg your pardon. Is this seat | taken | ?
      | occupied |
      | reserved |
      | reserved for somebody |

16. The restaurant is | up those stairs |
      | on the second floor |
      | down those stairs |
      | in the basement |

17. Isn't the restaurant | straight ahead | ?
      | around the corner |
      | in the middle of the next block |
      | right on the corner of Washington Street |

SUBSTITUTION DRILLS

1. 선생님
   아가씨
   나리
   대위님
   대령님

2. 피이치가
   음식점이
   우체국이
   비행장이
   철도역이

3. 앞으로 곧장 2 블록
   앞으로 곧장 2 마일
   길 건너편

4. 극장(에 가려면)
   우체국 (〃)
   대학교 (〃)
   은행 (〃)
   교회 (〃)

5. 오른편으로 도시오
   왼편으로 도시오
   곧 바로 앞으로 가시오
   오른편으로 가시오
   왼편으로 가시오

6. 말씀해 주실 수 있읍니까
   말씀해 주실 수 있읍니까
   말씀해 주실 수 있읍니까
   말씀해 주실 수 있읍니까

7. 한참 가야 됩니다.
   짧은 거리 입니다.
   조금만 걸으면 됩니다.
   한참 타고 가야 합니다.

8. 모퉁이를 돌면 바로
   그 블록 중앙에
   모퉁이에서 오른쪽에
   그 쪽 왼편 윗쪽에

9. (호텔)길 건너에
   (호텔)모퉁이를 돌아
   (호텔로 부터) 1 마일 되는 곳에
   (호텔에서) 잠깐 걸어가면

10. 전화번호를
    주소를
    직업을
    나이를
    신장과 체중을
    사무실 주소를

11. 그의
    그녀의
    죤의

12. 전화가
    병원이
    숙녀 화장실이
    신사 화장실이

13. 우체국이
    대학교가
    은행이
    비행장이

14. 두 블록
    한 두 블록
    2 마일 쯤

15. (앉은 사람)있읍니까
    (누가)차지한 겁니까
    맡아 놓은 자리입니까
    누군가가 맡아 놓은 자리입니까

16. 저 계단 위에
    2 층에
    저 계단 아래에
    지하실에

17. 바로 앞에
    모퉁이 근처에
    다음 블록 중간에
    와싱턴 가 모퉁이 오른쪽에

READING PRACTICE

Getting Information and Directions

Last week Bill had to go to New York. It was his first time there, and he didn't know his way around the city. He had a meeting at 10 o'clock, and he wanted to be on time. The meeting was in the Peterson Building on 34th Street, but Bill didn't know where that was. Seeing two men standing on a corner he asked them for directions.

"Pardon me," he said, "but can you tell me how to get to the Peterson Building on 34th Street?"

"Sure," answered one of the men. "You can get there in five minutes. Go to the next corner and turn left. Walk three blocks and there you are."

But the other man said: "There's a better way. Get on the bus here at this corner. It stops right near the Peters Building."

"Not Peters," Bill told him. "Peterson."

Then the first man said, "Oh, that's on *East* 34th Street, not *West* 34th. It's quite a distance from here. You'll have to take the subway."

But the second man told Bill: "No, don't go by subway. Take the crosstown bus. It goes to the Peterkin Building."

"Peterson. Not Peterkin." Bill looked at his watch. It was almost ten o'clock. "Thanks a lot," he said. "I think I'll take a taxi."

As he got into the taxi he saw the two men arguing and pointing in different directions. Next time he wanted to know how to get to a place, he'd ask a policeman!

Questions

1. Why did Bill have to go to New York?
2. What time was his meeting?
3. Who wanted to help Bill find the Peterson Building?
4. What did he finally do?
5. What did Bill want to do the next time he needed to ask directions?

READING PRACTICS

〔길 찾아 가는데 대한 대화〕

지난 주에 빌은 뉴욕에 가지 않으면 안되게 되었읍니다. 그는 거기에 처음 가는 것이어서, 시내의 지리를 잘 몰랐읍니다. 10시에 모임이 있어서 정시에 찾아가고 싶었읍니다. 그 모임은 34번가의 피터슨 빌딩에서 있었는데, 빌은 그 빌딩이 어디 있는지 몰랐읍니다. 길 모퉁이에 두 사람이 서 있는 것을 보고 그는 그들에게 방향을 알으켜 달라고 청했읍니다.

"실례지만" 그는 말했읍니다. "34번가의 피터슨 빌딩에 가려면 어떻게 가야 하는지 말 해 주시겠읍니까?"

"그러죠." 하고 한 사람이 대답했읍니다. "5분간 가면 그곳에 도착합니다. 다음 모퉁이까지 가서 왼편으로 도십시오. 그리고 세 블록을 걸어가십시오. 그러면 그곳에 이르를 것입니다."

그러나 다른 한 사람이 말했읍니다. "더 좋은 길이 있읍니다. 이 모퉁이에서 버스를 타세요. 버스가 피터스 빌딩 바로 가까이에서 정거합니다."

"피터스 빌딩이 아니라 피터슨 빌딩 입니다"라고 빌이 말했읍니다.

그러자 먼저 사람이 말했읍니다. "아, 그것은 동 34번가에 있지, 서 34번가에있지 않읍니다. 거긴 여기서 꽤 먼 거리 입니니. 지하철을 타야 할 겁니다."

그러나 두번째 사람은 빌에게 말했읍니다. "아뇨, 지하철로 가지 마세요. 시내 횡단 버스를 타면 됩니다. 그것이 피터킨 빌딩까지 가죠."

"피터슨 빌딩이지 피터킨 빌딩이 아닙니다."하며 빌은 그의 시계를 들여다 보았읍니다. 거의 10시가 되었읍니다. "매우 고맙습니다. 택시를 타고 갈 생각 입니다."하고 그는 말했읍니다.

그가 택시에 탔을 때 그는 두 사람이 서로 다른 방향을 가리키면서 다투는 것을 보았읍니다. 다음에 어떤 곳을 찾아 가고 싶을 때에는 순경에게 물어 봐야 되겠다고 그는 생각했읍니다.

＊ 새로 나온 단어와 어귀 ＊

his first time there 「그곳에 첫 나들이이다」 know his way around the city 「그 도시의 지리를 알다」 be on time 「정각에 가다」 Seeing two men standing~ 「~에 두 사람이 서 있는 것을 보고」 ask~ for ~ 「~에게 …을 청하다」 how to~ 「~하는 방법」 get to~ 「~에 도착하다」 ~and there you are. 「~하면 그곳입니다」 get on~ 「~을 타다」 take the subway 「지하철을 타다」 crosstown bus 「시내를 횡단하는 버스」 get into~ 「~을 타다」 arguing 「말다툼하고 있는」 pointing 「지적하고 있는」 in different directions 「각각 다른 쪽으로」 get there 「그 곳에 도착하다」

CONVERSATION

1. Getting directions

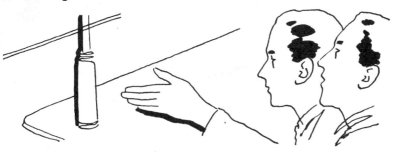

A: Excuse me. Can you tell me how to get to the post office?
B: Of course. It's very near here. Go to the corner and turn right. Walk one block and turn right again. Go across the street. The post office is on the corner. You can't miss it.
A: Thank you very much. I'm sure I'll find it.
B: There's one thing I forgot to tell you.
A: What's that?
B: Today is a holiday. The post office is closed.

2. Going to the movies

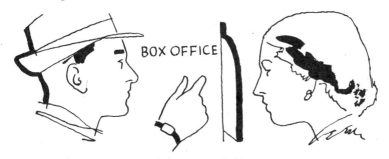

BOX OFFICE

A: What time does the complete show begin?
B: At seven o'clock. The first picture begins at seven-twenty.
A: How long does the complete program last?
B: The first show is finished at nine. The program lasts two hours.
A: Is the same picture on tomorrow night?
B: No. This is the last night.
A: Then I'll have to see it now. One ticket, please.

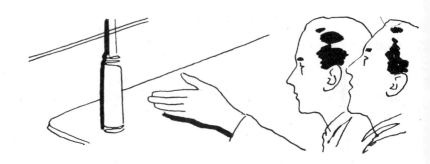

CONVERSATION

1. 방향을 묻는 말

   A. 실례합니다. 우체국은 어떻게 가야 하는지 말 해 주시겠읍니까?
   B. 그럽시다. 여기서 아주 가깝읍니다. 길 모퉁이로 가서 오른쪽으로 돌아
   가십시요. 한 구역을 걸어가서 다시 오른편으로 돌아가십시요. 그리고는
   길을 건너 가십시요. 우체국은 그 길 모퉁이에 있읍니다. 당신은 쉽게 찾
   아갈 수 있을 것입니다.
   A. 대단히 감사합니다. 틀림없이 찾아 가겠죠.
   B. 그런데 한 가지 잊은 것이 있읍니다.
   A. 무엇인데요?
   B. 오늘은 공휴일입니다. 우체국은 문을 안 열었을 겁니다.

2. 영화 구경

   A. 공연이 처음부터 시작 되는 건 몇시 입니까?
   B. 7시 입니다. 제 1 회 상영은 7 시20분에 시작합니다.
   A. 프로그램이 완전히 끝나려면 얼마나 걸립니까?
   B. 제 1 회 상영은 9 시에 끝납니다. 2 시간 걸리지요.
   A. 내일 밤도 같은 영화를 합니까?
   B. 아뇨. 오늘 밤이 마지막입니다.
   A. 그러면 지금 보아야겠군요. 표 한장만 주십시오.

✻ 새로 나온 단어와 어귀 ✻

   I'm sure 「나는 확신한다」 **one thing I forgot to tell you** 「너에게 얘기할
것을 잊어먹은 것 한 가지」 **is closed** 「문이 닫혀있다, 즉 휴무이다」
   complete show 「처음부터 끝까지 전부의 공연」 **last** 「계속되다」 **is finished** 「끝나다」 **Is the same show on～?** on은 be on이 되어 「상영되다」의 뜻.
The new picture is *on.* (새 영화가 상연 중이다) **one ticket** 「표 한장(주
쇼)」

EXERCISES

1. Use the right word.

far	miss	right
across	long drive	miles
straight ahead	corner	
way	taken	

a. Which _____ is it to the post office?

b. Go _____ for three blocks.

c. How _____ is it to the hotel?

d. Turn left and you can't _____ it.

e. The theater is _____ the street.

f. The airport is a _____ from here.

g. The bank is five _____ from the church.

h. Excuse me, is this seat _____?

i. I should turn _____ at this corner.

j. The house is around the _____.

Student A asks the following questions. Student B gives complete answers, using the information given in parentheses.

Example: Student A: Where are you going?
          Student B: (home) I'm going home.

a. A: Where is Peach Street?
   B: (two miles straight ahead)
b. A: How far is the bank?
   B: (five miles from here)
c. A: Where is the nearest restaurant?
   B: (across the street)
d. A: Which direction should I go to get to the post office?
   B: (to the right at the next corner)
e. A: Could you tell me where the nearest telephone is?
   B: (in the men's room or in the ladies' room)
f. A: Would you mind telling me where the school is?
   B: (in the middle of the next block)

g. A: Do you happen to know where the railroad station is?
   B: (*around the corner*)
h. A: Would you tell me where the National Theater is?
   B: (*right on the corner of Washington Street*)
i. A: How far is it from here to the airport?
   B: (*a long drive*)
j. A: Which direction is it to the university?
   B: (*about two miles to the left*)

3. Change the following sentences to questions beginning with the question words given.

   Examples: *He* is a student. Who *is a student?*
   He's going *to the university.* Where *is he going?*

   a. The church is *a long way* from here. How far _____?
   b. The bank is *across the street.* Where _____?
   c. This seat is reserved for *Mr. Cooper.* Who _____?
   d. I don't know my *neighbor's* address. Whose _____?
   e. We should turn *right* at the next corner. Which way _____?
   f. *The restaurant* is a short walk from the hotel. What _____?
   g. *The school* is around the corner. What _____?
   h. *The officer* gave me some information. Who _____?
   i. The National Theater is *straight ahead.* Which way _____?
   j. The telephone is *in the basement.* Where _____?
   k. The post office will open *at 8 a.m.* What time _____?
   l. Mr. Cooper is *sixty-one years old.* How old _____?
   m. The airport is *ten miles* from the town. How far _____?
   n. I'm going to school *this afternoon.* When _____?
   o. This table is reserved for Mr. Cooper *every day.* How often _____?
   p. This is *John's* telephone number. Whose _____?
   q. *The seat near the window* is occupied. Which seat _____?

WORD LIST

across	drive	railroad
airport	height	reserved
around	information	seat
bank	ladies' room	sir
basement	men's room	stairs
captain	miss	station
church	number	straight ahead
colonel	occupied	up
corner	officer	walk
direction	post office	way
down	profession	

Verb Forms	Expressions
happen to, happened to (*p. and p. part.*)	be taken
miss, missed (*p. and p. part.*)	I beg your pardon
turn, turned (*p. and p. part.*)	

Supplementary Word List
(Conversation and Reading Practice)

better	east	policeman
building	find	subway
bus	holiday	ticket
complete	last	west
crosstown	pointing	

UNIT *4* TALKING ABOUT FAMILY AND RELATIVES

346 Are you married?
347 No, I'm not married. I'm still single.
348 Your niece is engaged, isn't she?
349 My sister has been engaged for two months.
350 My grandfather got married in 1921.
351 When is your grandparents' wedding anniversary?
352 How long have they been married?
353 They've been married for quite a few years.
354 Who did George marry?
355 Do they have children?
356 They had a baby last month.
357 My son wants to get married in June.
358 They don't know when the wedding will be.
359 Their grandchildren are grown up now.
360 She's a widow. Her husband died last year.

UNIT 4 TALKING ABOUT FAMILY AND RELATIVES

346. 당신은 결혼하셨읍니까?
347. 아뇨. 결혼하지 않았읍니다. 나는 아직 독신입니다.
348. 당신의 질녀는 약혼했죠, 안 그래요?
349. 나의 누이는 약혼한지 2개월 됩니다.
350. 나의 할아버지는 1921년에 결혼하셨읍니다.
351. 당신의 조부모님의 결혼 기념일은 언제입니까?
352. 그들은 결혼한지 얼마나 됩니까?
353. 그들은 결혼한지 겨우 몇년됩니다.

354. 죠오지는 누구와 결혼했읍니까?·
355. 그들은 아이가 있읍니까?
356. 그들은 지난달에 애기를 낳았읍니다.
357. 내 아들은 6월에 결혼하고 싶어합니다.
358. 그들은 결혼 날짜가 언제가 될런지 아직 모릅니다.
359. 그들의 손자들이 이젠 어른이 되었읍니다.
360. 그녀는 과부입니다. 그녀의 남편은 작년에 죽었읍니다.

＊ 새로 나온 단어와 어귀 ＊

marry 「~와 결혼하다」 be married 「결혼 해 있다→결혼 생활 중이다」 single married의 반대. niece 「질녀, 여조카」 be engaged 「약혼해 있다→약혼 중이다」 grandfather 「조부」 get married 「결혼하다」 wedding 「결혼」 anniversary 「기념일」 baby 「아이, 애기」 grandchildren 「손자」 be grown up 「성인이 되어 있다→성인이다」 widow 「과부」 husband 「남편」

문 법

346. Are you married? : 「be+과거분사」는 수동태라 한다. 「어떤 동작을 행하다」를 능동태라 함에 반해서 「어떤 동작이 행해지다」라고, 동작을 받는 행위를 수동태라 한다.

수 동 태	능 동 태
read　　 (읽다)	be read　　 (읽히다)
see　　 (보다)	be seen　　 (보이다)
break　 (깨뜨리다)	be broken　 (깨어지다)

특히 동사가 수동이 되면 「상태」에 중점을 두게 되어, be married의 경우 「결혼해 있다→결혼생활 중이다→기혼이다」의 뜻을 갖게 되고, be engaged 의 경우 「약혼해 있다→약혼 중이다→약혼한 신분이다」의 뜻이 된다. 그러나 「get+과거분사」가 되면 「동작」에 중점을 두게 되어 get married「결혼하다」, get engaged 「약혼하다」의 뜻이 된다.

349. My sister has been engaged for two months. : 어떤 상태가 과거 어느 때부터 현재까지 계속되어 왔음을 나타내는 현재완료 용법이다. 게다가 수동태까지 겸한 문장이다. 이때 for~ months (days, weeks, years) 혹은 How long~? 이 주로 쓰인다.

How long have they been married?
(결혼한 상태가(오늘까지) 얼마나 오랫동안 계속되어 왔는가→결혼한지 얼마나 되었는가?)

They've been married *for quite a few years.*
(결혼한 상태가(현재까지) 몇년 동안 계속되어 왔다→결혼한지 몇년된다)

My sister has been married *for two months.*
(내 누이는 결혼한지 두 달이다)

How many years have they been married?
(그들이 결혼한지 몇년이 되었는가?)

354. Who did George marry? : 원래는 whom did George marry? 이어야 한다. 그러나 회화체에서는 문장 서두에서 whom 대신에 who가 주로 쓰인다.

358. They don't know when the wedding will be. : They don't know(그들은 알지 못한다)+when the wedding will be(결혼식이 언제가 될런지)

359. ~are grown up now. : 위에 말한 「상태」의 수동태로서 「자라 있다→인제는 어른이다」의 뜻.

INTONATION

346 Are you married?

347 No, I'm not married. I'm still single.

348 Your niece is engaged, isn't she?

349 My sister has been engaged for two months.

350 My grandfather got married in nineteen twenty-one.

351 When is your grandparents' wedding anniversary?

352. How long have they been married?

353 They've been married for quite a few years.

354 Who did George marry?

355 Do they have children?

356 They had a baby last month.

357 My son wants to get married in June.

358 They don't know when the wedding will be.

359 Their grandchildren are grown up now.

360 She's a widow. Her husband died last year.

VERB STUDY

1. **marry**
   a. Who did George marry?
   b. George married Elizabeth.
   c. He married her last year.

2. **be married**
   a. Are you married?
   b. No, I'm not married.
   c. My brother isn't married either.
   d. Was he married in California?

3. **get married**
   a. My grandfather got married in 1921.
   b. My son wants to get married in June.
   c. She's getting married tonight.

4. **be engaged (have been engaged)**
   a. Your niece is engaged, isn't she?
   b. I'm engaged.
   c. When I met her, she was engaged.
   d. My sister has been engaged for two months.
   e. How long have they been engaged?

5. **want to**
   a. My son wants to get married in June.
   b. Does she want to get married this year?
   c. I wanted to have breakfast at 6 o'clock this morning.
   d. We want to go home now.

6. **die**
   a. Her husband died last year.
   b. Did his cousin die last July?
   c. His grandfather died in California.

VERB STUDY

1. **marry** (결혼하다) ········능동
   a. 죠오지는 누구와 결혼 했읍니까?
   b. 죠오지는 엘리자벹과 결혼 했읍니다.
   c. 그는 작년에 그녀와 결혼 했읍니다.

2. **be married** (기혼이다) ········상태수동
   a. 당신은 기혼입니까?
   b. 아니오, 나는 기혼이 아닙니다.
   c. 나의 동생도 역시 기혼이 아닙니다.
   d. 그는 캘리포니아에서 결혼했읍니까?

3. **get married** (결혼하다) ········동작 수동
   a. 나의 할아버지는 1921년에 결혼하셨읍니다.
   b. 나의 아들은 6 월에 결혼하고 싶어 합니다.
   c. 그녀는 오늘 밤에 결혼합니다.

4. **be engaged**〔**have been engaged**〕 (약혼 중이다 〔지금까지 약혼 중이다〕)
   a. 당신의 질녀는 약혼 중이겠죠, 안 그래요?
   b. 나는 약혼 중입니다.
   c. 내가 그녀를 만났을 때 그녀는 약혼 중이었읍니다.
   d. 나의 누이는 약혼한지 2 개월이 됩니다.
   e. 그들은 약혼한지 얼마나 됩니까?

5. **want to** (…하고 싶다)
   a. 나의 아들은 6 월에 결혼하고 싶어합니다.
   b. 그녀는 금년에 결혼하고 싶어합니까?
   c. 나는 오늘 아침 6 시에 아침식사를 하고 싶었읍니다.
   d. 우리는 지금 집에 가고 싶읍니다.

6. **die** (죽다)
   a. 그녀의 남편은 작년에 죽었읍니다.
   b. 그의 사촌은 지난 7 월에 죽었읍니까?
   c. 그의 할아버지는 캘리포니아에서 돌아가셨읍니다.

＊ 새로 나온 단어와 어귀 ＊
Was he married～?는 get married와 거의 같은 뜻이다.

SUBSTITUTION DRILLS

1. My cousin is | still single |.
   | a bachelor |
   | an only child |

2. Your niece is | engaged | , isn't she?
   | married |

3. My sister has been | engaged | for two months.
   | married |

4. My | grandfather | got married in 1945.
   | grandmother |
   | grandson |
   | granddaughter |

5. | How long | have they been married?
   | Approximately how long |
   | How many years |
   | Exactly how many years |

6. I'm single, and my | cousin | is still single.
   | uncle |
   | nephew |
   | brother |

7. Is your | niece | married?
   | aunt |
   | cousin |
   | sister |

8. When did your | cousin | get married? Was it last year?
   | uncle |
   | aunt |
   | friend |

9. Who did | George | marry?
   | you |
   | she |
   | your cousin |
   | Mr. Cooper |

10. Do Mr. and Mrs. Cooper have

| children |
| any children |
| several children |
| a child |

?

11. They had

| a baby |
| a child |
| another child |

last month, didn't they?

12.

| My son |
| My daughter |
| His brother |
| Our grandchild |
| Their cousin |

wants to get married in June.

13. Their grandchildren are

| grown up |
| married |
| engaged |

now, aren't they?

14. She's a widow. Her husband

| died |
| passed away |

last year.

15.

| I'm |
| He's |
| She's |
| They're |

not married.

16. They don't know when the wedding

| will be |
| is going to be |
| is supposed to be |
| will take place |

17. They've been married for

| quite a few years |
| many years |
| quite a long time |
| years and years |

.

18. When is your

| grandparents' |
| parents' |
| friends' |
| brother's |

wedding anniversary?

SUBSTITUTION DRILLS

1. 독신
   미혼남자
   독자

2. 약혼(중입니다)
   결혼(중입니다)

3. 약혼(한 처지 입니다)
   결혼(″   )

4. 할아버지는
   할머니는
   손자는
   손녀는

5. 얼마나
   얼마쯤이나
   몇 년이나
   정확히 몇 년이나

6. 사촌은
   아저씨는
   조카는
   형님은

7. 질녀는
   아주머니는
   사촌은
   누이는

8. 사촌은
   아저씨는
   아주머니는
   친구는

9. 죠오지는
   너는
   그녀는
   너의 사촌은
   쿠우퍼 씨는

10. 애들을
    애들이 좀
    애들이 여럿
    아이를

11. 애기를
    아이를
    아이를 또 하나

12. 내 아들은
    내 딸은
    그의 동생은
    우리 손자는
    그들의 사촌은

13. 어른이 되(었죠)
    결혼하(″)
    약혼하(″)

14. 죽었읍니다
    사망했읍니다

15. 나는
    그는
    그녀는
    그들은

16. (언제) ~일지
    (″) ~일지
    (″) ~일지
    (″)행 할지

17. 꽤 몇 년
    여러해
    꽤 오래
    무척 여러해

18. 조부모님의
    부모님의
    친구의
    형님의

READING PRACTICE

Talking About Family and Relatives

A golden wedding anniversary is a celebration of fifty years of marriage. Usually there is a big party for all the friends and relatives of the married couple. Just think what a lot of people this can be! There are sons and daughters, nieces and nephews, brothers and sisters, cousins, grandchildren—even great-grandchildren. Of course many old friends come, too.

Frequently, members of the family from different towns don't see each other very often. They are glad to come to an anniversary party.

But it can be a time of confusion for the children. It's hard for them to remember the names of all their relatives. "Albert," one mother will say, "this is your cousin George. He's really your second cousin because he's Dorothy's son. Dorothy is my first cousin. Her mother is Aunt Helen, my father's sister."

At times there are stepsisters, half-brothers and nieces-in-law. There are "aunts" and "uncles" who aren't relatives at all, but good friends of the family! It can be very confusing, but everyone has a good time.

Questions

1. What is a golden wedding anniversary?
2. Have you ever been to this kind of celebration?
3. What do we call the children of grandchildren?
4. Name four types of relatives.
5. How many cousins do you have? Do you know them all by name?

READING PRACTICE

〔일가 친척에 대한 대화〕

금혼식이란 결혼 50주년을 축하하는 의식입니다. 보통 그 부부의 친구와 친척들의 큰 파아티가 열립니다. 금혼식에는 얼마나 많은 사람들이 모일까 생각해 보십시요. 아들, 딸, 조카, 질녀, 형제, 자매, 사촌, 손자 때로는 증손자까지도 있읍니다. 물론 옛 친구들도 옵니다.

흔히 각기 다른 고장에서 사는 일가들은 그리 자주 만나지를 못합니다. 그래서 그들은 기념 파아티에 기꺼이 옵니다.

그러나 아이들에게는 이때가 당혹한 때가 될 수도 있읍니다. 아이들이 모든 친척들의 이름을 기억하기는 어려울 테니까요. 어떤 어머니는 이렇게 말하기도 할 겁니다. "앨버트야, 얘가 네 사촌 죠오지다. 이 애는 도로디 아줌마의 아들이니까, 정말은 네 육촌형제다. 도로디 아줌마는 나하고 사촌간이야. 그 아줌마의 엄마는 네 외할아버지의 누이인 헬렌할머니이시다."

때로는 이복 자매들과 이복 형제들 그리고 처 조카들도 있읍니다. 그리고 친척은 결코 아니지만, 가족과 아주 친분있는 "아줌마"나 "아저씨"들도 있읍니다. 그래서 무척 어리벙벙할 수도 있겠지만 모두들 재미있는 시간을 보냅니다.

＊ 새로 나온 단어와 어귀 ＊

golden 「금으로 된」 **anniversary** 「기념일」 **golden wedding anniversary** 「금혼식」 **celebration** 「축하, 의식」 **relative** 「친척」 **couple** 「부부」 **married couple** 여기서는 금혼식 「당사자 부부」 **great-grandchildren** 「증손자」 **nephew** 「남자 조카」 **confusion** 「혼란, 당황」 **cousin** 「사촌」=first cousin **second cousin** 「육촌」 **because** 「왜냐하면」 **confusing** 「혼란시키는, 당황시키는」 **at times** 「때때로」 **stepsisters** 「이복누이」 **half-brother** 「이복형제」 **niece-in-law** 「처나 남편 쪽 조카」 **have a good time** 「즐거운 시간을 보내다」

CONVERSATION

Meeting relatives

JEAN: I just got a letter from Aunt Caroline. You remember her, don't you, David? My great-aunt. Grandma Allen's sister.

DAVID: Yes, I remember. She's the one who has been married twice. Her first husband died, didn't he?

JEAN: That's right. And she has children from each marriage. Uncle Jim, her second husband, was married before, too. He has four children from his first marriage. He and Aunt Caroline have three.

DAVID: Then they are all your cousins, aren't they?

JEAN: I call them all cousin. All of Aunt Caroline's children are my second cousins, but Uncle Jim's children from his first marriage are not relatives of mine.

DAVID: What are they to each other?

JEAN: Let's see. Aunt Caroline's sons and daughters from her first marriage are Uncle Jim's stepchildren. Aunt Caroline is his children's stepmother. The children are stepbrothers and stepsisters.

DAVID: I've never understood that. I thought they were half-brothers and half-sisters.

JEAN: No. Half-brothers and half-sisters have the same mother or the same father. Aunt Caroline's and Uncle Jim's children are half-brothers and half-sisters to the other children.

DAVID: It's very confusing. But what does Aunt Caroline say in her letter?

JEAN: They're all coming to visit us next week.

DAVID: What? I'll never know who is who!

CONVERSATION

(친척과의 해후)

Jean : 캐럴린 할머니로 부터 편지가 왔어, 데이비드. 너도 할머님을 알고 있지? 나의 대고모이고 알렌 할머니의 언니야.

David : 응, 나도 생각나. 그분은 재혼을 하셨지. 첫 남편이 돌아가시고, 그렇지 않어?

Jean : 맞아. 그분은 두 번째의 결혼에서 다 자식들이 있어. 두 번째 남편 짐도 전에 결혼한 적이 있는 분이야.
아저씨는 첫번째 결혼에서 네 아이를 낳았어. 그리고 캐럴린 할머니와의 사이에서 아이를 셋 낳으셨지.

David : 그럼 그분들이 모두 너의 사촌이지, 안 그래?

Jean : 나는 그들을 모두 사촌이라고 하지, 캐럴린 할머니의 애들은 모두 나와 육촌 간이야. 그러나 짐 대고모부가 먼저 부인한테서 낳은 자식들은 나와 친척이 아니지.

David : 그들은 서로 어떤 관계야?

Jean : 어디 보자. 캐럴린 할머니가 첫 남편과 낳은 자식들은 짐 대고모부 한테는 의붓자식이지. 캐럴린 할머니는 아이들의 의붓어머니구. 그리고 그 자식들끼리는 의붓형제 자매가 되는 거야.

David : 어떻게 되는 건지 도무지 모르겠어. 난 그들이 서로 이복 형제자매라고 생각했는데.

Jean: 아냐, 이복형제 자매란 어머니가 같거나, 아버지가 같아야지. 캐럴린 할머니와 짐 대고모부가 낳은 자식들은 그분 두 사람사이에서 난 세 자식들에겐 서로 이복형제 자매간이지.

David : 그것 참 어리벙벙하군. 어쨌던 캐럴린 할머니는 편지에 뭐라고 했어?

Jean : 그들은 다음 주에 여기를 방문하겠다는 거야.

David : 뭐? 난 누가 누군지 전혀 모를거야.

＊ 새로 나온 단어와 어귀 ＊

got a letter 「편지를 받았다」 **the one who has been married twice** 「결혼을 두 번 한분」 **call~…** 「~를 …라 부르다」 **each other** 「서로」 **who is who** 「누가 누구인지」 **step sister**—어머니와 아버지가 틀린 형제. **half brother**—어머니가 같거나 아버지가 같은 이복형제

EXERCISES

1. **Complete the sentences with the appropriate word from the list.**

grandparents   aunt   uncle
cousin   grandchildren   niece
nephew   brother   sister
grandmother   grandfather   husband

    a. My father's parents are my ———.

    b. My mother's sister is my ———.

    c. My mother's brother is my ———.

    d. My uncle's son is my ———.

    e. My sister's daughter is my ———.

    f. My brother's son is my ———.

    g. My son's children are my ———.

    h. My uncle is my father's ———.

    i. My aunt is my father's ———.

    j. My father's mother is my ———.

    k. My father's father is my ———.

    l. My father is my mother's ———.

2. **Use the possessive form of the pronoun in each of the following sentences.**

    Example: *My* brother had another child. (*I*)

    a. ——— children want to get married. (*We*)

    b. ——— cousin has been married for a long time. (*I*)

    c. When is ——— grandparents' wedding anniversary? (*you*)

    d. ——— grandchildren are grown up now. (*They*)

    e. ——— wedding will take place in June. (*He*)

    f. ——— husband passed away last year. (*She*)

3. Use contractions whenever possible in each sentence.

   Example: I am not married. *I'm not married.*

   a. She is a widow. Her husband died last year.
   b. He is engaged to be married.
   c. They are going to have a baby.
   d. You are still single.
   e. They do not know when the wedding will be.
   f. She did not get married last year.
   g. Mr. and Mrs. Cooper do not have any children, but they would like to.
   h. George is not a bachelor; he has been married for a long time.
   i. I am a bachelor, but I would like to get married.
   j. They have been married for approximately three years.
   k. I am going to get married in exactly three days.
   l. My sister has been engaged for two months.
   m. Today is my parents' anniversary.

4. Attach a tag question to each of the following sentences as shown in the examples.

   Examples: He wants to study, *doesn't he?*
   He's going to school, *isn't he?*

   a. Your nephew is engaged.
   b. Your granddaughter got married in 1945.
   c. You're still a bachelor.
   d. They had a child last month.
   e. Yesterday was your anniversary.
   f. They've been married for many years.
   g. She's been a widow since last year.
   h. Mr. and Mrs. Cooper have several children.
   i. Your wedding will take place in June.
   j. You're engaged now.
   k. Your niece is married.
   l. You got married last year.

WORD LIST

anniversary
approximately
baby
bachelor
engaged
grandchild, grandchildren

granddaughter
grandfather
grandmother
grandparent
grandson
grown up

married
nephew
niece
single
wedding
widow

Verb Forms

die, died (*p. and p. part.*)
marry, married (*p. and p. part.*)
pass away, passed away
   (*p. and p. part.*)
take place, took place (*p.*),
   taken place (*p. part.*)

Expressions

be supposed to
get married

Supplementary Word List

(Conversation and Reading Practice)

because
call
celebration
confusing
confusion
golden

great-aunt
great-grandchildren
half-brothers
half-sisters
marriage
members

nieces-in-law
stepbrothers
stepchildren
stepmother
stepsisters

UNIT 5 TALKING ABOUT NEIGHBORS AND FRIENDS

361   Where did you grow up?
362   I grew up right here in this neighborhood.
363   My friend spent his childhood in California.
364   He lived in California until he was seventeen.
365   There have been a lot of changes here in the last 20 years.
366   There used to be a grocery store on the corner.
367   All of those houses have been built in the last ten years.
368   They're building a new house up the street from me.
369   If you buy that home, will you spend the rest of your life there?
370   Are your neighbors very friendly?
371   We all know each other pretty well.
372   A young married couple moved in next door to us.
373   Who bought that new house down the street from you?
374   An elderly man rented the big white house.
375   What beautiful trees those are!

UNIT **5** TALKING ABOUT
NEIGHBORS
AND FRIENDS

361. 당신은 어디서 성장했읍니까?

362. 나는 바로 이 이웃에서 자랐
읍니다.

363. 나의 친구는 어린 시절을 캘리
포니아에서 보냈읍니다.

364. 그는 17살까지 캘리포니아에
서 살았읍니다.

365. 이곳은 지난 20년 동안에 많
은 변화가 있었읍니다.

366. 그 모퉁이에는 식료잡화점이
있었읍니다.

367. 저 집들은 모두 지난 10년 사
이에 지어진 집들 입니다.

368. 그들은 나의 집 길 위 쪽에
새 집을 짓고 있읍니다.

369. 만일 당신이 그 집을 살 수 있다
면 당신은 거기서 여생을 보낼
것입니까?

370. 당신의 이웃들은 아주 친절합
니까?

371. 우리들은 모두 서로 잘 아는 사
이입니다.

372. 한 젊은 부부가 우리 옆 집에
이사 왔읍니다.

373. 당신 집 길 아래 쪽에 있는 새집
은 누가 샀읍니까?

374. 한 중년 남자가 그 큰 하얀 집에
세 들었읍니다.

375. 저것들은 얼마나 아름다운 나무
들입니까!

✽ 새로 나온 단어와 어귀 ✽

grow up「자라다」 **grew**=grow의 과거 **right here**「바로 여기」 **neighborhood**
「이웃」 **spent**=spend「보내다」의 과거. **childhood**「어린 시절」 **until ~**「~때까
지」 **change**「변화」 **last**「지나간」 **used to**「…였었다」 **grocery store**「식
료 잡화점」 **built**=build「짓다」의 과거·과거분사 **buy**「사다」 **if**「만일 …하면」
rest「나머지 전부」 **the rest of your life**「나머지 여생」 **neighbor**「이웃 사람」
friendly「친절한」 **pretly well**=very well「대단히 잘」 **married couple**「결혼
부부」 **move in**「이사하다」 **bought**=buy의 과거·과거분사. **rent**「빌리다, 세들
다」 **tree**「나무」

361. Where did you grow up?:

> You grew up *there.*
>
> <u>*Where*</u> did you grow up?

364. He lived in California until he was seventeen. : He lived in California(그는 캘리포니아에 살았다) + until he was seventeen(그가 17세가 될 때 까지)

366. There used to be a grocery store on the corner. : There was a store. 는 「가게가 있었다」는 사실을 말하고 있을뿐으로, 지금은 그대로 있는지 없는지와는 상관없다.

There used to be a store. 는 「늘 가게가 있었는데(지금은 없다)」는 뜻으로 현재와 관련되는 표현이다.

한편 on the corner 의 on 은 그 「주변」이란 뜻이고, at the corner의 at 는 바로 그 「지점」임을 나타낸다.

368. ~up the street from me.:

> *up* the street from me   (내 집에서 길 위쪽으로)
>
> *down* the street from me (내 집에서 길 아래쪽으로)

이 이외에 across the street, around the corner, on the corner, around the city 도 다 같은 표현이다.

369. If you buy that home, will you spend~? : If you buy that home(당신이 그 집을 사면) + will you spend~ (~을 보내시렵니까?) 이와 같이 문장을 거느리고 있는 if를 접속사라 한다. 접속사에는 이 이외의 after, before, since, and 등이 있다.

> *If* you purchase that home, will you spend the rest of your life there?
> (당신이 그 집을 사시면, 그곳에서 여생을 보내시렵니까?)
>
> *If* you rent that home, will you spend the rest of life there?
> (당신이 그 집에 세를 드시면 그곳에서 여생을 보내시렵니까?)
>
> We began to work *after* breakfast was over.
> (우리는 조반이 끝난후 일을 시작했다)
>
> My father died *before* I was born.
> (나의 아버지는 내가 태어나기 전에 돌아가셨다)
>
> *It* is three years *since* we began to learn English.
> (우리가 영어를 배우기 시작한지 3년이 되었다)
>
> He studied *and* I played. (그는 공부하고 나는 놀았다)

373. Who bought that new house~? : 이런 who를 의문대명사라 한다. 이 외에 what, why, how, where, when, which 등이 있다.

Who is he ? (그는 누구입니까?)

What makes you sad ? (무엇이 당신을 슬프게 만들고 있읍니까?)

Who gave you that ? (누가 그것을 당신에게 주었읍니까?)

When did you meet her ?

　(그 여자를 언제 만났읍니까?)

Why do you like him ?

　(왜 그를 좋아하세요?)

How did it happen ?

　(어떻게 해서 그런 일이 일어났죠?)

375. What beautiful trees those are ! : 감정을 강하게 나타내기 위해 쓰는 표현으로서 감탄문이라 한다. 감탄문은 what이나 how 를 써서 만드는데, 어느 것을 써야 할지는 형식상의 차이에 따라야 한다. 예를 들면 This is very long 과 This is a very long river. 의 경우 is 다음에 명사가 있느냐 없느냐에 따라서, 명사가 있는 경우 what를, 없는 경우 how 를 써서 만든다. 이를테면

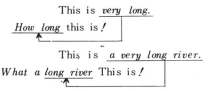

This is *very long.*

How long this is !

This is *a very long river.*

What a long river This is !

이와 같이 만든다.

Those are *very beautiful trees.*

What beautiful trees those are !

It is *a very lvely day.*

— *What a lovely day* it is ! (참으로 아름다운 날이로구나 !)

It is *very cold.*

— *How cold* it is ! (참으로 춥구나 !)

You look *very healthy.*

— *How healthy* you look. !

　　(당신은 무척 건강해 보입니다 !)

INTONATION

361   Where did you grow up?

362   I grew up right here in this neighborhood.

363   My friend spent his childhood in California.

364   He lived in California until he was seventeen.

365   There have been a lot of changes here in the last 20 years.

366   There used to be a grocery store on the corner.

367   All of those houses have been built in the last ten years.

368   They're building a new house up the street from me.

369   If you buy that home, will you spend the rest of your life there?

370   Are your neighbors very friendly?

371   We all know each other pretty well.

372   A young married couple moved in next door to us.

373   Who bought that new house down the street from you?

374   An elderly man rented the big white house.

375   What beautiful trees those are!

VERB STUDY

1. **grow up**
   a. Where did you grow up?
   b. I grew up here in this neighborhood.
   c. I've grown up here in this city.

2. **spend (one's) childhood**
   a. My friend spent his childhood in California.
   b. Where did you spend your childhood?

3. **build (be building)**
   a. They built a new house.
   b. They're building a new house up the street from me.
   c. Are you building a new house this year?

4. **be built (have been built)**
   a. Those houses were built last year.
   b. All of those houses have been built in the last 10 years.
   c. When were those houses built?

5. **move in (be moving in)**
   a. A young married couple moved in next door.
   b. When did they move in?
   c. You moved in yesterday, didn't you?
   d. They're moving in today.

6. **buy**
   a. Who bought that house?
   b. If you buy that house, will you live there several years?
   c. If he buys that house, will he live there several years?

7. **know (each other)**
   a. We all know each other pretty well.
   b. Do they know each other very well?
   c. Did they know each other last year?
   d. We knew each other in California several years ago.

8. **there has been, there have been**
   a. There have been many changes in the last 20 years.
   b. There has been a change in John in the last few days.
   c. Have there been many changes here in the last five years?

░VERB STUDY░

1. grow up (자라다, 어른이 되다)
  a. 당신은 어디서 자랐읍니까?
  b. 나는 이 이웃에서 자랐읍니다.
  c. 저는 이 도시에서 자랐읍니다.

2. spend (one's) childhood (어린 시절을 보내다)
  a. 나의 친구는 캘리포니아 에서 어린 시절을 보냈읍니다.
  b. 당신은 어린 시절을 어디서 보냈읍니까?

3. build [be building] 집을 짓다 [집을 짓고 있다]
  a. 그들은 새 집을 지었읍니다.
  b. 그들은 우리집에서 길 위쪽에 새 집을 짓고 있읍니다.
  c. 당신은 올해에 새 집을 지으십니까?

4. be built [have been built] (집이 지어지다, 집이 지어져 있다)
  a. 저 집들은 작년에 지어졌읍니다.
  b. 저 집들은 모두 지난 10년 새에 지어진 것들입니다.
  c. 저 집들은 언제 지어졌읍니까?

5. move in [be moving in] (…으로 이사하다 [이사하고 있다])
  a. 젊은 부부가 옆 집에 이사왔읍니다.
  b. 그들은 언제 이사했읍니까?
  c. 당신은 어제 이사를 하셨지요? 그렇지 않읍니까?
  d. 그들은 오늘 이사를 합니다.

6. buy (사다)
  a. 누가 그 집을 샀읍니까?
  b. 당신이 그 집을 산다면 몇년간은 거기서 사시겠지요?
  c. 그가 그 집을 산다면 그는 몇년간은 거기서 살테지요?

7. know [each other] (서로 알다)
  a. 우리는 서로 매우 잘 아는 사이입니다.
  b. 그들은 서로 매우 잘 아는 사이입니까?
  c. 그들은 작년에 서로 아는 사이였읍니까?
  d. 우리는 몇해 전 캘리포니아 에서 서로 알게 된 사이였읍니다.

8. there has been, there have been (있었다, 있어 왔다)
  a. 지난 20년 사이에 많은 변화가 있었읍니다.
  b. 지난 며칠 사이에 존에게는 좀 변화가 있었다.
  c. 지난 5년 사이에 이곳에는 많은 변화가 있었읍니까?

✳ 새로 나온 단어와 어귀 ✳

several 「여러…, 몇」 **several years** 「몇년」 **there has(have) been** ~은
There is (are) ~의 현재완료형.

SUBSTITUTION DRILLS

1. Where did | you / she / he / Peter and John / they | grow up?

2. I grew up | in this neighborhood / in this city / on a farm / in a little country town | . Where did you grow up?

3. My friend spent his | childhood / early childhood / early years / childhood years | in California.

4. He lived in | California / Texas / New York / Virginia | until he was seventeen.

5. There have been a lot of | changes / developments / improvements | here in the last 20 years.

6. There used to be a | grocery store / drugstore / department store / movie theater | on the corner.

7. | All / Some / A few / Many / Almost all | of those houses have been built in the last 10 years.

8. They're building a new | house / apartment house / building / office building | up the street from me.

9. If you | buy / purchase / rent | that home, will you spend the rest of your life there?

10. Are your neighbors very | friendly / kind / quiet / noisy | ?

11. | We all / Some of us / A few of us / Most of us / Three or four of us | know each other pretty well.

12. A young married couple | moved in / has moved in / is moving in / is going to move in | next door to us.

13. Who bought that new house | down the street / up the street / across the street / around the corner / two blocks | from you?

14. An elderly man | rented / has rented / is renting / is going to rent | the big white house.

15. What beautiful | trees / flowers / homes / trees and flowers | those are!

16. We all | know each other pretty well / see each other often / talk to each other every day / help each other all the time | . We're neighbors.

SUBSTITUTION DRILLS

3. 너는
   그녀는
   그는
   피터와 존은
   그들은

2. 이 이웃에서
   이 도시에서
   어떤 농장에서
   어느 작은 시골 마을에서

3. 어린 시절을
   아주 어린 시절을
   어린 시절을
   초년 시절을

4. 캘리포니아(에서)
   텍사스(″)
   뉴욕(″)
   버지니아(″)

5. 변화가
   발전이
   향상이

6. 식료잡화점이
   약국이
   백화점이
   영화관이

7. 모두
   어떤 것은
   몇 몇은
   많은 집들은
   거의 모두가

8. 집을
   아파아트를
   빌딩을
   사무용실 빌딩을

9. 산다(면)
   산다(″)
   빌린다(″)

10. 친절한
    친절한
    조용한
    소란한

11. 우리들 모두는
    우리들 중 몇 몇은
    우리들 중 두 세 명은
    우리들 대부분은
    우리들 중 서넛은

12. 이사왔읍니다
    (방금)이사왔읍니다
    이사를 하고 있읍니다
    이사를 오려고 합니다

13. 길 아래쪽에 있는
    길 위쪽에 있는
    길 건너에 있는
    모퉁이를 돌아서 있는
    2 블록 떨어져 있는

14. 빌렸읍니다
    (방금)빌렸읍니다
    빌리고 있읍니다
    빌리려고 합니다

15. 나무들
    꽃들
    집들
    나무와 꽃들

16. 서로 아주 잘 아는 사이입니다
    서로 자주 만납니다
    서로 매일 이야기 합니다
    언제나 서로 돕습니다

READING PRACTICE

Talking About Neighbors and Friends

Last summer, my wife Jane and I went to visit the town where we both grew up. We hadn't been there since we were married ten years ago.

First, we went to the neighborhood where my wife spent her childhood. It hadn't changed very much. The house where she was born was still there, but it was now a different color. The same neighbors still lived next door. They were very glad to see Jane, and asked us to come in and have a cup of coffee. We learned about all the neighbors, old and new. Jane had a very good time. As fast as one question was answered, she would ask the next. "What happened to the Dunbars who used to have the little yellow house on the corner?" "Who bought the old Johnson place in the next block?" "Do Fred and Martha Alberts still live down the street?" "What about Miss Burton who lived alone in that extremely big house around the corner?"

Then we went to see the neighborhood where I grew up. What a disappointment! It was all changed. All the old houses I remembered were gone and in their place were some very modern ones. I didn't know any of the people who lived there.

Someone has said that you can't go home again. Jane might not think so, but I believe this is true.

Questions

1. How long had it been since Jane and her husband visited their hometown?
2. Had Jane's neighborhood changed very much?
3. How did she learn all the news about her neighborhood?
4. Was Jane's husband's neighborhood the same as when he lived there?
5. Is it true that "you can't go home again"?

READING PRACTICE
〔이웃과 친구에 관한 대화〕

지난 여름, 아내 제인과 나는 우리가 함께 자랐던 읍을 방문하러 갔읍니다. 우리는 10년전 결혼한 후로 아직껏 가본 적이 없었읍니다.

먼저, 우리는 내 아내가 어린시절을 보냈던 마을 부근으로 갔읍니다. 그곳은 많이 변하지 않았읍니다. 아내가 태어난 집은 아직도 그대로 있었지만 집 색깔이 지금은 다르게 칠해져 있었읍니다. 그때의 이웃 사람들은 아직도 옆집에 살고 있었읍니다. 그들은 제인을 보고 매우 기뻐하였고, 우리에게 들어와서 커피 한잔 마시라고 했읍니다. 우리는 옛날의 이웃들과 새로운 이웃들의 이야기를 모두 들었읍니다. 제인은 아주 즐거운 시간을 보냈읍니다. 하나의 질문에 대한 대답이 끝나는 것 만큼이나 빨리 그녀는 다음 질문을 또 하곤 했읍니다. "모퉁이의 조그만 노란집에 살던 던바 네는 어떻게 됐나요?" "요 다음 구역에 있던 그 낡은 존슨관은 누가 샀나요?" "프레드와 마아더 앨버츠 네는 아직도 길 아래쪽에 살고 있나요?" "모퉁이를 돌아 있는 아주 큰 집에서 외로이 살던 미스 버튼은 어떻게 됐나요?"

그리고 나서 우리는 내가 자라난 마을 부근을 보러 갔읍니다. 얼마나 큰 실망을 했는지! 그곳은 완전히 변해 있었읍니다. 내가 기억하는 오래된 집들은 모조리 없어졌고, 그 자리에 아주 현대적인 집들이 들어서 있었읍니다. 그곳에서 살고있는 사람들은 어느 누구도 내가 아는 사람이 아니었읍니다.

누군가 사람이란 다시 고향에 갈 수는 없는 것이라고 말한 사람이 있읍니다. 제인은 그렇게 생각하지 않을런지 모르지만 나는 이말이 사실이라고 믿고 있읍니다.

✻ 새로 나온 단어와 어귀 ✻

had been there 「그곳에 가본 적이 있다」neighborhood where my wife spent her childhood 「내처가 어린 시절을 보냈던 마을 근처」 the house where she was born 「처가 태어난 집」 were glad to see~「~을 보고 기뻐했다」 as~as…「…만큼 ~ 하게」 as fast as one question was answered 「하나의 질문에 답해지는 것만큼 빨리 → 하나의 질문에 답해지자 마자」 What happened to~「~에게 무엇이 일어났는가? → ~는 어떻게 되었는가?」 the Dunbars who used to have~「~을 갖고 있었던 던바 네」 What about~?「~는 어떻게 되었는가?」 Miss Burton who lived alone 「혼자 살던 미쓰 버튼」 disappointment 「실망」 all the houses I remembered 「내가 기억하고 있는 모든 집들」 were gone 「사라지고 없었다」 the people who lived there 「그곳에 살고 있는 사람들」

CONVERSATION

I. Looking for a new house

SALESMAN: I think I have exactly the house you are looking for, Mr. James. It's in a very good neighborhood.

MR. JAMES: Fine. Is it near a shopping center?

SALESMAN: Yes, it is. The shopping center is just a short walk. And the school, too.

MR. JAMES: Good. Is the house very old? I'd like a new one.

SALESMAN: All the houses here are very modern. None of them are over five years old.

MR. JAMES: I'd like to see the house. From what you tell me it is just what I want.

SALESMAN: I can take you to see it now.

2. Neighborhood friends

MABEL: Have you met our new neighbors yet? They moved in last Saturday.

KITTY: No, I haven't. I understand they are renting the house. They aren't buying it.

MABEL: That's right. I've talked to one of the children. He's the same age as my son. There are five in the family: the parents, two sons, and a daughter.

KITTY: Let's go and welcome the new family to the neighborhood. I'm sure they'd like that.

MABEL: That's a good idea. Perhaps there is something we can do for them.

KITTY: Everyone was very kind when I moved here two years ago. It's good to feel welcome in a new neighborhood.

CONVERSATION

1. 새 집을 찾아서
   Salesman : 제임즈 씨, 저는 당신이 찾고 계시는 바로 그런집을 갖고있
             읍니다(→ 소개할 수 있읍니다). 이웃들이 아주 좋읍니다.
   Mr. James : 좋읍니다. 그 집은 쇼핑 센터에서 가깝읍니까?
   Salesman : 네, 그렇죠. 쇼핑센터는 바로 조금만 걸으면 있는걸요. 학교
             도 그렇고요.
   Mr. James : 좋읍니다. 오래된 집인가요? 나는 새 집을 원하는데.
   Salesman : 여기에 있는 집들은 모두 아주 현대식 이예요. 어느것도 5년
             이상 된 것은 없어요.
   Mr. James : 그집을 보고 싶군요. 당신이 내게 이야기하는 내용으로 보아
             바로 내가 원하던 집인것 같군요.
   Salesman : 지금 그 집을 보여드릴 수 있읍니다.

2. 이웃 친구들
   Mabel : 당신은 새로 온 우리 이웃을 벌써 만나 보셨나요? 그들은 지
           난 토요일에 이사를 왔어요.
   Kitty : 아뇨, 아직 못 만나 봤는데요. 저는 그들이 그 집에 세를 들
           고 있는 것으로 알고 있어요. 그들은 그 집을 사지 않았어요.
   Mabel : 그래요, 저는 어린애들 중 한 아이와 이야기를 했었어요. 그
           애는 우리 애와 동갑입니다. 식구는 다섯인데 부부와 아들 둘,
           그리고 딸 하나래요.
   Kitty : 가서 이웃에 사는 새로운 가족들을 환영 합시다. 그들도 좋아
           할거예요.
   Mabel : 좋은 생각이예요. 우리가 그들을 도와 줄만한 일이 있을지도
           몰라요.
   Kitty : 제가 2년전 여기로 이사해 왔을 때 모든 사람들은 아주 친
           절 했었어요. 새로운 동네에서 환영 받는다는 느낌은 좋은 일이
           예요.

* 새로 나온 단어와 어귀 *
the house you are looking for「당신이 찾고 있는 집」 look for「찾다」
shopping center「상점가」 over five years old「5년 이상 된」 from what
you tell me「당신이 내게 이야기하는 것으로 미루어 보아」 it is just what I
want「내가 바로 원하는 것이다」
the same age as my son 「내 아들과 같은 나이」 welcome「환영하다」
feel welcome「환영받는다고 느끼는 것」

EXERCISES

1. Use the right form of "grow up."
   Example: I *grew up* in Texas.

   a. Children _____ fast.

   b. John _____ in California.

   c. Where did they _____?

   d. They _____ in New York.

   e. Boys _____ to be men.

   f. A girl _____ to be a woman.

2. Use the right form of "wake up."
   Example: I *wake up* at 7 o'clock every day.

   a. Yesterday morning I _____ at ten o'clock.

   b. I usually _____ at eight.

   c. My family often _____ before 6:30.

   d. My brother _____ on time this morning.

   e. Last night they _____ at midnight.

3. Use the right form of "spend."
   Example: I *spend* every day at work.

   a. John _____ his childhood in New York.

   b. Will you _____ the night at my house?

   c. Yes, I'll _____ the night.

   d. I _____ last week in California.

   e. My sister _____ her childhood in Texas.

4. Complete the sentences with the correct word from the list.

on	up
from	until
of	in

   a. There have been a lot _____ improvements here.

b. I grew _____ in a small country town.

c. There used to be a grocery store _____ the corner.

d. A young married couple moved _____ next door.

e. We bought the new house two blocks _____ you.

f. He lived in Texas _____ he was seventeen.

g. An elderly man rented the house _____ us.

h. I spent my childhood _____ a farm.

i. Many of those houses have been built _____ the last ten years.

j. The movie theater is _____ the street from me.

5. Change the following sentences to exclamations as shown in the examples.

      Examples: That tree is large.
                What a large tree that is!

                Those are beautiful trees.
                What beautiful trees those are!

a. That is a large building.
b. Those flowers are beautiful.
c. You have quiet neighbors.
d. He had a happy childhood.
e. This neighborhood is noisy.
f. That couple is friendly.

6. Answer the following questions. Give short answers as shown in the example.

Example: Do you live in Virginia? *Yes, I do.*

a. Did Peter grow up on a farm? Yes, _____.

b. Did you spend your childhood in California? Yes, _____.

c. Has an elderly woman rented that new house? Yes, _____.

d. Do you know that couple next door? No, _____.

e. Are you building a new house next month? Yes, _____.

f. Has Mr. Jones bought that office building yet? No, ____.

g. Will Mrs. Jones buy a new house? No, ____.

h. Did Mary know Mrs. Jones last month? Yes, ____.

i. Have there been a lot of improvements in this neighborhood?

Yes, ____.

j. Are those neighbors very friendly? Yes, ____.

WORD LIST

beautiful	each other	kind
building	elderly	new
change	farm	noisy
childhood	flower	quiet
couple	friendly	the rest of
department store	grocery store	tree
development	improvement	until
drugstore		

Verb Forms

buy, bought (*p. and p. part.*)
build, built (*p. and p. part.*)
grow up, grew up (*p.*),
    grown up (*p. part.*)
move in, moved in (*p. and p. part.*)
purchase, purchased
    (*p. and p. part.*)
rent, rented (*p. and p. part.*)
spend, spent (*p. and p. part.*)

Expressions

all the time
know (someone)
spend (one's) childhood

Supplementary Word List

(Conversation and Reading Practice)

again	modern
alone	shopping center
changed	true
disappointment	welcome
idea	

REVIEW ONE

UNITS 1-5

1. Conversation Review and Practice

a. Weighing things

A: How much does that book weigh?
B: I don't know. Let's weigh it.
A: It weighs nearly two pounds.
B: This dark blue book weighs just as much as that green book.
A: How much does that table weigh? Can you tell me?
B: It's not awfully heavy, but I don't know the exact weight.
A: It must weigh about forty or fifty pounds.
B: I'd say it weighs nearly seventy pounds.
A: Can you tell me how much that typewriter weighs?
B: No, I can't. I don't know what the weight of the typewriter is.
A: How much do you weigh?
B: I don't know how much I weigh. Maybe I weigh about two hundred pounds.
A: Does your brother know his exact weight?
B: No, he doesn't. He doesn't know how much he weighs.

b. Measuring things

A: Will you please measure that window to see how wide it is?
B: It's twenty-eight inches wide.
A: How high is that window? Will you measure it?
B: It's not very high. It's forty-one inches in height.
A: This window is just as wide as that one, isn't it?
B: Yes, it is. But this window is higher than that one.
A: What's the width of those walls?
B: These walls are exactly two inches thick.
A: How wide is Jones Boulevard? Do you know?
B: I'd say it's about seventy-five feet wide.
A: Jones Boulevard is wider than Baltimore Avenue, isn't it?
B: Yes, it is. Baltimore Avenue is only fifty feet wide.

c. Asking for help

A: Will you please do me a favor?
B: Yes. What can I do?
A: Please bring me those magazines.
B: Here they are. They're not very heavy.
A: Now, would you help me move this heavy box?
B: Yes. Oh, this box is very heavy!
A: Yes, it is. Now, I have to wrap the box.
B: Let's put the box down on the table.
A: Fine. Get me a yardstick from the kitchen, will you?
B: Yes. What color is the yardstick?
A: The yardstick is yellow. And get me a hammer, too, will you?
B: Yes, I will. Here you are.
A: Would you mind mailing this package for me this afternoon?
B: I can't. I won't have time to mail the package.

d. Getting help

A: Would you please tell Mr. Cooper that I'm here?
B: Mr. Cooper is very busy right now.
A: Would you please ask him to call me tomorrow?
B: I'll ask him to call you.
A: Please bring me my coat. I hung it up in the closet.
B: Here's your coat. Is this your hat, too?
A: Yes, it is. Put my hat down on the table, will you please?
B: Yes. Would you mind doing a favor for me?
A: What can I do for you?
B: Would you mind mailing this letter for me?
A: I'll mail the letter for you. I'm not very busy today.
B: Thank you very much. If you're able to, please mail this
   package, too.

2. **Review Exercises**

Use the proper verb form.

a. How much does this typewriter _____? (*weigh*)

b. I _____ the suitcase this morning. (*weigh*)

c. I _____ last night's movie very much. (*like*)

d. This material _____ soft, doesn't it? (*feel*)

e. Last year Mr. Cooper _____ a good automobile. (*own*)

f. Does he _____ a dark blue book? (*have*)

g. My friend _____ the window to see how wide it was. (*measure*)

h. I don't know the weight of that book, but this one _____ two pounds. (*weigh*)

i. I already _____ John to help you. (*ask*)

j. Is he _____ you? (*bother*)

k. He _____ my coat in the closet an hour ago. (*hang up*)

l. Would you mind _____ this package? (*wrap*)

m. Would you do me the favor of _____ this milk into that glass? (*pour*)

n. They're _____ a new house up the street from me. (*build*)

o. You _____ yesterday, didn't you? (*move in*)

p. My friend _____ his childhood in California. (*spend*)

q. If he _____ that house, will he live there several years? (*buy*)

r. There _____ be a department store on the corner. (*use to*)

s. I _____ in a little country town not far from here. (*grow up*)

t. Who _____ that new house down the street from you? (*buy*)

u. What beautiful homes these _____! (*be*)

v. Would you mind _____ me how far it is to the university? (*tell*)

w. Could you tell me where the nearest telephone _____? (*be*)

x. My grandfather _____ in 1931. (*get married*)

y. Her husband _____ last year. (*die*)

z. My daughter _____ get married next June. (*want to*)

3. Answer the questions

a. What size suitcase do you own?

b. What street do you live on?

c. What's your address?

d. Do you know where Jones Boulevard is?

e. Have you ever measured a window to see how wide it was?

f. How much does a typewriter weigh?

g. Do you write many letters?

h. Do you happen to know Mr. Cooper's telephone number?

i. By the way, who is Mr. Cooper? Do you know him?

j. Are you married?

k. Do you know when your grandfather got married?

l. Where did you grow up?

m. Are your neighbors very friendly?

4. Conversation Practice

You are looking for Peach Street and the university, and a man gives you directions.

First you ask for information.

You:

The man:

You want to find Peach Street, and the man tells you where to go.

You:

The man:

Then you ask the man where the university is, and he tells you.

— — —

You thank the man and say good-bye to him.

— — —

5. Review Sentences

Study and review Base Sentences 301 to 375.

UNIT 6 TALKING ABOUT FUTURE ACTIVITIES

376 What time are you going to get up tomorrow morning?
377 I'll probably wake up early and get up at 6:30.
378 What will you do then?
379 After I get dressed, I'll have breakfast.
380 What will you have for breakfast tomorrow morning?
381 I'll probably have eggs and toast for breakfast.
382 After breakfast, I'll get ready to go to work.
383 I'll leave the house at 8:00 and get to the office at 8:30.
384 I'll probably go out for lunch at about 12:30.
385 I'll finish working at 5:30 and get home by 6 o'clock.
386 Are you going to have dinner at home tomorrow night?
387 Do you think you'll go to the movies tomorrow night?
388 I'll probably stay home and watch television.
389 When I get sleepy, I'll probably get ready for bed.
390 Do you think you'll be able to go to sleep right away?

UNIT 6 TALKING ABOUT FUTURE ACTIVITIES

376. 당신은 내일 아침 몇시에 일어 나려고 하십니까?

377. 나는 아마 일찍 잠을 깨어서, 6시30분에는 일어나게 될 것 입니다.

378. 그 다음에는 무엇을 하시겠읍 니까?

379. 나는 옷을 입은 다음에 조반을 먹을것 입니다.

380. 내일 조반에는 무엇을 드시겠 읍니까?

381. 나는 아마 조반에 몇 개의 달 걀과 토스트를 먹을 것입니다.

382. 아침 식사 후에 나는 일하러 갈 준비를 할 것입니다.

383. 나는 8시에 집을 떠나 8시30 분에는 사무실에 도착 할 것입 니다.

384. 아마 12시30분경에 점심 식 사 하러 나갈 것입니다.

385. 5시30분에 일을 끝마치고 6시 까지 집에 돌아올 것입 니다.

386. 당신은 내일 밤 집에서 저녁 을 들려고 합니까?

387. 당신은 내일 밤 영화를 보러 갈려고 생각하고 있읍니까?

388. 나는 아마 집에서 텔레비젼 을 보고 있을 것입니다.

389. 나는 졸리울땐 잘 준비를 하 게 될 것입니다.

390. 당신은 곧 잠이 들 수 있다 고 생각하십니까?

＊ 새로 나온 단어와 어귀 ＊

be going to~「~하려고 하다, ~할 것이다」 **probably**「아마도」 **get dressed**「옷을 입다」 **egg**「달걀」 **get ready to~**「~할 준비를 하다」 **by 6 o'clock**「6시까지는」 **stay home**「집에 있다, 외출하지 않다」 **get sleepy**「졸리워 지다」 **get ready for~**「~에 대한 준비를 하다」 **be able to~**「할 수 있다」 **right away**「즉시, 곧」

문 법

376. **What time are you going to get up~?:** be going to~는 「간다」는 뜻 이외에 「~하려고 한다, 할 작정이다」와 같은 미래의 뜻을 갖기도 한다.

What time *is* she *going to* get up? (그녀는 몇시에 일어나려 합니까?)

What time *is* he *going to* get up? (그는 몇시에 일어나려 합니까?)

What *are* you *going to* have for breakfast?

(조반으로 무얼 드시려 합니까?)

I'm going to have eggs and toast for breakfast.

(조반에 달걀과 토스트를 먹으려 합니다)

I'm not *going to* get up at 8 o'clock.

(8 시에는 일어나려 하지 않습니다)

377. **I'll probably wake up early~:** I'll 은 I shall이나 I will 의 단축형으로 서 「~할 것이다, ~하겠다」는 미래의 동작을 나타낸다.

378. **What will you do then?:** will you~는 「~하려 합니까?」라는 뜻. then은 「그러면, 그리고 나선, 그땐」의 뜻.

What *will you* do then? (그리고 나선 무엇을 하렵니까?)

What *will you* do at that time? (그때에는 무엇을 하렵니까?)

What *will you* do after that? (그후에는 무엇을 하렵니까?)

What *will you* do next? (그 다음에는 무엇을 하렵니까?)

379. **After I get dressed, I'll have breakfast.:** After I get dressed (옷을 입은후) +I'll have breakfast. (아침을 먹겠읍니다)

382. **~I'll get ready to go~:** get ready to~나 get dressed는 「동작」을 나 타내고 한편 be ready to~나 be dressed는 「상태」를 나타낸다.

get dressed (옷을 입다) \   *be dressed* (입고 있다)

get ready (준비하다)   *be ready* (준비가 되어 있다)

385. **~by 6 o'clock:** by 가 시간 앞에서는 「~까지는」의 뜻이다.

Can you finish this work *by tomorrow*?

(내일까지는 이 일을 마칠 수 있읍니까?)

I'll be here *by four*. (4 시까지는 여기에 있읍니다)

387. **Do you think you'll go to the movies~?:** Do you think (생각합니까?) + you'll go to the movies (영화관에 갈 것이라고)

389. **When I get sleepy, I'll probably get ready~:** When I get sleepy (내 가 졸리울 땐) + I'll probably get ready (나는 아마도 준비를 할 것이다)

INTONATION

376 What time are you going to get up tomorrow morning?

377 I'll probably wake up early and get up at six thirty.

378 What will you do then?

379 After I get dressed, I'll have breakfast.

380 What will you have for breakfast tomorrow morning?

381 I'll probably have eggs and toast for breakfast.

382 After breakfast, I'll get ready to go to work.

383 I'll leave the house at eight and get to the office at eight thirty.

384 I'll probably go out for lunch at about twelve thirty.

385 I'll finish working at five thirty, and get home by six o'clock.

386 Are you going to have dinner at home tomorrow night?

387 Do you think you'll go to the movies tomorrow night?

388 I'll probably stay home and watch television.

389 When I get sleepy, I'll probably get ready for bed.

390 Do you think you'll be able to go to sleep right away?

VERB STUDY

1. **get up**
   a. What time are you going to get up tomorrow?
   b. I got up at 6 o'clock yesterday.
   c. She gets up at 7:30 every day.
   d. I'm getting up right now.

2. **wake up, go to sleep**
   a. I'll probably wake up early tomorrow.
   b. I woke up at 6 o'clock yesterday morning.
   c. My brother wakes up at 9 o'clock every day.
   d. Do you think you'll be able to go to sleep right away?
   e. He goes to sleep at 11:30 every night.

3. **get dressed**
   a. I get dressed at 9 o'clock every day.
   b. He got dressed at 8 o'clock yesterday morning.
   c. She gets dressed at 7 o'clock every day.
   d. Did you get dressed before breakfast this morning?

4. **stay**
   a. I'll probably stay home tonight.
   b. He stays home every night.
   c. She stayed home last night.

5. **watch**
   a. I watch television after dinner every night.
   b. He watches television after breakfast each day.
   c. We watched television last night until midnight.
   d. Did you watch television last Sunday?

6. **do**
   a. What will you do then?
   b. What are you doing now?
   c. She does the same thing every day.

7. **leave**
   a. I'll leave the house at 8 o'clock tomorrow.
   b. He left the house at 9 o'clock yesterday morning.
   c. She leaves the house at 10 o'clock every day.

8. **be able to**
   a. Do you think you'll be able to sleep immediately?
   b. I'm always able to go to sleep immediately.
   c. Were you able to talk with Mr. Cooper yesterday?

VERB STUDY

1. **get up** (일어나다)
   a. 내일 몇 시에 일어날 예정입니까?
   b. 나는 어제 6시에 일어났읍니다.
   c. 그녀는 매일 7시 30분에 일어납니다.
   d. 나는 방금 일어나는 중입니다.

2. **wake up, go to sleep** (잠이 깨다, 잠 들다)
   a. 나는 아마 내일 일찌기 잠이 깰 것입니다.
   b. 나는 어제 아침 6시에 잠이 깼읍니다.
   c. 나의 형은 매일 9시에 잠에서 깹니다.
   d. 당신은 곧 잠이 들수 있다고 생각하십니까?
   e. 그는 매일 밤 11시30분에 잠에 듭니다.

3. **get dressed** (옷을 입다)
   a. 나는 매일 9시에 옷을 입읍니다.
   b. 그는 어제 아침 8시에 옷을 입었읍니다.
   c. 그녀는 매일 7시에 옷을 입읍니다.
   d. 당신은 오늘 아침, 아침 식사 전에 옷을 입었읍니까?

4. **stay** (머무르다)
   a. 나는 아마 오늘 밤에 집에 있을 것입니다.
   b. 그는 매일 밤 집에 있읍니다.
   c. 그녀는 어젯밤 집에 있었읍니다.

5. **watch** (〔주의깊게〕 지켜보다, 구경하다)
   a. 나는 매일 밤 식사 후에 텔레비젼을 봅니다.
   b. 그는 매일 아침 식사 후에 텔레비젼을 봅니다.
   c. 우리들은 어젯밤 한·밤 중 까지 텔레비젼을 보았읍니다.
   d. 당신은 지난 일요일에 텔레비젼을 보았읍니까?

6. **do** (어떤 일을 하다)
   a. 그 다음에는 무엇을 하시겠읍니까?
   b. 지금 무엇을 하고 있읍니까?
   c. 그녀는 매일 같은 일을 하고 있읍니다.

7. **leave** (떠나다, 출발하다)
   a. 나는 매일 8시에 집을 출발할 것입니다.
   b. 그녀는 어제 아침 9시에 집을 떠났읍니다.
   c. 그녀는 매일 10시에 집을 출발합니다.

8. **be able to** (…할수 있다)
   a. 당신은 곧 잘수 있을 것이라고 생각하십니까?
   b. 나는 언제나 곧 잠들 수 있읍니다.
   c. 당신은 어제 쿠우퍼 씨와 이야기 할 수 있었읍니까?

✱ 새로 나온 단어와 어귀 ✱

until midnight 「재 밤중까지, 자정까지」 the same thing 「똑 같은 것」 immediately 「즉시, 곧」=right away were able to~=be able to~의 과거

SUBSTITUTION DRILLS

1. What time

are	you
---	we
	they
is	she
	he

going to get up tomorrow morning?

2.

| I'll |
| We'll |
| You'll |
| They'll |
| She'll |
| He'll |

probably wake up early tomorrow morning.

3. What will you do

| then |
| at that time |
| after that |
| next |

? Will you get dressed?

4. After

I	get
you	
she	gets
he	

dressed, it will be time for breakfast.

5. After John gets dressed, he'll

| have breakfast |
| go to work |
| leave the house to go to work |
| read the newspaper |

6. What

| will you |
| are you going to |
| do you think you'll |

have for breakfast tomorrow morning?

7. After breakfast, I'll get ready to

| go to work |
| leave the house |
| write some letters |

8.

| I'll leave |
| I'm going to leave |
| Every day I leave |
| Yesterday I left |
| I used to leave |

the house at 8 o'clock.

9. | He'll get | home by 6 o'clock.
    | He's going to get |
    | Every day he gets |
    | Yesterday he got |
    | He used to get |

10. I'll finish | working | at 5:30.
    | eating dinner |
    | .writing letters |
    | reading the newspaper |

11. Do you think | you'll go | to the movies tomorrow
    | John will go | night?
    | Peter and John will go |

12. Do you think | you'll | be able to go to sleep right away?
    | John will |
    | your friend will |

13. What time are you going to get up | tomorrow morning | ?
    | the day after tomorrow |
    | next Tuesday morning |
    | a week from Saturday |
    | morning |

14. I'll be able to go to sleep | right away | .
    | immediately |

15. Will Mr. Cooper be able to | have breakfast | with us?
    | go out for lunch |
    | eat dinner |
    | watch television |
    | speak French |

16. Do you think you'll go to the movies | tomorrow night | ?
    | Saturday night |
    | next week |
    | next weekend |
    | a week from today |

17. John will probably wake up | early tomorrow morning | .
    | late this afternoon |
    | in the middle of the night |
    | at the crack of dawn |

SUBSTITUTION DRILLS

1.

너는	~입니까
우리들은	~입니까
그들은	~입니까
그녀는	~입니까
그는	~입니까

2.
나는
우리들은
너는
그들은
그녀는
그는

3.
그 때에
그 때에
그 다음에
다음 번에

4.

나는	~한 후
너는	~한 후
그녀는	~한 후
그는	~한 후

5.
아침 식사를 할(겁니다)
일하러 갈(〃)
일하러 가기 위하여 집을 출발할(〃)
신문을 읽을(〃)

6.
너는 ~하려 합니까
너는 ~하려 합니까
너는 ~할 생각입니까

7.
일하러 갈~
집을 떠날~
편지 몇 통을 쓸~

8.
나는 출발하려고 합니다
나는 출발하려고 합니다
매일 나는 출발합니다
어제 나는 출발했읍니다
나는 출발하곤 하였읍니다

9.
그는 도착할 것 입니다.
그는 도착하려고 합니다
매일 그는 도착합니다
어제 그는 도착했읍니다
그는 도착하곤 하였읍니다

10.
일을
저녁 먹기를
편지 쓰기를
신문 읽기를

11.
당신은 가려고
쫀은 갈 것이라고
피터와 쫀은 갈 것이라고

12.
너는
쫀은
너의 친구는

13.
내일 아침
모래
다음 화요일 아침에
토요일 아침부터 일주일 동안

14.
곧 바로
즉시

15.
아침식사를 할~
점심하러 나갈~
저녁을 먹을~
텔레비젼을 볼~
프랑스 어를 말할~

16.
내일 밤
토요일 밤
다음 주
다음 주말에
오늘부터 일주일 후

17.
내일 아침 일찍
오늘 오후 늦게
한 밤중에
새벽에

READING PRACTICE

Talking About Future Activities

Marie works hard in an office all week. On Saturday and Sunday she has a very busy social life. This weekend she's going to Boston. She has never been there and she wants to see as much as she can while she is there. This is Marie's plan:

When she finishes work on Friday afternoon, she'll take a taxi to the airport and fly to Boston. She'll go to her hotel and leave her suitcase there. Then she'll have dinner with some friends who live in Boston.

Marie's friends know Boston very well. They are going to take her to all the interesting places. Friday evening after dinner they are going to drive around the city in their car. That way Marie will be able to see Boston at night.

On Saturday morning Marie will get up early. After she has breakfast, her friends are going to drive her to the historic towns of Concord and Lexington. They will have lunch at a restaurant in Concord. Then they will visit Harvard University, which is in Cambridge, across the river from Boston. By that time it will be evening. Marie and her friends are going to go to a concert by the Boston Symphony Orchestra. There will be two symphonies by Beethoven on the program.

On Sunday, after visiting other interesting parts of the city, Marie will go to the airport and fly home. She knows she will have a good time in Boston. She'll probably want to visit it again some day.

Questions

1. Where is Marie going for the weekend? Has she been there before?
2. When is she leaving? How will she go to Boston?
3. What are Marie's plans for Friday evening?
4. Where will she go on Saturday?
5. Does Marie have any plans for Saturday evening? What are they?
6. Have you ever been to Boston?

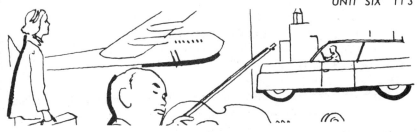

READING PRACTICE

〔미래의 동작에 관한 대화〕

마리는 사무실에서 1주일 내내 열심히 일합니다. 토요일과 일요일은 매우바쁜 사교적인 생활을 합니다. 이번 주말에 그녀는 보스턴으로 갈 예정입니다. 그녀는 그곳에 한번도 가 본 적이 없어서 그곳에 머무르는 동안 될 수 있는한 많이 구경하기를 원합니다. 마리의 계획은 이렇읍니다.

그녀는 금요일 오후 일을 끝 마친 후 택시를 타고 공항으로 나가 보스턴으로 비행할 것입니다. 그녀는 호텔에 들러 여행용 가방을 그곳에 맡겨 놓고, 그리고 나서 보스턴에 사는 몇몇 친구들과 저녁을 같이 먹을 것입니다.

마리의 친구들은 보스턴을 잘 압니다. 그들은 그녀를 온갖 재미 있는 곳으로 데리고 다닐 것입니다. 금요일 저녁 식사를 마친 다음 그들은 그들의 차로 시가지 주위를 드라이브 할 것입니다. 그런 방법으로 마리는 보스턴의 야경을 볼 수 있을 것입니다.

토요일 아침에 마리는 일찍 일어날 것입니다. 아침 식사 후에 그녀의 친구들은 그녀를 데리고 콩코오드와 렉싱턴의 역사적인 도시로 드라이브할 예정입니다. 그들은 콩코오드의 한 식당에서 점심을 먹을 것입니다. 그리고 나서 하버드 대학을 방문할 것입니다. 그 대학은 보스턴에서 강 건너인 케임브리지에 있읍니다. 그때 쯤이면 저녁 때가 될 것입니다. 마리와 그녀의 친구들은 보스턴 교향악단이 연주하는 음악회에 갈 것입니다. 연주 곡목에는 베토오벤의 교향곡이 두가지나 있을 것입니다.

일요일에 그 도시의 딴 재미있는곳 들을 찾아 보고 나서 마리는 공항으로 나가 비행기를 타고 돌아올 것입니다. 그녀는 보스톤에서 즐거운 시간을 보낼 것임을 압니다. 그녀는 아마도 언젠가 다시 한번 방문 하기를 바랄 것입니다.

✻ 새로 나온 단어와 어귀 ✻

all week「일주일 내내」 busy「바쁜」 social life「사교생활」 has been「가본적이 있다」 as much as she can「가능한 많이」 take a tax「택시를 타고 ~에 가다」 fly to~「비행기를 타고 ~에 가다」 leave her suitcase「가방을 맡겨 놓다」 friends who live in Boston「보스톤에 살고 있는 친구들」 take her to~「그녀를 ~로 데리고 가다」 drive around the city「그 도시 주변으로 드라이브를 하다」 interesting「재미있는」 that way「그런 식으로」 historic「역사적인, 유서 깊은」 which is in Cambridge=Havard University is in Cambridge. by that time「그때 까지는」 symphony「교향곡」 on the program「푸로에 따라서」

CONVERSATION

Detectives at work

DETECTIVE A: We don't have much time, so listen to me. I'll tell you what we are going to do.

DETECTIVE B: I'll write it down while you're talking.

A: The man we want does everything at exactly the same time every evening. I've watched him for three days.

B: You don't think he'll change his plan tonight, do you?

A: I'm sure he won't. At 7 o'clock he'll come down those stairs and go into the restaurant next door.

B: Are you sure he'll eat in that restaurant and not in another one?

A: He'll eat in that one. He'll get a steak, a baked potato, and a tossed green salad.

B: Where will he sit?

A: He'll take the first table by the window. And he'll look out at the street.

B: We'll have to be careful when we go into the restaurant to get him.

A: We won't go into the restaurant. We don't want him to see us.

B: What will we do?

A: We'll wait for him in the street. We'll get him when he finishes eating and leaves the restaurant.

B: Look! There he is now. Let's go.

CONVERSATION

근무 중인 형사들

형사 A : 우리는 시간이 많지 않네. 그러므로 내 말을 듣게. 자네에게 우리들이 하려하는 일을 말 하겠네.

형사 B : 나는 자네가 말하는 동안에 그것을 적겠네.

형사 A : 우리가 찾는자는 매일 저녁 틀림없이 똑같은 시간에 모든 일을 하네. 나는 3일간 그를 감시 해 왔어.

형사 B : 자네는 그가 오늘밤 계획을 변경 하리라고는 생각하지 않겠지 ?

형사 A : 그는 그럴리 없어. 7시에 이 계단을 내려와서 이웃집 식당으로 들어갈 걸세.

형사 B : 자네는 그가 딴 곳이 아닌 저 식당에서 식사 하리라고 확신하나 ?

형사 A : 그는 저 집에서 먹을 걸세 그는 스테이크와 구운 감자 그리고 비빔야채 샐러드를 먹을걸세.

형사 B : 그는 어디에 앉나 ?

형사 A : 그는 창가의 첫번째 테이블을 차지할 걸세. 그리고 그는 거리를 내다볼 걸세.

형사 B : 우리가 그를 체포하러 식당 안으로 들어갈 때 조심해야 되겠군.

형사 A : 식당 안으로 들어가지 말아야지. 그가 우리를 보는 것은 원치 않네.

형사 B : 어떻게 하나 ?

형사 A : 우리는 거리에서 그를 기다려야 하네, 그가 식사를 끝내고 식당을 나올 때 체포 해야지.

형사 B : 보게, 저기 그가 있군, 자아 가보세.

✻ 새로 나온 단어와 어귀 ✻

detective「탐정, 형사」 what we are going to do「우리가 하려 하는 것」 write down「기록하다」 while you are talking「네가 말하는 동안」 the man we want 「우리가 원하는 자 → 우리가 잡고자 하는 자」 change「바꾸다, 변경하다」 stairs 「층계」 bake「굽다」 potato「감자」 by the window「창가의」 careful「조심스러운」 to get him「그를 체포하려고」

EXERCISES

1. Complete the sentences with the correct form of the verb in parentheses.

   Examples: Yesterday I *went* to school. (*go*)

   I *go* to school every day. (*go*)

   I *will go* to school tomorrow. (*go*)

   a. Yesterday I _____ the house at 8:00. (*leave*)

   b. I _____ the house at 8:00 every day. (*leave*)

   c. I _____ the house at 8:00 tomorrow. (*leave*)

   d. I _____ to work last week. (*go*)

   e. I _____ to work today. (*go*)

   f. I _____ to work tomorrow morning. (*go*)

   g. I _____ late yesterday. (*be*)

   h. If I don't hurry, I _____ late today. (*be*)

   i. John _____ in the middle of last night. (*wake up*)

   j. John _____ at the crack of dawn tomorrow. (*wake up*)

   k. I _____ television last Saturday. (*watch*)

   l. I _____ television next Tuesday morning. (*watch*)

2. Use contractions wherever possible in the following sentences.

   Examples: I will go to school tonight. *I'll go to school tonight.*

   I will not go to school tonight.

   I won't go to school tonight.

   a. John will probably wake up soon.

   b. He will have breakfast after he wakes up.

   c. Then he will get ready to go to work.

   d. After that he will leave the house.

e. He will read the newspaper on the way to work.

f. John will not wake up in the middle of the night.

g. He will not go out for breakfast.

h. He will not leave the house before breakfast.

i. He will not finish working until 5:30.

j. He will not get home by 6:30.

k. He will get home at 7:00.

l. He will be able to eat dinner with us.

m. Next he will probably watch television.

n. After that he will go to sleep.

3. Change each of the following to a question beginning "Do you think . . . ?" Follow the examples. Use contractions wherever possible.

   Examples: Will John go to school tonight?
   Do you think John'll go to school tonight?

   Did he go to school last night?
   Do you think he went to school last night?

a. Will you finish reading the newspaper at 5:30?

b. Did he get home by 6:00 yesterday?

c. Will John go to the movies with us?

d. Will she be able to go out for lunch?

e. Did they wake up early yesterday morning?

f. Did he use to leave the house at 8 o'clock?

g. Will you be able to make some phone calls after breakfast?

h. Did they write some letters after breakfast?

i. Will we finish working at 5:30?

j. Will I be able to get home by 6 o'clock?

k. Did your friend go to sleep right away?

l. Did John make some phone calls early this morning?

m. Will she be ready to go to work right away?

n. Will Mr. Cooper be able to eat dinner with us a week from today?

WORD LIST

egg
probably
weekend

Verb Forms	**Expressions**
stay, stayed (*p. and p. part.*)	crack of dawn
	get ready
	get sleepy

Supplementary Word List

.(Conversation and Reading Practice)

baked potato	drive	social
careful	fly	steak
change	historic	symphonies
concert	plan	tossed salad
detectives	river	

UNIT 7 TALKING ABOUT THE WEATHER

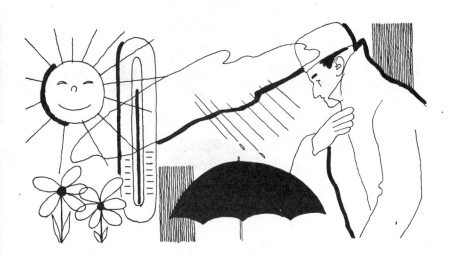

391 How is the weather today?
392 The weather is nice today.
393 What was the weather like yesterday?
394 Yesterday it rained all day.
395 What will the weather be like tomorrow?
396 It's going to snow tomorrow.
397 It's quite cold today.
398 It's been cloudy all morning.
399 Is it raining now?
400 It'll probably clear up this afternoon.
401 The days are getting hotter.
402 Today is the first day of spring.
403 What's the temperature today?
404 It's about seventy degrees Fahrenheit this afternoon.
405 There's a cool breeze this evening.

UNIT 7 TALKING ABOUT THE WEATHER

391. 오늘은 날씨가 어떻읍니까?
392. 오늘은 날씨가 좋읍니다.
393. 어제 날씨는 어떠했읍니까?
394. 어제는 종일 비가 왔읍니다.
395. 내일 날씨는 어떨까요?
396. 내일은 눈이 올 것입니다.
397. 오늘은 꽤 춥읍니다.
398. 오전 내내 구름이 껴 있었읍니다.
399. 지금 비가 오고 있읍니까?

400. 오후에는 아마 개일것입니다.
401. 날씨가 점점 더 더워지고 있읍니다.
402. 오늘은 봄의 첫 날 입니다.
403. 오늘은 몇 도 입니까?
404. 오늘 오후에는 화씨 약 70도 입니다.
405. 오늘 저녁에는 시원한 산들바람이 붑니다.

---

* 새로 나온 단어와 어귀 *

weather「날씨」 nice「멋있는, 훌륭한」 be like「~와 같다」 rain「비가 오다」 snow「눈이 오다」 cold「추운」 cloudy「구름 낀」 clear up「개이다」 get hotter「더욱 더 더워지다」 temperature「온도」 degree「…도」 Fahrenheit「화씨」 cool「시원한」 breeze「산들바람」

문 법

391. How is the weather today? : 날씨를 물을 경우 How is the weather?
와 What is the weather like? 두가지가 있다. What is the weather like
? 는 is like what(무엇과 같은가?)의 의미이다.
가령 what is it? 는 「그것은 무엇인가?」
What is it like? 는 「그것은 무엇과 같은 모습인가?」와 같은 의미상의 차
이가 있다.

394. ~it rained~. It rained. 는 「비가 왔다」 It snowed. 「눈이 왔다」의 뜻
으로서,

현재형 { It *rains.* / It *snows.* }   진행형 { It *is raining* / It *is snowing* }

현재완료형 { It *has rained.* / It *has snowed.* }   부정형 { It *does not rain.* / It *does not snow.* }

396. It's going to snow tomsrrow. : It'll snow tomorrow와 같다.
It's *going to* rain tomorrow. (내일 비가 올 것이다)
It's *going to* sleet tomorrow. (내일 진눈개비가 올 것이다)
It's *going to* hail tomorrow. (내일 싸락눈이 올 것이다)
It's *going to* drizzle tomorrow. (내일 이슬비가 내릴 것이다)

397. It's quite cold today. : 날씨·시간·거리등을 나타낼 때 막연히 it 를
주어로 한다. quite는 「상당히, 꽤」의 뜻.
날씨 — *It* is fine today. (오늘 날씨가 좋읍니다)
     It is cloudy today. (오늘은 구름이 끼었읍니다)
시간 — *It* is five o'clock. (5시입니다)
     It is Sunday today. (오늘은 일요일 입니다)
거리 — How far is *it* from here to the station?
     (여기서 정거장까지 거리가 얼마입니까?)
     It is a short drive.
     (차를 타고 조금만 가면 되는 거리입니다)

400. It'll clear up~ : clear up 「날씨가 개이다」 It 는 역시 「날씨」의 주어.

401. The days are getting hotter. : get는 뒤에 형용사가 오면 「…되다」의
뜻이 된다.
get better (더 좋아지다, 더 건강해지다)
get colder (더 추워지다)   *get* tired (피곤해지다)

403. What's the temperature today? : 이에 대한 대답 역시 「날씨」의 주어 it
를 주어로 해서 대답한다.
It is about 70 degrees Fahrenheit. (약 화씨 70도 입니다)
It is about three degrees centigrade. (약 섭씨 3도입니다)
Fahrenheit는 「화씨」, centigrade 는 「섭씨」

INTONATION

391 How is the weather today?

392 The weather is nice today.

393 What was the weather like yesterday?

394 Yesterday it rained all day.

395 What will the weather be like tomorrow?

396 It's going to snow tomorrow.

397 It's quite cold today.

398 It's been cloudy all morning.

399 Is it raining now?

400 It'll probably clear up this afternoon.

401 The days are getting hotter.

402 Today is the first day of spring.

403 What's the temperature today?

404 It's about seventy degrees Fahrenheit this afternoon.

405 There's a cool breeze this evening.

VERB STUDY

1. **rain**

   a. Yesterday it rained all day.
   b. Is it raining now?
   c. Do you think it will rain tomorrow?
   d. How hard did it rain last night?

2. **snow**

   a. It's going to snow tomorrow.
   b. It snowed all day yesterday, didn't it?
   c. Is it snowing now?

3. **clear up**

   a. It'll probably clear up this afternoon.
   b. It cleared up at about 3 o'clock yesterday afternoon.
   c. It clears up every day before 12 o'clock noon.
   d. It's clearing up now, isn't it?
   e. Has it cleared up yet?

4. **get (hotter), be getting (hotter)**

   a. The days are getting hotter.
   b. The days get hotter every week.
   c. Are the days getting much hotter?
   d. The days have gotten hotter, haven't they?

5. **have been**

   a. It's been cloudy all morning.
   b. Has it been cloudy all morning?
   c. I have been very well, thank you.
   d. Has she ever been in California?

6. **be like**

   a. What will the weather be like tomorrow?
   b. What was it like yesterday?
   c. The weather is nice today. It's just like a spring day.
   d. What is the weather like in Florida?

VERB STUDY

1. rain (비가 오다)
    a. 어제는 종일 비가 왔읍니다.
    b. 지금 비가 오고 있읍니까?
    c. 내일 비가 오리라고 생각합니까?
    d. 어제 밤에는 비가 얼마나 심하게 왔읍니까?

2. snow (눈이 오다)
    a. 내일 눈이 올 것입니다.
    b. 어제는 종일 눈이 왔죠, 그렇지 않읍니까?
    c. 지금 눈이 오고 있읍니까?

3. clear up (개이다)
    a. 오늘 오후에는 아마 개일 것입니다.
    b. 어제 오후 3시쯤에 개였읍니다.
    c. 매일 정오 12시 전에 개입니다.
    d. 지금 개이고 있죠?
    e. 벌써 개였읍니까?

4. get(hotter), **be getting**(hotter)　(더 더워지다, 더 더워지고 있다)
    a. 날씨가 점점 더워지고 있읍니다.
    b. 날씨가 매주 차츰 더워집니다.
    c. 날씨가 무척 더 더워지고 있읍니까?
    d. 날씨가 차츰 더워졌읍니다. 그렇죠?

5. have been (계속 …했다 ; …에 갔다 왔다)
    a. 오전 내내 흐려 있었읍니다.
    b. 오전 내내 흐렸읍니까?
    c. 그동안 건강했읍니다, 감사합니다.
    d. 그 여자는 캘리포니아에 갔던 적이 있읍니까?

6. be like (…와 같다)
    a. 내일 날씨는 어떨까요?
    b. 어제 날씨는 어떠했읍니까?
    c. 오늘은 날씨가 좋읍니다. 마치 봄 날씨와 같읍니다.
    d. 플로리다에서는 날씨가 어떻읍니까?

SUBSTITUTION DRILLS

1. How is the weather today | in California | ?
   | in New York |
   | in Florida |

2. The weather is | nice | today.
   | fine |
   | beautiful |
   | perfect |

3. What was the weather like yesterday? Was it | nice | ?
   | sunny |
   | stormy |
   | cloudy |

4. Yesterday it | rained | all day.
   | snowed |

5. The weather was | nice | last week.
   | terrible |
   | awful |
   | miserable |

6. What will the weather be like | tomorrow | ?
   | the day after tomorrow |
   | next Sunday |

7. It's going to | snow | tomorrow.
   | rain |
   | sleet |
   | hail |
   | drizzle |

8. It's | cold | today. What will the weather be like tomorrow?
   | hot |
   | sunny |
   | cloudy |
   | windy |
   | foggy |

9. It's been | cloudy | all morning.
                 foggy
                 chilly
                 warm

10. How's the weather? Is it | raining | now?
                             snowing
                             sleeting
                             hailing
                             drizzling

11. It'll probably | clear up | this afternoon.
                    rain
                    snow

12. The days are getting | hotter | .
                      colder
                      warmer
                      cooler
                      longer
                      shorter

13. Today is the first day of | spring | .
                         summer
                         winter
                         fall

14. There's a | cool breeze | this evening, isn't there?
              strong wind
              gusty wind

15. It's | cold | today. What's the temperature?
        hot
        cool
        warm
        freezing

16. The temperature is about | 70 degrees
                          70 degrees Fahrenheit
                          32° F.
                          zero degrees centigrade
                          3° C.

SUBSTITUTION DRILLS

1. 캘리포니아에서는
   뉴욕에서는
   플로리다에서는

2. 훌륭한
   좋은
   아름다운
   더할 나위없는

3. 좋은
   해가 쨍쨍한
   폭풍우가 치는
   구름이 낀

4. 비가 왔읍니다
   눈이 왔읍니다

5. 좋은
   고약한
   나쁜
   비참한

6. 내일
   모레
   다음 일요일

7. 눈이 내릴(겁니다)
   비가 내릴(〃)
   진눈깨비가 내릴(〃)
   싸라기가 내릴(〃)
   궂은 비가 내릴(〃)

8. 추운
   더운
   해가 난
   구름이 낀
   바람이 부는
   안개가 낀

9. 구름이 낀
   안개가 낀
   쌀쌀한
   따뜻한

10. 비가(내립니까)
    눈이(〃)
    진눈깨비가(〃)
    우박이(〃)
    궂은 비(〃)

11. 개일(겁니다)
    비가 올(〃)
    눈이 올(〃)

12. 더 더워지고(있읍니다)
    더 추워지고(〃)
    더 따뜻해지고(〃)
    더 선선해지고(〃)
    더 길어지고(〃)
    더 짧아지고(〃)

13. 봄
    여름
    겨울
    가을

14. 시원한 바람이
    세찬 바람이
    돌풍이

15. 추운
    더운
    시원한
    따뜻한
    무척 추운

16. 70도
    화씨 70도
    화씨 32도
    섭씨 영도
    섭씨 3도

READING PRACTICE

Talking About the Weather

As the American author, Mark Twain, once said, "Everybody talks about the weather, but nobody does anything about it." It is true that everybody talks about the weather; it's the most common subject of conversation there is. "Isn't it a nice day?" "Do you think it will rain?" "I think it's going to snow." These are common ways of starting a conversation.

Many people think they can tell what the weather is going to be like. But they hardly ever agree with each other. One man may say, "Do you see how cloudy it is in the east? It's going to rain tomorrow." Another man will say, "Yes, it's cloudy in the east. We're going to have fine weather tomorrow."

People often look for the weather they want. When a farmer needs water, he looks for something to tell him it's going to rain; he won't believe anything else. When friends have a picnic, they are so sure the weather is going to clear up very quickly that they sit eating their lunch while it rains.

Almost everyone listens to what the weatherman says. But he doesn't always tell us what we want, and once in a while he makes a mistake. Still, he probably comes closer to being correct than anyone else.

Questions

1. What did Mark Twain say about the weather?
2. What is the most common subject of conversation?
3. Do people usually agree about the weather?
4. Do you believe that the weatherman usually gives us the correct weather news?
5. What is the weather going to be like tomorrow?

READING PRACTICE

〔날씨에 관한 이야기〕

언젠가 미국의 작가 마아크 트웨인이 말한것 처럼 "모든 사람이 날씨 이야기를 하지만, 아무도 날씨에 관해서 이렇다 할 행동을 하는 사람은 없읍니다" 모든 사람이 날씨에 관해 이야기하는 것은 사실입니다. 날씨는 가장 흔한 화제인 것입니다. "날씨가 좋군요" "비가 올까요?" "눈이 올 것 같아요" 이것이 회화를 시작하는 흔한 방법들 입니다.

날씨가 어떻게 될런지 알수 있다고 생각하는 사람들이 많읍니다. 그러나 의견은 여간해서 일치하지 않읍니다. 어떤 사람은 이렇게 말 할 것입니다. "동쪽에 구름이 많이 꼈죠? 내일 비가 올거예요" 다른 사람은 이렇게 말 할 것 입니다. "예, 동쪽에 구름은 꼈읍니다만 내일은 날씨가 좋을 걸요"

사람들은 흔히 자기가 바라는 날씨를 기대합니다. 농부가 물이 필요할 때는 비가 올 것 이라고 말 해 주는 것을 찾읍니다. 그밖의 것은 통 믿으려고 하지 않읍니다. 친구들이 소풍을 가게되면 그들은 날씨가 빨리 개일것 이라고 너무나 믿는 나머지 비를 맞으며 점심을 먹읍니다.

거의 모든 사람이 일기예보자의 말을 듣읍니다. 그러나 그가 언제나 우리가 원하는 예보를 해 주는 것은 아니고, 가끔은 실수를 하곤 합니다. 그렇기는 해도 그는 아마도 어느 누구 보다도 정확에 더 가까웁곤 합니다.

✻ 새로 나온 단어와 어귀 ✻

as~「~처럼」 American author와 Mark Twain은 동격. author「작가」 common「공통의」 subject of conversation「화제」 ways of starting~「~을 시작하는 방법들」 agree with~「~와 의견이 일치하다」 look for~「~을 찾다, 기대하다」 weatherman「일기예보하는 사람」 once in a while「가끔」 makes a mistake「실수」 come loser to~「~에 보다 가까웁다」 correct「정확한」

CONVERSATION

1. Talking about the weather

BOB: We're having a picnic tomorrow. Why don't you come with us?

LOUISE: I'd like to, but I think it's going to rain. The weatherman says it is.

BOB: I don't think he's right. It hasn't rained for a week and it isn't cloudy today, either.

LOUISE: But he's usually correct in his weather news.

BOB: The temperature is 80 degrees this afternoon. I'm sure we'll have fine weather for our picnic.

LOUISE: Well, I'll go, but I'll take my umbrella with me.

2. Winter weather

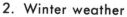

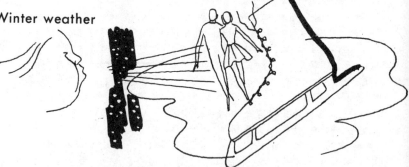

DICK: Look! It's snowing! Winter is here at last.

LARRY: It's really cold today. I'm glad I have my overcoat on.

DICK: There's ice on the lake, too. We'll be able to go skating this weekend.

LARRY: Not if it's too windy. Come on! I'm freezing.

DICK: You'll just have to learn to like it. The weather's going to be like this for the next three months.

LARRY: Then I'm going to Florida!

CONVERSATION

1. 날씨에 관한 대화

Bob : 우리는 내일 소풍을 갑니다. 같이 안 가시렵니까?

Louise : 가고는 싶지만 비가 올 것 같아요. 일기 예보자가 그러던데요.

Bob : 그 사람이 틀릴겁니다. 일주일 동안 비가 안 온데다가 오늘은 흐린 날씨도 아니지 않읍니까?

Louise : 그렇지만 그 사람의 예보가 대게 맞던 걸요.

Bob : 오늘 오후 기온은 80도 예요. 소풍 가기 좋은 날씨가 틀림 없을 거예요.

Louise : 글쎄요, 저도 가죠. 허지만 우산을 가지고 갈래요.

2. 겨울 날씨

Dick : 저것 봐, 눈이 오네. 드디어 겨울이야.

Larry : 오늘은 정말 추운데, 오버 코오트를 입은게 다행이야.

Dick : 호수에는 얼음도 얼었어. 이번 주말엔 스케이트도 타러 갈 수 있을 거야.

Larry : 바람이 너무 불면 못 가지. 가자구 얼어 죽겠어.

Dick : 추위를 좋아하지 않을 수 없을 거예요. 날씨가 앞으로 석달 동안 이럴테니까.

Larry : 그럼 난 플로리다로 갈테야.

＊ 새로 나온 단어와 어귀 ＊

umbrella 「우산」 have ～on 「～을 입고 있다」 overcoat 「오바 코오트」 lake 「호수」 windy 「바람부는」

EXERCISES

1. Answer the following questions with short answers as shown in the example.

   Example: Is it cold today? *Yes, it is.*

   a. Did it rain yesterday? Yes, _____.

   b. Is it snowing now? No, _____.

   c. Is it cold this morning? Yes, _____.

   d. Has it cleared up yet? No, _____.

   e. Has it been cloudy all day? Yes, _____.

   f. Is it going to snow tomorrow? No, _____.

   g. Is it raining now? Yes, _____.

   h. Was it sunny yesterday? No, _____.

   i. Does it usually snow in Florida? No, _____.

   j. Is there a cool breeze today? Yes, _____.

   k. Are the days getting hotter every summer? Yes, _____.

2. Use the right word.

   Example: It's *raining.* (*rain, raining*)

   a. Yesterday it _____ all night. (*hailed, hail*)

   b. It's _____ now. (*snow, snowing*)

   c. The weather's getting _____. (*hotter, more hotter*)

   d. Is it _____? (*rain, raining*)

   e. The weather was very _____. (*nicer, nice*)

   f. It'll probably be _____ all afternoon. (*drizzle, drizzling*)

   g. There's a strong _____ this evening. (*wind, windy*)

   h. The weather will be _____ tomorrow. (*cloudy, clouds*)

   i. Has it _____ yet? (*clearing up, cleared up*)

   j. The weather was _____ last week. (*terribly, terrible*)

3. Student A adds tag questions to the following statements and Student
B gives short, affirmative answers. Follow the examples.

Examples: It's been beautiful this spring.
Student A: *It's been beautiful this spring, hasn't it?*
Student B: *Yes, it has.*

There's a cool breeze today.
Student A: *There's a cool breeze today, isn't there?*
Student B: *Yes, there is.*

a. It's cold today.
b. Today is the first day of spring.
c. There's a strong wind this evening.
d. The temperature will be about 70 degrees today.
e. It'll probably clear up this afternoon.
f. It's been cloudy all morning.
g. The weather was miserable last week.
h. It snowed all day yesterday.
i. It's been cold all winter.
j. There was a terrible storm in New York.

4. Use the appropriate subject in the following sentences.

there	I
we	you
it	she
they	he

a. _____ will probably rain soon.
b. _____ don't like this freezing weather, do you?
c. _____ is a gusty wind this evening, isn't there?
d. Mary is happy. _____ has been in California where it is warm.
e. My friends and I don't like snow. _____ like warm weather.
f. Peter doesn't like the rain. _____ hopes it will clear up soon.
g. The days are long and _____ are getting longer.
h. _____ am happy to hear that the days are getting warmer.

WORD LIST

awful	freezing	sunny
breeze	gusty	temperature
centigrade	like	terrible
chilly	miserable	warm
cloudy	nice	wind
cool	perfect	windy
degree	spring	winter
Fahrenheit	stormy	zero
fall	strong	
foggy	summer	

Verb Forms

clear up, cleared up (*p. and
   p. part.*)
drizzle, drizzled (*p. and p. part.*)
hail, hailed (*p. and p. part.*)
rain, rained (*p. and p. part.*)
sleet, sleeted (*p. and p. part.*)
snow, snowed (*p. and p. part.*)

Measures

32° = thirty-two degrees
32° F. = thirty-two degrees
   Fahrenheit
0° C. = zero degrees centigrade

Supplementary Word List

(Conversation and Reading Practice)

agree	nobody
author	picnic
common	skating
conversation	true
ice	umbrella
lake	weatherman

UNIT 8 TALKING ABOUT SICKNESS AND HEALTH

406 How are you feeling today?

407 I don't feel very well this morning.

408 I was sick yesterday, but I'm better today.

409 My fever is gone, but I still have a cough.

410 My brother has a bad headache.

411 Which of your arms is sore?

412 My right arm hurts. It hurts right here.

413 What's the matter with you?

414 I've got a pain in my back.

415 Which foot hurts? Is it the left one?

416 How did you break your leg?

417 I slipped on the stairs and fell down. I broke my leg.

418 Your right hand is swollen. Does it hurt?

419 It's bleeding. You'd better go see a doctor about that cut.

420 I hope you'll be well soon.

UNIT 8 TALKING ABOUT SICKNESS AND HEALTH

406. 오늘 기분이 어떠세요?

407. 오늘 아침에는 썩 좋지는 않군요.

408. 어제는 아팠는데, 오늘은 좀 나았어요.

409. 열은 없어졌지만(내렸지만), 여전히 기침이 납니다.

410. 내 동생은 두통이 매우 심합니다.

411. 어느쪽 팔이 아픈가요?

412. 오른쪽 팔이 아픕니다. 바로 여기가 아파요.

413. 어찌된 일입니까?

414. 등에 통증이 있읍니다.

415. 어느 발이 아픕니까? 왼쪽 발 인가요?

416. 어떻게 하다가 다리를 부러뜨렸지요?

417. 층계에서 미끄러 떨어져 다리를 부러뜨렸어요.

418. 당신 오른 손이 부었군요. 아픈가요?

419. 피가 납니다. 의사한테 가서 상처를 치료 받는게 좋겠읍니다.

420. 곧 나아 지시기를 빕니다.

✳ 새로 나온 단어와 어귀 ✳

feel「느끼다」 feel well「건강하다, 기분이 좋다」 sick「병든, 아픈」 better =well의 비교급「더 건강한」 fever「열」 be gone「사라지고 없다」 cough 「기침」 headache「두통」 arm「팔」 sore「상처가 아픈」 hurt「아프다, 고통을 느끼다」 matter「문제, 난처한 일」 pain「고통」 back「등」 foot 발(복수 feet) break「부러뜨리다」 leg「다리」 slip「미끄러지다」 fell =fall의 과거 fall down「넘어지다」 broke=break의 과거 swollen =swell swelled의 과거분사 「부어오른」 bleed「피가 나다」 cut「벤 자리, 상처」 hope「희망하다, 바라다」 soon「곧」

문 법

406. How are you feeling today? : How are you? 가 만났을 때의 인사임에 대해서, How are you feeling~?은 아픈 사람에게 묻는 말이다. 이 이외에 Aren't you feeling well? Don't you feel well? Are you feeling any better ?등도 마찬가지 뜻이다.

How are they *feeling* today? (그들은 오늘 좀 어떠하시죠?)
How is John *feeling* today? (존은 오늘 좀 어떤가요?)

407. I don't feel very well~. : feel에 여러가지 형용사를 써서 여러가지 기분을 나타낼 수가 있다.

I *feel* chilly.　　　(오싹오싹 춥다)
I *feel* wonderful.　 (기분이 상쾌하다)
I *feel* low.　　　　(기분이 저조하다)
I *feel* feverish.　　(열이 좀 있읍니다)
I *feel* sleepy.　　　(졸리웁군요)
I *feel* bad.　　　　(기분이 좋지 않읍니다)

408. I was sick yesterday, but I'm better~. : 「아프다」는 표현을 영국 영어에서는 I am ill. 미국 영어에서는 I am sick. 가 주로 쓰인다. 특히 sick에는 특별한 뜻이 많다. homesickness 「향수병」 seasickness 「뱃멀미」등이다. I am better. 는 I am well. (건강하다)의 비교급으로 더 「건강해졌다」는 뜻.

409. My fever is gone, but I still have a cough. : be gone은 「사라지고 지금은 없다」의 뜻. 또한 「어떤 병에 걸렸다」든가 「증세가 있다」등의 경우 have 동사를 잘 쓴다.

I *have* a sore throat.　　　　　I *have* a bad cold.
(나는 인두염을 앓고 있다)　　　(독감에 걸렸다)
I *have* pains in my chest.　　　I *have* a bad headache.
(가슴이 결린다)　　　　　　　(두통이 심하다)

411. Which of your arms is sore? : Which~is 사이의 「of+명사」구는 「…중에서」라 번역한다.

Which *of your hands* is sore?
(너의 손 중에서 어느 것이 아픕니까?)
Which *of your legs* is sore?
(너의 다리 중에서 어느 것이 아픕니까?)
Which *of your feet* is sore?
(너의 발 중에서 어느 쪽이 아픕니까?)

413. What's the matter with you? : 「불평·고통·불행등을 물을 경우」What's the matter with~?라 묻는다. 「…은 어떠냐?, …어찌 되었느냐?」의 뜻.

What's the matter with him?
(그는 어떠냐?)

What's the matter with her?
(그 여자는 어떠니?)
What's the matter with them?
(그들은 어찌 되었느냐?)
이 이외에 What's wrong with~?가 있다.

414. I've got a pain in my back. : have got는 「have+과거분사=현재완료형」으로 보이지만, 단지 have의 뜻에 지나지 않는다. 이것은 특히 미국 영어에만 있는 현상으로서 주로 구어이다.

I've got money in my pocket.
(주머니에 돈이 있다)
I've got a slight pain in my back.
(등이 좀 아프다)
I've got a terrible pain in my back.
(등이 지독히 아프다)

419. You'd better go see a doctor ~. : 남에게 이렇게, 저렇게 「하는 것이 좋을 거다」라고 권할 때 「had better+원형동사」의 표현을 쓴다. 주로 better의 단축형을 쓴다. 특히 친한 사이에는 better만을 쓰기도 한다.

You'*d better cosult* a doctor.
(의사의 진찰을 받는 것이 좋을거요)
You'*d better marry* him.
(그와 결혼하는 것이 좋을 겁니다)
부정문이 되면 better다음에 not를 놓는다.
You'd better *not* consult a doctor.
You'd better *not* marry him.
한편 go see a doctor는 go to see a doctor가 원칙이지만 미국 영어에서는 흔히 to를 생략한다.

420. I hope you 'll be well soon. : I hope (…이기를 바란다)+you'll be well soon. (네가 곧 건강해질 것을)

INTONATION

406 How are you feeling today?

407 I don't feel very well this morning.

408 I was sick yesterday, but I'm better today.

409 My fever is gone, but I still have a cough.

410 My brother has a bad headache.

411 Which of your arms is sore?

412 My right arm hurts. It hurts right here.

413 What's the matter with you?

414 I've got a pain in my back.

415 Which foot hurts? Is it the left one?

416 How did you break your leg?

417 I slipped on the stairs and fell down. I broke my leg.

418 Your right hand is swollen. Does it hurt?

419 It's bleeding. You'd better go see a doctor about that cut.

420 I hope you'll be well soon.

VERB STUDY

1. **hurt**
   - *a.* My right arm hurts.
   - *b.* Does your back hurt?
   - *c.* Yesterday my right arm was hurting.
   - *d.* My head hurt last night.
   - *e.* I hurt my hand.
   - *f.* How did you hurt your hand?
   - *g.* She hurt her leg yesterday.

2. **break**
   - *a.* How did you break your leg?
   - *b.* I broke my leg yesterday afternoon.
   - *c.* He breaks his leg frequently.
   - *d.* I have never broken my leg.
   - *e.* Has she ever broken her arm?

3. **slip**
   - *a.* I slipped on the stairs.
   - *b.* Did you slip on the stairs this morning?
   - *c.* I won't slip on the stairs.

4. **fall down**
   - *a.* I slipped on the stairs and fell down.
   - *b.* Did you fall down?
   - *c.* He often slips on the stairs and falls down.
   - *d.* I have slipped on the stairs and fallen down many times.

5. **hope, hope to**
   - *a.* I hope you'll be well soon.
   - *b.* He hopes you'll be well soon.
   - *c.* I hope to go with you tomorrow.
   - *d.* He hoped to go with us today.

6. **be bleeding**
   - *a.* Your hand is bleeding.
   - *b.* My hand was bleeding last night.
   - *c.* His hand isn't bleeding.

VERB STUDY

1. **hurt** (아프다, 다치다)
   a. 오른 팔이 아픕니다.
   b. 등이 아픕니까?
   c. 어제는 오른 팔이 아팠읍니다.
   d. 지난 밤에는 머리가 아팠읍니다.
   e. 손을 다쳤읍니다.
   f. 당신 손은 어떻게 하다 다쳤지요?
   g. 그녀는 어제 다리를 다쳤읍니다.

2. **break** (부러뜨리다, 탈구하다)
   a. 어떻게 하다가 다리를 부러뜨렸는지요?
   b. 나는 어제 오후에 다리를 부러뜨렸읍니다.
   c. 그는 번번히 다리를 부러뜨리곤 합니다.
   d. 나는 한번도 다리를 부러뜨린 적이 없읍니다.
   e. 그녀는 팔을 부러뜨린 적이 있읍니까?

3. **slip** (미끄러 지다)
   a. 층계에서 미끄러졌읍니다.
   b. 오늘 아침에 층계에서 미끄러졌읍니까?
   c. 나는 층계에서 미끄러지진 않아요.

4. **fall down** (넘어지다, 쓰러지다)
   a. 나는 층계에서 미끄러져, 넘어졌읍니다.
   b. 넘어졌어요?
   c. 그는 종종 층계에서 미끄러져 넘어집니다.
   d. 나는 여러번 층계에서 미끄러져 넘어졌읍니다.

5. **hope, hope to** (바라다, 기대하다)
   a. 곧 나아지기를 바랍니다.
   b. 그는 당신이 곧 회복되기를 바랍니다.
   c. 내일 당신과 같이 가고 싶읍니다.
   d. 그는 오늘 우리와 같이 가기를 바라고 있읍니다.

6. **be bleeding** (피가 나고 있다)
   a. 당신 손에서 피가 납니다.
   b. 내 손에서는 어젯밤 피가 났읍니다.
   c. 그의 손에서는 피가 나지 않읍니다.

* 새로 나온 단어와 어귀 *

frequently「빈번히, 자주」   **many times**「여러번」

SUBSTITUTION DRILLS

1. How

are	you
	they
	Mr. and Mrs. Cooper
is	John
	Mary

feeling today?

2.

I	don't
They	
He	doesn't
She	

feel very well this morning.

3. I was

| sick |
| ill |

yesterday, but I'm better today.

4. My fever is gone, but I still have

| a cough |
| a sore throat |
| pains in my chest |
| a bad cold |

.

5. My brother has a bad

| headache |
| toothache |
| backache |

.

6. Which of your

| arms |
| hands |
| legs |
| feet |

is sore?

7 My right

| arm |
| leg |
| hand |
| foot |
| ear |
| eye |

hurts. It hurts right here.

8. What's the matter with

| you |
| him |
| her |
| them |

?

9. I've got a | pain / slight pain / terrible pain | in my back.

10. How did you break your | leg / arm / wrist / ankle | ?

11. I slipped on the stairs and fell down. I broke my | leg / arm / ankle / wrist | .

12. Your | right hand / thumb / finger / toe | is swollen. Does it hurt?

13. I've got a pain in my | back / neck / stomach / knee | .

14. It's bleeding. | You'd better / You better / You ought to / You should | go see a doctor about that.

15. I don't feel very well. My arm | hurts / aches | .

16. My brother is | very well / very sick / not well / healthy | .

17. I'm not feeling very well today. My | head / back / left shoulder / arm / leg | aches.

SUBSTITUTION DRILLS

1.
너는	~입니까
그들은	~입니까
쿠우퍼씨 부처는	~입니까
죤은	~입니까
메어리는	~입니까

2.
나는	~하지 않읍니다
그들은	~하지 않읍니다
그는	~하지 않읍니다
그녀는	~하지 않읍니다

3.
아픈
병이 든

4.
기침 (이 납니다)
목구멍이 쓰립(니다)
가슴이 아픕(니다)
감기가 지독(합니다)

5.
두통
치통
등의 통증

6.
팔
손
다리
발

7.
팔이
다리가
손이
발이
귀가
눈이

8.
너는
그는
그녀는
그들은

9.
아픕(니다)
약간 아픕(〃)
지독히 아픕(〃)

10.
다리를
팔을
손목을
발목을

11.
다리를
팔을
발목을
손목을

12.
오른 손이
엄지 손가락이
손가락이
발가락이

13.
등에
목에
위에
무릎에

14.
너는 ~하는 게 좋겠읍니다
너는 ~ 〃 좋겠읍니다
너는 ~해야만 합니다
너는 ~해야만 합니다

15.
아픕니다
쑤십니다

16.
매우 좋은
매우 아픈
좋지 않은
건강한

17.
머리가
등이
왼쪽 어깨가
팔이
다리가

READING PRACTICE

Talking About Sickness and Health

Bobby Adams was very quiet as Dr. Smith examined him. The doctor looked at the boy's throat, took his temperature and listened to his heart. Finally, he asked Bobby's mother a few questions.

"When did Bobby begin to feel ill?"

"This morning when he got up. He said he felt too sick to go to school today."

"What did he eat for breakfast?"

"He had orange juice, two pieces of buttered toast, dry cereal, and milk."

"I see." The doctor asked Bobby, "How do you feel now, my boy?"

Bobby answered, "Terrible. I think I'm going to die."

The doctor said, "You won't die. In fact, you'll be fine by dinner time."

"Oh, Doctor! Do you really think so?" Bobby's mother looked very glad.

Dr. Smith answered, "Mrs. Adams, your son has a sickness that is very common to boys at a time like this. It comes and goes very quickly."

Mrs. Adams said, "But I don't understand."

"Today," the doctor told her, "the most important baseball game of the year is on television. If Bobby feels well enough to watch television this afternoon, and I think he does, he will be fine when the game is finished. It's the only cure I know for this sickness. Now, if you'll excuse me, I must go across the street to see the Morton's boy, Alfred. He seems to have the same thing Bobby has today."

Questions

1. How did Dr. Smith examine Bobby?
2. What had Bobby eaten for breakfast?
3. Did the doctor think Bobby would get well?
4. How did Bobby say he felt?
5. Have you ever had a sickness like Bobby Adams'?

READING PRACTICE
〔병과 건강에 관한 대화〕

보비 애덤즈는 스미드 의사가 그를 진찰 할 때 아주 조용히 있었읍니다. 의사는 소년의 목젖을 들여다 보고, 체온도 재고, 심장의 고동도 들었읍니다. 마침내 의사는 보비의 어머니에게 몇 가지 질문을 했읍니다.

"보비가 언제부터 아프다고 했읍니까?"

"오늘 아침 일어났을 때예요. 그 애는 너무나 아파서 학교에 갈 수가 없다고 그랬어요."

"아침에는 무엇을 먹었읍니까?"

"오렌지 쥬스하고, 버터 바른 토스트 두 조각하고, 드라이 시리얼하고 밀크를 먹었지요."

"알겠읍니다."하고 의사는 보비에게 물었읍니다. "애야, 지금은 기분이 어떠냐?"

보비는 "굉장히 아파요, 아파서 죽을 것 같아요"하고 대답했읍니다.

의사는 이렇게 말했읍니다. "죽기는, 이제 봐라. 저녁때면 썩 좋아질거다."

"아, 선생님! 정말 그렇게 생각하세요?"하고 보비의 어머니는 희색이 만면해졌읍니다.

스미드 의사가 대답했읍니다. "애덤즈 부인, 아드님은 이맘때의 아이들에게 흔히 있는 병에 걸려 있읍니다. 쉽게 걸리고 쉽게 낫는 병입니다."

애덤즈 부인이 말했읍니다. "전 잘 모르겠는데요."

"오늘,"의사가 부인에게 말했읍니다. "가장 중요한 야구 경기가 텔레비젼으로 중계됩니다. 오늘 오후 쯤에 보비가 텔레비젼을 볼 수 있을 정도로 나아지면, 저는 그렇게 되리라 생각합니다만, 경기가 끝날 때 쯤에는 다 나아 있을 겁니다. 이것이 이런 종류의 병에 대해 제가 알고있는 단 한 가지 치료법입니다. 자, 괜찮으시다면, 저는 이제 길 건너로 모오튼 댁 앨프레드 란 아이를 보러 가 봐야겠읍니다. 그 애도 오늘 보비와 똑 같은 증세를 갖고 있는 것 같아 보이는군요."

✻ 새로 나온 단어와 어귀 ✻

quiet 「조용한」 as~ 「~할 때」 examine 「진찰하다」 look at~ 「~을 보다」 throat 「인후, 목구멍」 temperature 「체온」 take one's temperature 「체온을 재다」 heart 「심장」 finally 「드디어, 마침내」 too~ to… 「너무나~해서 …할 수 없다」 answer 「답변하다」 terrible 「무시무시한, 지독한」 die 「죽다」 in fact 「사실은」 look glad 「기쁜 표정이 되다」 sickness 「병」 common 「흔한」 a sickness that is common to~ 「~에 흔한 병」 on television 「텔레비젼에 중계되다」 be finished 「끝나다」 the only cure I know for~ 「~에 대해서 알고 있는 유일한 치료법」 if you'll excuse me 「저를 용서해 주신다면→실례지만」 the same ~as… 「…와 같은~」

CONVERSATION

1. Appointment with the doctor

NURSE: The doctor will see you in a minute, Mr. Lewis. While you're waiting, you can answer some questions.

MR. LEWIS: But, nurse, you don't understand. I only want to see the doctor about . . .

NURSE: I know you want to see the doctor, Mr. Lewis. **And** you will in just a few minutes. But first I must ask you about your health.

MR. LEWIS: I'm very healthy.

NURSE: You are? Then why are you here?

MR. LEWIS: I want to pay the doctor for my wife's operation last month.

NURSE: You do? Why didn't you say so? Go right in!

2. A broken left arm

MOTHER: Billy! What's the matter? Are you hurt?

BILLY: I slipped on the stairs and fell down. I think my **arm is broken.**

MOTHER: Oh! I hope not. Which arm is it?

BILLY: The left one. It hurts right here.

MOTHER: Let me see. I don't think it's broken but we're **going to** see the doctor right now.

BILLY: I'm glad it wasn't my right arm. That's the one I **need for** baseball.

CONVERSATION

1. 의사와의 약속

Nurse : 의사선생님께서 곧 당신을 면담하실 거예요, 루이스 씨. 기다리
시는 동안에 몇 가지 질문에 대답해 주세요.

Mr. Lewis : 헌데, 간호원. 잘못 알고 있소. 나는 단지 의사 선생을 만나보
고 싶을 뿐인데…

Nurse : 당신이 의사 선생님을 보고 싶어 하시는 걸 알아요, 루이스 씨.
몇분만 기다리시면 돼요. 그런데 먼저 당신의 건강에 관해서 여
쭤 봐야 되겠군요.

Mr. Lewis : 나는 아주 건강하오.

Nurse : 그래요? 그렇다면 어째서 여기엔 오셨지요?

Mr. Lewis : 지난 달에 내 안 사람이 수술을 받았는데, 의사 선생님께 그 돈
을 내려 하는 거요.

Nurse : 그래요? 왜 그럼 진작 그렇게 말씀 안 하셨죠? 좋아요, 들어
가세요 !

2. 부러진 왼쪽 팔

Mother : 빌리 ! 어찌 된 일이냐? 어디 아프냐?

Billy : 층계에서 미끄러져 넘어졌어요. 팔이 부러진 것 같아요.

Mother : 저런 ! 그렇지 않으면 좋겠구나. 어느 쪽 팔이냐?

Billy : 왼쪽 팔 이예요. 바로 여기가 아파요.

Mother : 어디 보자. 내가 보기에 부러진 것 같지는 않지만, 아무튼 의
사 선생님한테 가서 보여야겠다.

Billy : 오른쪽 팔이 아닌 것이 다행 이어요. 오른 팔은 야구 할 때 써
야 하니까요.

＊ 새로 나온 단어와 어귀 ＊

nurse 「간호원」 **health** 「건강」 **pay～for…** 「…의 값을 ～에게 내다」
operation 「수술」
Let me see 「좀 보자」 **the one I needed** 「내가 필요로 하는 것」

EXERCISES

1. Complete the following sentences.

   Example: How are you *feeling* today? (*feeling, feel, do*)

   a. I _____ feel well today. (*doesn't, don't, am not*)

   b. My headache _____ gone. (*are, do, is*)

   c. My sister _____ a fever. (*have, has, makes*)

   d. My arm _____. (*hurt, hurts, do hurt*)

   e. Did you _____ your arm? (*broke, breaks, break*)

   f. I _____ and fell down. (*slip, slips, slipped*)

   g. She often _____ and falls. (*slip, slips, slipped*)

   h. Mary _____ you'll feel better soon. (*hope, hopes, hopes to*)

   i. My leg _____ bleeding. (*are, is, aren't*)

   j. Have you ever _____ your leg? (*break, broke, broken*)

   k. I _____ go with her. (*hope to, hopes to, hopes*)

   l. I've _____ a pain in my back. (*get, got, getting*)

   m. You'd _____ go see a doctor. (*good, better, well*)

   n. Your thumb is _____. (*swells, swell, swollen*)

2. Complete the sentences with the appropriate word from the list.

coughing	better	sick	matter
had to	sore throat	ached	pains

   a. I felt very _____ yesterday.

   b. I was _____ a great deal and I had a _____.

   c. I _____ call a doctor.

   d. He asked me what was the _____.

   e. I told him my throat and my head _____.

   f. I'm feeling a little _____ today.

   g. My fever is gone and so are the _____ in my throat.

3. Complete these sentences with the appropriate word from the list below.

fell   pain   break   hurts
swollen   bleeding   ought to

a. My friend slipped and _____ down the stairs.

b. His leg was _____ and _____.

c. I told him he _____ see a doctor.

d. He said to the doctor, "My leg _____ very much."

e. "I hope I didn't _____ it."

f. He feels better today, but he still has a _____ in his leg.

4. Use contractions in the following sentences.

Example: I have got a headache. *I've got a headache.*

    a. I have got a terrible toothache.

    b. He has got a broken leg.

    c. You had better see a doctor about that.

    d. She does not feel well this morning.

    e. He should not go to work with a bad cold.

    f. I do not feel better today.

    g. My fever is gone.

    h. My arm is broken.

5. Change the following to negative sentences.

Example: I feel well. I *don't* feel well.

    a. John has a fever.

    b. I've got a headache.

    c. I hurt my leg when I fell down.

    d. Have you ever had a sore throat?

    e. Did you have a toothache yesterday?

    f. Are you feeling sick today?

    g. Should you see a doctor about that?

    h. Did she feel better this morning?

WORD LIST

ankle
arm
back
backache
bad
chest
cold
cough
cut
ear
eye
fever

finger
foot, feet
hand
head
headache
healthy
ill
knee
leg
neck
pain
shoulder

sick
slight
soon
sore
stomach
swollen
throat
thumb
toe
toothache
which of
wrist

Verb Forms

ache, ached (*p. and p. part.*)
bleed, bled (*p. and p. part.*)
break, broke (*p.*), broken
   (*p. part.*)
fall down, fell down (*p.*),
   fallen down (*p. part.*)
hurt, hurt (*p. and p. part.*)
slip, slipped (*p. and p. part.*)

Expressions

be better
feel well
had better
have got, has got

Supplementary Word List

(Conversation and Reading Practice)

baseball
common
cure
enough
examined

game
heart
important
operation
pay

UNIT 9 TALKING ABOUT DAILY HABITS

421   I get out of bed about 7 o'clock every morning.

422   After getting up, I go into the bathroom and take a shower.

423   Then, I shave, brush my teeth and comb my hair.

424   After brushing my teeth, I put on my clothes.

425   After that, I go downstairs to the kitchen to have breakfast.

426   After eating breakfast, I go back upstairs again.

427   Then, it's usually time to wake up my little brother.

428   He can't dress himself yet because he's too young.

429   I wash his face and hands, and then I dress him.

430   He tries to button his own shirt, but he can't do it.

431   My little brother takes a bath before he goes to bed at night.

432   He always forgets to wash behind his ears.

433   I'm always tired when I come home from work.

434   At bedtime, I take off my clothes and put on my pajamas.

435   I get into bed at about 11:30, and go right off to sleep.

UNIT 9 TALKING ABOUT DAILY HABITS

421. 나는 매일 아침 7시경에 일
    어납니다.
422. 일어난 후 나는 목욕실로 가
    서 샤워를 합니다.
423. 그리고서 면도를 하고 이를
    닦고 머리를 빗습니다.
424. 이를 닦은 후 나는 옷을 입
    읍니다.
425. 그리고 나서 아침 식사를 하
    려고 부엌으로 내려 갑니다.
426. 아침 식사 후 나는 윗층으로
    다시 올라 갑니다.
427. 그리고나면 내 동생을 깨울
    시간이 되는게 보통입니다.
428. 그는 아직 너무 어려서 혼자

옷을 입을 수가 없읍니다.
429. 나는 그의 얼굴과 손을 씻겨주고
    옷을 입힙니다.
430. 그는 혼자서 샤쓰의 단추를 끼려
    고 하지만 할 수가 없읍니다.
431. 내 꼬마 동생은 밤에 자기 전에
    목욕을 합니다.
432. 그는 언제나 귀 뒤쪽을 씻기를
    잊곤 합니다.
433. 나는 직장에서 돌아오면 언제나
    피로합니다.
434. 취침 시간엔 옷을 벗고 잠옷을
    입읍니다.
435. 나는 11시 30분쯤에 잠자리에 들
    어서, 곧 잠이 듭니다.

* 새로 나온 단어와 어귀 *

get out of bed 「잠자리에서 일어나다」 **go into~** 「~로 들어가다」 **bathroom**
「목욕실」 **shower** 「샤워」 **take a shower** 「샤워를 하다」 **shave** 「면도를 하다」
brush 「닦다」 **teeth** 「이」 **comb** 「빗질을 하다」 **hair** 「머리칼」 **put on** 「입다」
clothes 「옷」 **go downstairs** 「아랫층으로 내려가다」 **kitchen** 「부엌」 **back** 「도
로, 다시」 **go upstairs** 「윗층으로 올라가다」 **It's time to~** 「~할 시간이다」
wake up 「깨우다」 **dress himself** 「스스로 옷을 입다」 **wash** 「씻다」 **face** 「얼굴」
dress 「옷을 입히다」 **tries**⟨try to~ 「~하려고 하다」 **button** 「단추를 채우다」
his own~ 「자기 자신의~」 **shirt** 「샤쓰」 **bath** 「목욕」 **take a bath** 「목욕하다」
behind~ 「~뒤」 **ear** 「귀」 **tired** 「피곤한」 **at bedtime** 「취침시간에」 **take off**
「옷을 벗다」 **pajama** 「잠옷」 **get into bed** get out of bed의 반대.

:::::: 문 ── 법 ::::::

422. After getting up, I go into the bathroom~ : after I got up(과거시제 내가 일어난 후)나 after I get up(현재시제 : 내가 일어난 후)를 줄여서 after getting up이라 할 수가 있다. before의 경우도 마찬가지다.

after I brush my teeth=*after brushing*
after I eat breakfast=*after eating* breakfast
before he goes to bed=*before going* to bed
before he combs his hair=*before combing* his hair

424. ~I put on my clothes. : put on은 「입다, 신다, 쓰다」등의 동작을 나타 내는 뜻인데 대해서 have~on은 「입고 있다」라는 상태를 뜻한다. put on 의 반대의 뜻은 take off 「벗다」이다.

425. After that, I go~ : after that은 422번에서 설명한 after getting up과 같은 원리이다.

after breakfast (아침 식사 후)
after supper (저녁 먹은 후)
after school (방과 후)

427. ~it's usually time to wake up~~ : It's time to~ (~해야 할 때이 다)라는 뜻으로 it's 역시 「시간」의 it 이므로 번역되지 않는다.
It's usually *time to* dress my little brother.
(보통 동생에게 옷을 입혀야 할 시간이다)
It's usually *time to* get my little brother up.
(보통 동생을 일으켜야 할 시간이다)
It's usually *time to* give my little brother a bath.
(보통 동생에게 목욕을 시켜야 할 시간이다)

428. He can't dress himself yet because he's too young. : He can't dress himself yet (아직은 스스로 옷을 입을 수가 없다)+because he's too young. (아직은 너무 어리기 때문에)

430. He tries to button his own shirt~. : He tries to~ 는 I나 you의 경 우에는 I try to~, you try to~의 꼴을 취한다. 뜻은 「~하려고 노력하다」
I try to get out of bed about 7 o'clock every morning.
(나는 매일 아침 7시경에 잠자리에서 일어나려고 노력한다)
You try to get into bed at about 11 : 30.
(너는 11시 30분에 잠자리에 들려고 노력한다)
He tries to take a bath before going to bed.
(그는 잠자리에 들기 전에 목욕을 하려고 노력한다)
한편 his own~은, own 앞에 my, your, his, their, her 등을 써서 소유 의 뜻을 강조하는 용법이다.
my own shirts   *your own* pants
her own coat   *their own* sweaters

433. I'm always tired when I come home from work. : I'm always tired(나 는 언제나 피곤하다)+when I come home from work(일터에서 집으로 귀가 했을 때)

INTONATION

421 I get out of bed about 7 o'clock every morning.

422 After getting up, I go into the bathroom and take a shower.

423 Then, I shave, brush my teeth and comb my hair.

424 After brushing my teeth, I put on my clothes.

425 After that, I go downstairs to the kitchen to have breakfast.

426 After eating breakfast, I go back upstairs again.

427 Then, it's usually time to wake up my little brother.

428 He can't dress himself yet because he's too young.

429 I wash his face and hands, and then I dress him.

430 He tries to button his own shirt, but he can't do it.

431 My little brother takes a bath before he goes to bed at night.

432 He always forgets to wash behind his ears.

433 I'm always tired when I come home from work.

434 At bedtime, I take off my clothes and put on my pajamas.

435 I get into bed at about eleven thirty, and go right off to sleep.

VERB STUDY

1. **get out of bed, get into bed**
   a. I get out of bed at about 7 o'clock every morning.
   b. My brother gets out of bed at 11 o'clock in the morning.
   c. I got out of bed at 7 o'clock yesterday morning.
   d. I get into bed at about 11:30 every night.
   e. John gets into bed at midnight every night.

2. **put on, take off**
   a. After brushing his teeth, he puts on his clothes.
   b. Yesterday I put on my clothes at about 7 o'clock.
   c. At bedtime, I take off my clothes and put on my pajamas.
   d. After he takes a bath, he puts on his pajamas.

3. **shave**
   a. I shave every morning.
   b. I've already shaved twice today.
   c. I shaved after breakfast yesterday morning.
   d. He shaves every Monday morning.
   e. He's shaving right now.

4. **brush (one's) teeth**
   a. I brush my teeth every morning.
   b. Last night I brushed my teeth after dinner.
   c. He brushes his teeth after breakfast, lunch, and dinner.
   d. I've brushed my teeth three times today.
   e. She's brushing her teeth right now, isn't she?

5. **comb (one's) hair**
   a. After I brush my teeth, I comb my hair.
   b. I combed my hair three times yesterday.
   c. She combs her hair many times each day.
   d. I've combed my hair this way for a long time.
   e. He's combing his hair right now.

6. **dress (one's self)**
   a. He can't dress himself yet, because he's too young.
   b. Their little daughter dresses herself already.
   c. He dressed himself, and then he combed his hair.

7. **button**
   a. He tries to button his shirt, but he can't do it.
   b. He buttoned his shirt, and then he combed his hair.

VERB STUDY

1. **get out of bed, get into bed** (일어나다, 자리에 들다)
   a. 나는 매일 아침 7시경 일어납니다.
   b. 내 동생은 아침 11시에 일어납니다.
   c. 나는 어제 아침 7시에 일어났읍니다.
   d. 나는 매일 밤 11시30분경에 자리에 듭니다.
   e. 존은 매일 밤 자정에 자리에 듭니다.

2. **put on, take off** (옷을 입다, 옷을 벗다)
   a. 양치질을 하고 나서 그는 옷을 입는다.
   b. 나는 어제 7시경에 옷을 입었다.
   c. 취침시간에 나는 옷을 벗고 파자마를 입는다.
   d. 목욕을 한 후 그는 파자마를 입는다.

3. **shave** (면도하다)
   a. 나는 매일 아침 면도 합니다.
   b. 나는 오늘 벌써 2번 면도했읍니다.
   c. 나는 어제 아침 식사 후 면도했읍니다.
   d. 그는 매 월요일 아침에 면도합니다.
   e. 그는 지금 바로 면도 중 입니다.

4. **brush (one's) teeth** (양치질 하다, 이를 닦다)
   a. 나는 매일 아침 양치질을 합니다.
   b. 엊저녁 나는 식사 후에 양치질 했읍니다.
   c. 그는 아침, 점심, 그리고 저녁 식사 후에 양치질 합니다.
   d. 나는 오늘 세번 양치질 했읍니다.
   e. 그녀는 지금 바로 양치질 하고 있지요?

5. **comb (one's) hair** (머리를 빗다)
   a. 양치질을 한다음, 나는 머리를 빗읍니다.
   b. 나는 어제 세번 머리를 빗었읍니다.
   c. 그녀는 매일 여러번 빗질을 합니다.
   d. 나는 오래전 부터 이렇게 머리를 빗읍니다.
   e. 그는 지금 바로 머리를 빗고 있읍니다.

6. **dress (one's self)** (옷을 입다)
   a. 그는 너무 어려서 아직 옷을 입을줄 모릅니다.
   b. 그들의 꼬마 딸은 벌써 혼자 옷을 입어요.
   c. 그는 옷을 입고 머리를 빗습니다.

7. **button** (단추를 채우다)
   a. 그는 샤쓰 단추를 끼우려고 합니다. 그러나 할 수가 없읍니다.
   b. 그는 샤쓰 단추를 끼우고서 머리를 빗었읍니다.

SUBSTITUTION DRILLS

1. I | get out of bed / jump out of bed / get up | at about 7 o'clock every morning.

2. After getting up, | I go / he goes / John goes | into the bathroom.

3. John goes into the bathroom and | takes a shower / takes a hot shower / takes a cold shower / takes a bath / bathes |.

4. After | getting up / taking a shower / combing my hair / getting dressed / bathing |, I shave and brush my teeth.

5. After taking a shower, John shaves and | brushes his teeth / combs his hair / puts on his clothes |.

6. After | taking a shower / brushing his teeth / combing his hair / washing his face and hands |, John puts on his clothes.

7. After that, | I / we / they | go / | she / John | goes | downstairs to the kitchen to have breakfast.

8. John goes downstairs to the
| kitchen |
| dining room |
| living room |

9. After eating breakfast,
| I go back |
| she goes back |
| John goes back |
upstairs again.

10. Then it's usually time to
| wake up my little brother |
| dress my little brother |
| get my little brother up |
| give my little brother a bath |
| wash my little brother's face and hands |

11. Then it's usually time to wake up
| my |
| his |
| her |
| their |
| John's |
little brother.

12. He tries to button his own
| shirt |
| pants |
| coat |
| sweater |
| jacket |
| raincoat |
, but he can't do it.

13. I'm always
| tired |
| sleepy |
| happy |
| sad |
| hungry |
when I come home from work.

14. He can't
| dress himself |
| bathe himself |
| brush his own teeth |
| comb his own hair |
| fix his own breakfast |
yet because he's too young.

15.

He	can't dress	himself	yet because	he's	too young.
She		herself		she's	
They		themselves		they're	
You		yourself		you're	
I		myself		I'm	
We		ourselves		we're	

16. At bedtime,

I take off my	clothes and	put on my	pajama:
he takes off his		puts on his	
she takes off her		puts on her	
they take off their		put on their	
you take off your		put on your	

17.

I get	into bed at about 11:30, and	go	right off to sleep.
He gets		goes	
She gets		goes	
They get		go	
You get		go	
We get		go	

18. I'm always tired

when I come home
after work
at bedtime

19.

After breakfast	, I wake up my brother.
After that	
Then	

20. I'm

always	hungry when I get up in the morning.
usually	
sometimes	
almost always	
hardly ever	
never	

SUBSTITUTION DRILLS

1. 잠자리에서 일어 납니다
   벌떡 일어 납니다
   일어 납니다

2. 나는 (들어) 갑니다
   그는 (〃) 갑니다
   죤은 (〃) 갑니다

3. 샤워를 합니다
   뜨거운 물로 샤워를 합니다
   찬 물로 샤워를 합니다.
   목욕을 합니다
   목욕을 합니다

4. 일어난 (후)
   샤워를 한 (〃)
   머리를 빗은 (〃)
   옷을 입은 (〃)
   목욕을 한 (〃)

5. 이를 닦읍니다
   머리 빗읍니다
   옷을 입읍니다

6. 샤워를 한 (후)
   이를 닦은 (〃)
   머리를 빗은 (〃)
   세수를 한 (〃)

7. 나는 갑니다
   우리는 갑니다
   그들은 갑니다
   그녀는 갑니다
   죤은 갑니다

8. 부엌 (으로)
   식당 (으로)
   거실 (로)

9. 나는 도로 갑니다
   그녀는 도로 갑니다
   죤은 도로 갑니다

10. 내 꼬마 동생을 깨워야 할
    내 꼬마 동생을 옷 입혀야 할
    내 꼬마 동생을 일으켜야 할
    내 꼬마 동생을 목욕시켜야 할
    내 꼬마 동생의 얼굴과 손을 씻어줘야 할

11. 나의
    그의
    그녀의
    그들의
    죤의

12. 샤쓰
    팬츠
    코우트
    스웨터
    자켓
    비옷

13. 피곤한
    졸리운
    행복한
    슬픈
    배고픈

14. 혼자 옷을 입을
    혼자 목욕할
    혼자 이를 닦을
    혼자 머리빗을
    혼자 아침을 먹을

15.
그는	그 자신	그는 ~이다
그녀는	그녀 자신	그녀는 ~이다
그들은	그들자신	그들은 ~이다
너는	너 자신	너는 ~이다
나는	나 자신	나는 ~이다
우리는	우리자신	우리는 ~이다

16. 나는 나의 ~를 벗고 입읍니다
    그는 그의 ~를 벗고 입읍니다
    그녀는 그녀의 ~를 벗고 입읍니다
    그들은 그들의 ~를 벗고 입읍니다
    너는 너의 ~를 벗고 입읍니다

17.
나는 (잠자리에듭니) 다	(잠듭) 니다
그는 (〃) 니다	(〃) 니다
그녀는 (〃) 니다	(〃) 니다
그들은 (〃) 니다	(〃) 니다
너는 (〃) 니다	(〃) 니다
우리는 (〃) 니다	(〃) 니다

18. 나는 집에 오면
    일이 끝난 후에는
    취침 시간에는

19. 아침 식사 후
    그 후
    그리고 나서

20. 항상
    대개
    이따금
    대개는 늘
    별로 ~않읍니다
    결코 ~않읍니다

READING PRACTICE

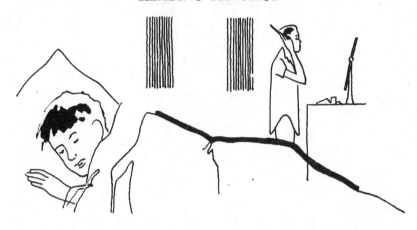

Talking About Daily Habits

I think the most terrible thing in life for my little brother is getting up in the morning. He is almost sick when my mother calls, "Herbert! It's seven o'clock! Get up!"

Herby answers, "I'm coming!" and goes right back to sleep.

I'm not at all like my brother. I don't like to go to bed at night but I don't mind getting up in the morning. I usually wake up before my mother calls me. I jump out of bed and go into the bathroom to take my shower. I get dressed, brush my teeth, comb my hair, and get ready to go downstairs for breakfast as soon as my mother calls.

But not Herby. He just sleeps. A military band in our bedroom could not wake him up. I call him and say, "Get up! Mom will be up here to pull you out of bed if you don't get up immediately!"

But he just sleeps. After calling a few more times my mother has to come upstairs and pull Herby out of bed. He always says, "I was going to get up in another minute. Really I was."

It's that way every day with my little brother. Perhaps some day he'll learn to get up on time, but I really don't think so.

Questions

1. What doesn't Herby like to do?
2. What doesn't his brother like to do?
3. What does Herby's brother do before his mother calls in the morning?
4. What does Herby say when his mother pulls him out of bed?
5. Are you like Herby or his brother?

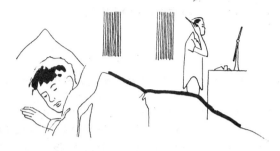

READING PRACTICE
〔일상 습관에 관한 대화〕

나는, 내 꼬마 동생이 세상에서 가장 싫어하는 일은 아침에 일어나는 일이라고 생각합니다. 그래서, 어머니가 "허버트야 일곱시다. 일어나거라."하고 소리칠 때 마다 동생은 병이 날 지경입니다.

"예, 갈께요"하고 허버트는 대답하고 다시 잠이 듭니다.

나는 내 동생과는 딴판 입니다. 나는 밤에 잠자기가 싫지만, 아침에 일어나는 것은 싫지 않읍니다. 나는 대개 어머니가 일어나라고 부르기 전에 일어납니다. 나는 벌떡 일어나서 목욕실로 가서 샤워를 합니다.

나는 옷을 갈아 입고, 양치질을 하고, 머리를 빗고, 어머니가 부르시면 즉시 아침 식사를 하러 아래층으로 내려갈 준비를 하고 있읍니다.

그러나 허버트는 그렇지 않읍니다. 그는 깊이 잠이 든채 입니다. 침실안에 군악대가 있대도 그를 깨울 수는 없을 겁니다. 내가 "일어나, 네가 일어나지 않으면 엄마가 올라와서 침대에서 너를 끌어낼 거야."라고 그에게 말합니다.

그래도 그는 그냥 잠만 잡니다. 몇번 더 부르고 난 후 엄마가 이층까지 올라와서 침대에서 끌어냅니다. "금방 일어나려든 참인데, 참."이라고 그는 항상 말합니다.

내 동생은 매일 그런식입니다. 아마 언젠가는 그도 제 시간에 일어나겠지만, 참말은 그럴것 같지 않기도 합니다.

---

* 새로 나온 단어와 어귀 *

I'm coming 우리'말로 「갈께요!」라는 말은 영어로는 "I'm going!"이 아니고 "I'm coming!"이다. 이것은 상대방을 위주로 생각하는 사고방식에서 나온 것이라 할 수 있다. "I'm going!" 이라 하면 「나 외출합니다!」하는 뜻이 된다. **not at all** 「조금도…아니다」 **mind getting up** 「일어나기를 꺼리다, 싫어하다」 **jump out of bed** 「뛰어 일어나다」 **as soon as**~ 「~하자마자」 **military band** 「군악대」 **be up here** 「여기로 올라오다」 **pull~out of** … 「…에서 ~을 끌어내다」 **It's that way**~ 「그식이다」 **with my little brother** 「내 동생에게는」

CONVERSATION

Bedtime

MOTHER: Children! It's your bedtime. Go upstairs and go to bed.

MARY: Oh, Mother! Do we have to? It's still early.

BEN: Yes, and it's Friday night. There's no school tomorrow.

MOTHER: Yes, but tomorrow we have to get up early and go shopping.

MARY: I forgot that. Okay, I'll go to bed without arguing. I like to shop.

BEN: Do I have to take a bath tonight, Mom?

MOTHER: Of course you do. And don't forget to wash behind your ears.

MARY: Do I have clean pajamas, Mother?

MOTHER: Yes. They're in your closet. Be sure to brush your teeth, Mary.

MARY: I will. And I'll comb my hair, too.

BEN: Good night, everybody. See you tomorrow.

MOTHER: Good night. Don't forget to open your bedroom window before you go to sleep.

MARY: We won't. Good night, Mom.

CONVERSATION

취침시간

Mother : 애들아 ! 잠잘 시간이다. 위층으로 올라가 자거라.

Mary : 어마나 ! 벌써 자야 돼요 ? 아직 이른데요.

Ben : 그래요. 더구나 금요일 밤인데요. 내일은 학교가지 않는데.

Mother : 그래도 내일은 일찍 일어나서 쇼핑을 가야돼.

Mary : 그렇군요. 그럼 엄마 말씀대로 가서 자겠어요. 난 쇼핑이 좋아요.

Ben : 엄마, 오늘 저는 목욕을 해야잖아요 ?

Mother : 물론이지, 귀 뒤를 꼭 씻도록 해라.

Mary : 엄마, 깨끗한 잠옷 있어요 ?

Mother : 그래, 그건 네 장속에 있다. 그리고 이를 꼭 닦도록 해, 메리야.

Mary : 예, 그리고 머리도 빗지요.

Ben : 안녕히 주무세요.

Mother : 안녕. 잠들기 전에 침실 창문을 꼭 열어라.

Mary : 예. 알았어요, 안녕 !

✱ 새로 나온 단어와 어귀 ✱

go shopping 「장보러가다」 **forgot**＝forget 「잊다」의 과거. **without~** 「~하지 않고」 **arguing** 「주장, 논쟁」 **be sure to~** 「반드시 ~하다」

EXERCISES

1. Student A asks the following questions, and Student B gives complete answers, using the information in parentheses.

Examples: Student A: When do you go to school? (*at 9:00*)
Student B: *I go to school at 9:00.*

Student A: When do you go to work? (*after I eat breakfast*)
Student B: *I go to work after I eat breakfast.*

a. What time do you get out of bed every morning? (*at about 7 o'clock*)

b. When do you brush your teeth? (*after taking a shower*).

c. When do you go downstairs? (*after I put on my clothes*)

d. Where do you eat breakfast? (*downstairs in the kitchen*)

e. Why can't your brother dress himself yet? (*because he's too young*)

f. How do you feel when you come home from work? (*tired and hungry*)

g. When do you put on your pajamas? (*at bedtime*)

h. What time do you get into bed? (*about 11:30*)

2. Complete the following sentences with the appropriate words from the list.

put on	go off	wake up	get out
go into	getting up	get into	take off

a. I _____ of bed at 7 a.m.

b. After _____, I take a shower.

c. After that, I _____ my clothes.

d. Before I leave the house, I _____ my brother.

e. When he is dressed, we _____ the kitchen for breakfast.

f. At bedtime, I _____ my clothes and put on my pajamas.

g. After that, I go upstairs and _____ bed.

h. I usually _____ right _____ to sleep.

3. Insert the word in parentheses in the proper position in the sentence. Follow the examples.

   Examples: My brother can't button his jacket. (*still*)
   My brother still can't button his jacket.

   My brother can't fix his own breakfast. (*yet*)
   My brother can't fix his own breakfast yet.

   I shave every day. (*always*)
   I always shave every day.

   I eat breakfast at 7 o'clock. (*usually*)
   I usually eat breakfast at 7 o'clock.

   a. My little brother can't dress himself. (*still*)

   b. My little brother can't bathe himself. (*yet*)

   c. I get up at 7:00 every morning. (*always*)

   d. He brushes his teeth after he shaves. (*usually*)

   e. He hasn't combed his hair. (*still*)

   f. He hasn't washed his face and hands. (*yet*)

   g. I'm hungry when I wake up. (*always*)

   h. I'm tired when I come home from work. (*usually*)

4. Complete the sentences with the proper form of the pronoun from the list.

himself	yourself	her	I	they
herself	my	their	he	you
themselves	his	your	she	we

   a. I take off _____ clothes before I go to bed.

   b. My little brother tried to button _____ own shirt.

   c. He can't dress _____ yet.

   d. She usually combs _____ own hair.

   e. She still cannot bathe _____.

   f. The children tried to put their jackets on _____.

g. You can dress _____, can't you?

h. In the morning the children took off _____ own pajamas.

i. Do you eat _____ breakfast in the dining room?

j. After the boys get up, _____ shave and brush their teeth.

k. John goes downstairs where _____ fixes breakfast.

l. After John and I get dressed, _____ eat breakfast together in the kitchen.

m. Then _____ go back upstairs to wake up my sister.

n. I help her get dressed because _____ is still too young to dress herself.

o. You help your little brother, don't _____?

5. **Use the right verb to complete the sentences.**

   Example: I *get* dressed. (*get, give*)

   a. I _____ my teeth. (*brush, button*)

   b. I _____ my hair. (*comb, shave*)

   c. I _____ breakfast. (*fix, put*)

   d. I _____ my shirt. (*give, button*)

   e. I _____ my face. (*comb, shave*)

   f. I _____ my clothes. (*wash, bathe*)

   g. I _____ a shower. (*wash, take*)

   h. I _____ into bed. (*jump, take*)

   i. I _____ on my pajamas. (*put, take*)

   j. I _____ off my jacket. (*put, take*)

WORD LIST

again	herself	pants
bathroom	himself	raincoat
because	hungry	sad
bed	jacket	sweater
bedtime	living room	teeth
behind	myself	themselves
clothes	off	tired
downstairs	ourselves	upstairs
face	own	yourself
hair	pajamas	

Verb Forms

bathe, bathed (*p. and p. part.*)
brush, brushed (*p. and p. part.*)
button, buttoned (*p. and p. part.*)
comb, combed (*p. and p. part.*)
fix, fixed (*p. and p. part.*)
go back, went back (*p.*),
   gone back (*p. part.*)
jump, jumped (*p. and p. part.*)
put on, put on (*p. and p. part.*)
shave, shaved (*p. and p. part.*)
take off, took off (*p.*),
   taken off (*p. part.*)
try, tried (*p. and p. part.*)
wash, washed (*p. and p. part.*)

Expressions

fix breakfast
get into bed
get out of bed
give a bath
jump out of bed
take a bath
take a shower

Supplementary Word List

(Conversation and Reading Practice)

bedroom
military band
pull
shop

GETTING OTHER PEOPLE'S OPINIONS AND IDEAS

436   What do you think? Is that right?

437   Certainly. You're absolutely right about that.

438   I think you're mistaken about that.

439   I like hot weather best.

440   Personally, I prefer winter weather.

441   Do you think it's going to rain tomorrow?

442   I don't know whether it will rain or not.

443   In my opinion, that's an excellent idea.

444   Why is Mr. Cooper so tired? Do you have any idea?

445   He's tired because he worked hard all day today.

446   What do you think of my children?

447   I think you have very attractive children.

448   Please give me your frank opinion.

449   Do you really want to know what I think?

450   Of course I want to know what your opinion is!

UNIT 10 GETTING OTHER
PEOPLE'S
OPINIONS AND
IDEAS

436. 어떻게 생각합니까? 그것은
옳읍니까?
437. 물론이지요, 당신은 그것에
대해 절대로 옳읍니다.
438. 나는 당신이 그것에 대해 잘
못 생각하고 있다고 생각합니
다.
439. 나는 더운 날씨를 제일 좋아
합니다.
440. 개인적으로, 나는 겨울 날씨
를 오히려 좋아합니다.
441. 당신은 내일 비가 올것 이라
고 생각합니까?
442. 나는 비가 올지 안 올지 모
르겠읍니다.
443. 내 생각에는, 그것은 훌륭한

생각입니다.
444. 왜, 미스터 쿠우퍼는 그렇게 피
곤합니까? 당신은 알고 있읍
니까?
445. 그는 오늘 하루 종일 일을 열심
히 했기 때문에 피곤합니다.
446. 나의 애들을 어떻게 생각합니까?
447. 당신은 매우 귀여운 아이들을 가
졌다고 생각합니다.
448. 당신의 솔직한 의견을 나에게 알
려 주세요.
449. 당신은 내가 생각하고 있는 것을
정말 알고 싶읍니까?
450. 물론, 나는 당신의 의견이 어떠
한 것인지 알고 싶읍니다.

* 새로 나온 단어와 어귀 *

think 「생각하다」 right 「옳은」 cértainly 「확실히, 물론」 absolutely 「절대적
으로, 전적으로」 be mistaken 「그릇된, 잘못된」 hot 「더운」 weather 「날씨」
like~best 「~을 가장 좋아하다」 personally 「개인적으로」 prefer 「오히려 …을
좋아하다」 whether 「…인지 …아닌지」 opinion 「견해, 생각」 in my opinion 「내
생각에는」 excellent 「훌륭한」 idea 「생각, 관념」 tired 「피로한」 children=
child 「아이」의 복수. attractive 「매력적인」 frank 「솔직한」 give an opinion
「의견을 알려주다」 of course 「물론」

::::::: 문 법 :::::::

436. What do you think? : 상대방의 의견을 물어서 「어떻게 생각하십니까?」 라고 물을 때 쓰는 표현이다. 우리말로 「어떻게?」라고 한다고 해서 How do you think? 라고는 하지 않는다.

437. Certainly. You're absolutely right. : Is that right? 에 대한 대답이다. 묻는 말에 대한 긍정적인 답변에는 여러가지가 있다. certainly 는 Yes, 보다 강한 뜻으로 「물론 그렇죠」라는 뜻이다. 이외에도 of couse, naturally 도 마찬가지 뜻이다.

Certainly.
Of course. } You're right.
Naturally.   (물론. 당신 말이 맞읍니다)

한편 absolutely right 는 absolutely 가 right 를 수식해서 「전적으로 옳다」라는뜻.

439. I like hot weather best. : best 는 well 「잘, 무척, 대단히」의 최상급으로서 「가장~」라고 번역한다. 비교급은 better 「~보다 더」라 번역한다.

I like hot weather *well.*   (나는 더운 날씨를 무척 좋아한다)
I like hot weather *better* than cold weather.
    (나는 추운 날씨보다 더운 날씨를 더 좋아한다)
I like winter weather *best.*   (나는 겨울날씨를 가장 좋아한다)
I like summertime *best.*   (나는 여름을 가장 좋아한다)

440. Personally, I prefer winter weather. : Personally 는 「개인적으로, 개인적인 생각으로」의 뜻. prefer 는 원래 prefer A to B 「B보다 A를 더 좋아하다」의 뜻으로서, 위의 문장은 I prefer winter weather to summer weather. (나는 여름 날씨 보다 겨울 날씨를 더 좋아한다)와 같은 표현에서 to~ 이하가 쓰이지 않은 것이다.

442. I don't know whether it will rain or not. : whether 는 「…인지 아닌지」의 뜻으로서 it will rain~이라는 문장을 거느리고 있다. 위의 문장을 I don't know whether or. not it will rain. 이라 쓸 수도 있다.

I don't know *whether John will leave to day or not.*
(존이 오늘 떠날지 안 떠날지 모른다)
I don't know *whether I will see him or not.*
(내가 그를 만나게 될지 안 될지 모른다)
I don't know *whether I'll enjoy the movie or not.*
(그 영화가 재미 있을지 없을지 모르겠다)

443. In my opinion, : in my opinion 은 personally 나 I think 와 같은 뜻이다.

446. What do you think of my children? : What do you think? 는 막연히 「어떻게 생각하느냐?」의 뜻이고, 이에 덧붙여 「~에 대해서 어떻게 생각하느냐?」라고 물을 때는 What do you think of~? 라고 한다.

What do you think *of my pet dog?*
(내 귀여운 개에 대해서는 어떻게 생각하세요?)
What do you think *of my garden?*
(내 정원에 대해서는 어떻게 생각하세요?)
What do you think *of my story?*
(내 이야기에 대해서는 어떻게 생각하세요?)

INTONATION

436 What do you think? Is that right?

437 Certainly. You're absolutely right about that.

438 I think you're mistaken about that.

439 I like hot weather best

440 Personally, I prefer winter weather.

441 Do you think it's going to rain tomorrow?

442 I don't know whether it will rain or not.

443 In my opinion, that's an excellent idea.

444 Why is Mr. Cooper so tired? Do you have any idea?

445 He's tired because he worked hard all day today.

446 What do you think of my children?

447 I think you have very attractive children.

448 Please give me your frank opinion.

449 Do you really want to know what I think?

450 Of course I want to know what your opinion is!

VERB STUDY

1. think

    a. What do you think?
    b. He thinks you're absolutely right about that.
    c. He thought you were right about that.
    d. We think you're mistaken about that.
    e. Do you really want to know what I think?

2. think of

    a. What do you think of my children?
    b. I think a lot of Mr. Cooper.
    c. You thought a lot of Mr. Cooper, didn't you?
    d. What does she think of my French accent?

3. prefer

    a. Personally, I prefer winter weather.
    b. She prefers summer weather.
    c. He likes winter weather best, but she prefers summer weather.
    d. Which do you prefer?
    e. Which does he prefer?

4. work

    a. He worked hard all day.
    b. He always works hard every day.
    c. I work hard , too.
    d. My friends work eight hours every day.
    e. I've worked in New York for ten years.
    f. Yesterday she worked at home all day.
    g. Last year he was working in California.
    h. Has she always worked in New York?

5. be mistaken

    a. I think you're mistaken about that.
    b. We thought you were mistaken about that.
    c. Isn't he mistaken about that?
    d. I'm mistaken about that.

VERB STUDY

1. **think** (생각하다)
   a. 당신은 어떻게 생각합니까?
   b. 그는 당신이 그것에 대해 절대로 옳다고 생각합니다.
   c. 그는 당신이 그것에 대해 옳았다고 생각했었다.
   d. 우리는 네가 그것에 대해 실수를 했다고 생각한다.
   e. 당신은 정말 내가 생각한 것을 알고 싶읍니까?

2. **think of** (…에 대해서 생각하다)
   a. 나의 애들에 대해서 어떻게 생각하십니까?
   b. 나는 쿠우퍼 씨를 무척 많이 생각한다.
   c. 당신은 쿠우퍼 씨를 대단히 많이 생각했었죠, 그렇지요?
   d. 그녀는 나의 불란서어 액센트를 어떻게 생각합니까?

3. **prefer** (오히려 …을 좋아하다)
   a. 개인적으로, 나는 오히려 겨울 날씨를 좋아한다.
   b. 그녀는 오히려 여름 날씨를 좋아한다.
   c. 그는 겨울날씨를 제일 좋아한다. 그러나 그녀는 오히려 여름
      날씨를 좋아 한다.
   d. 너는 어느 쪽을 좋아합니까?
   e. 그녀는 어느 쪽을 좋아합니까?

4. **work** (일하다)
   a. 그는 온 종일 열심히 일했다.
   b. 그는 항상 매일 열심히 일한다.
   c. 나도 역시 열심히 일한다.
   d. 나의 친구들은 매일 8시간 일한다.
   e. 나는 뉴욕에서 10년동안 일해 왔다.
   f. 어제 그녀는 하루 종일 집에서 일했다.
   g. 작년에 그는 캘리포니아에서 일하고 있었다.
   h. 그녀는 뉴욕에서 일을 해 왔읍니까?

5. **be mistaken** (틀리다, 실수를 하다)
   a. 나는 네가 그것에 대해 실수를 했다고 생각한다.
   b. 우리는 네가 그것에 대해 실수를 했다고 생각했다.
   c. 그는 그것에 대해 틀리지 않았는가?
   d. 나는 그것에 대해 틀렸다.

＊ 새로 나온 단어와 어귀 ＊
   thought＝think의 과거.

SUBSTITUTION DRILLS

1. What do you think? Is that

right
wrong
correct
incorrect

?

2.

Certainly
Of course
Naturally

. You're absolutely right about that.

3.

I think
She thinks
John thinks

you're mistaken about that.

4.

You're
You're not
You aren't
He's
He's not
He isn't

mistaken about that.

5.

Aren't you
Isn't she
Isn't John

mistaken about that?

6. I like

hot weather
winter weather
summertime
sunshine

best.

7. Personally, I

prefer
love
like
enjoy

winter weather.

8. Do you

think
suppose
feel
believe

it's going to rain tomorrow?

9. I don't know whether

| it will rain |
| John will leave today |
| I will see him |
| I'll enjoy the movie |

or not.

10. In my opinion, that's

| an excellent |
| a wonderful |
| a marvelous |
| a good |

idea.

11. Why is Mr. Cooper so

| tired |
| happy |
| sad |
| excited |
| angry |
| healthy |

? Do you have any idea?

12. I don't know why. Maybe it's because he

| worked hard all day |
| finished working early today |
| finished working late today |
| got a letter from his friend |
| didn't have lunch today |
| always eats good food |

.

13. What do you think of my

| children |
| pet dog |
| garden |
| story |
| poem |

?

14.
| I think |
| Personally, I think |
| In my opinion |
| Personally, I'm of the opinion that |

you have very attractive children.

15. Please give me your
| frank |
| honest |
| medical |
opinion.

16. Do you really want to know what
| I think |
| she thinks |
| John thinks |
?

17. Of course I want to know what your
| opinion |
| judgment |
| conclusion |
| recommendation |
is.

18. I like geography, but I prefer
| history |
| art |
| literature |
| music |
| medicine |
| mathematics |
| religion |

19. Mr. Cooper is happy because today is
| his birthday |
| his wedding anniversary |
| the first day of spring |
| a holiday |
.

SUBSTITUTION DRILLS

1. 옳은
   그른
   맞는
   틀린

2. 확실히
   물론
   당연히

3. 나는 생각한다
   그녀는 생각한다.
   존은 생각한다

4. 당신은 ~입니다
   너는 ~않읍니다
   너는 ~않읍니다
   그는 ~입니다
   그는 ~않읍니다
   그는 ~않읍니다

5. 당신은 ~않읍니까
   그녀는 ~않읍니까
   존은 ~않읍니까

6. 더운 기후를
   겨울 기후를
   여름철을
   햇볕을

7. 오히려 좋아합니다
   사랑합니다
   좋아합니다
   즐깁니다

8. 생각합(니까)
   추측합(니까)
   느낌이 듭(니까)
   믿읍(니까)

9. 비가 올것인지
   존이 오늘 떠날지
   내가 그를 만나게 될지
   내가 영화를 즐기게 될지

10. 훌륭한~
    경탄할 만한~
    신기한~
    좋은~

11. 피로한
    행복한
    슬픈
    흥분한
    화가난
    건강한

12. 하루 종일 고되게 일했 (으므로)
    오늘 일을 일찌기 끝냈(으므로)
    오늘 일을 늦게 끝냈(으므로)
    친구에게서 편지를 받았(으므로)
    오늘 점심을 못 먹었 (으므로)
    항상 좋은 음식을 먹었 (으므로)

13. 아이들
    애완용 개
    정원
    이야기
    시

14. 나는 생각합니다
    개인적으로 나는 생각합니다
    내 의견으로는
    개인적으로 나는 ~라는 생각입니다

15. 솔직한
    거짓없는
    의학적인

16. 나는 생각합니다
    그녀는 생각합니다
    존은 생각합니다

17. 의견이
    판단이
    결론이
    충고가

18. 역사를
    미술을
    문학을
    음악을
    의학을
    수학을
    종교를

19. 그의 생일
    그의 결혼 기념일
    입춘
    휴일

READING PRACTICE

Getting Other People's Opinions and Ideas

When I was a child there were some people whose ideas I respected. My Uncle John, I thought, knew everything about the world; he had traveled and seen all there was to see. I believed anything he told me about places like Japan, Australia, and Brazil. When I wanted to know anything about baseball I asked our neighbor, Mr. Fulton; there wasn't anything he didn't know about that game. My teacher, Miss Ellis, was an expert on nature and I always believed all of the things she told our class about plants and animals.

When I was sixteen years old I got the idea that my parents, while they were very nice people and I loved them, really didn't know very much. I, of course, knew everything. Then, when I was eighteen, I realized my mother and father had learned a lot in just two years. I now respected their opinions on different subjects. It took two years of growing up for me to realize that they had had these opinions and ideas all the time.

Some people have an opinion on every subject. Others have none. The best kind is the person who studies the subject before giving an answer to the question, "What do you think?"

Questions

1. What do you think of a person who has an opinion on every subject?
2. Do you think Uncle John knew everything about the world?
3. Do you suppose that Miss Ellis was really an expert on nature?
4. Why did the boy think his parents had learned a lot in two years?
5. Do you like to give your opinion on different subjects?

READING PRACTICE
〔남의 의견과 생각을 듣는 이야기〕

내가 어린애 였을 때 그들의 의견이 존중 할만한 사람들이 있었읍니다. 나의 아저씨 존은 세상일에 대해서 무엇이든지 알고 있다고 나는 생각했읍니다. 그 아저씨는 여행을 해 왔고 볼만한 것은 모두 보았읍니다. 나는 그 아저씨가 일본, 오스트레일리아, 브라질과 같은 곳에 대해 나에게 이야기 해 준 것은 무엇이든 믿었읍니다.

내가 야구에 관해서 무엇이고 알고 싶었을 때 나는 이웃분인 풀톤 씨 에게 물어 보았읍니다. 그 경기에 관해서 그 아저씨는 모르는 것이 없었읍니다. 나의 선생 미스 엘리스는 자연에 관해 전문가 였으며, 나는 그녀가 우리 학급에서 식물 이라든지 동물에 관해서 이야기해 주는 것은 늘 무엇이든지 다 믿었읍니다)

내가 열여섯살 적에 나는 부모님들이 매우 훌륭한 분들이고 또 나는 그분들을 사랑하고 있기는 하였지만 사실상 그분들은 아는 것이 그리 많지 않다는 생각이 들게 되었읍니다. 나는 물론 무엇이든지 알고 있었읍니다. 그 다음 내가 열 여덟살 적에 나는 어머니와 아버지가 불과 2년 동안에 많은 것을 공부해 왔다는 것을 알아 차렸읍니다. 그 때 나는 여러 가지 문제들에 관해서 그들의 의견을 존중 하였읍니다. 그들이 항상 이러한 의견과 생각들을 지녀왔었다는 것을 깨달을 만큼 성장하기 까지는 나는 2년이 걸렸읍니다.

몇몇 사람들은 모든 문제에 관해서 의견을 가지고 있읍니다. 전혀 가지고 있지 않은 사람들도 있읍니다. 가장 바람직한 사람이란 "당신은 어떻게 생각하십니까?"라는 질문에 대해 대답을 말하기 전에 문제를 연구하는 사람입니다.

---

* 새로 나온 단어와 어귀 *

respect「존경하다」 people whose ideas I respected「생각이 존경받을 사람들」
travel「여행하다」 seen=see의 과거 분사. baseball「야구」 game「시합」
expert「숙련자, 능숙한 사람」 nature「자연, 본성」 plants「식물들」 animals
「동물들」 realized「깨달았다」 subject「문제」

CONVERSATION

INTERVIEWER: Mr. Smith, we are very happy to have you on our television program this evening.

MR. SMITH: I am glad to be here.

INTERVIEWER: Miss Fisher and I both have questions for you. We'd like to know your opinion. Miss Fisher, do you want to ask the first question?

MISS FISHER: Thank you. Mr. Smith, what do you think of our morning newspaper? Would you say it gives us all the latest news?

MR. SMITH: Yes, I would say so. I think it is a very good newspaper.

INTERVIEWER: What is your opinion of television? Do you think that all the programs are good?

MR. SMITH: No, I don't. Some of the programs are interesting, but others could be better.

MISS FISHER: Please give me your frank opinion about our schools, Mr. Smith. Do you believe our teachers are doing a good job?

MR. SMITH: Yes, I do. I believe our schools are excellent.

INTERVIEWER: What about music? What do you think of modern music?

MR. SMITH: I guess some of it is good. I don't always understand it. Personally, I prefer the symphonies of Beethoven.

INTERVIEWER: We'd like to talk more, Mr. Smith, but we have no time. Miss Fisher and I want to thank you for being with us on our program this evening.

MISS FISHER: I am sure our television audience has enjoyed listening to your opinions. Thank you, and good night.

MR. SMITH: It was my pleasure.

CONVERSATION

Interviewer : 스미드 씨, 우리는 오늘 저녁 당신을 우리 텔레비젼 프로에 모시게 된 것을 매우 기쁘게 생각합니다.

Mr. Smith : 나는 여기에 나오게 되어 기쁩니다.

Interviewer : 피셔 양과 저는 당신에게 여쭈어 볼것이 있읍니다. 우리는 당신의 의견을 알고 싶읍니다. 피셔 양, 처음 질문은 당신이 묻고 싶읍니까?

Miss. Fisher: 고맙읍니다, 스미드 씨, 당신은 우리 조간신문을 어떻게 생각하십니까? 그것은 우리에게 최신 뉴우스를 전해 준다고 말 할수 있겠읍니까?

Mr. Smith : 예, 나는 그렇게 말하고 싶읍니다. 나는 그것이 매우 좋은 신문이라고 생각합니다.

Interviewer : 텔레비젼에 관한 당신의 의견은 어떻읍니까? 당신은 모든 프로가 다 좋다고 생각하십니까?

Mr. Smith : 그렇게는 생각지 않읍니다. 프로 중 몇가지는 재미가 있읍니다. 그러나 딴 것 들은 더 나아져야 되겠읍니다.

Miss. Fisher : 우리 학교에 대해서 솔직한 의견을 말씀해 주십시오, 스미드 씨. 당신은 우리 선생들이 좋은 일을 하고 있다고 믿으십니까?

Mr. Smith : 예, 그렇읍니다. 나는 우리 학교가 훌륭한 학교라고 믿읍니다.

Interviewer : 음악에 관해서는 어떻읍니까? 당신은 현대 음악을 어떻게 생각 하십니까?

Mr. Smith : 좋은 것도 있다고 생각합니다. 나는 반드시 그것을 알고 있지는 못합니다. 개인적으로는 오히려 나는 베에토벤의 교향곡을 좋아합니다.

Interviewer : 우리는 더 이야기를 하고 싶읍니다만 시간이 없군요, 스미드 씨 피셔 양과 저는 당신이 오늘 저녁 우리와 함께 우리들의 프로에 나와 주신 데 대해 감사를 드리고 싶읍니다.

Miss Fisher : 우리 텔레비젼 시청자들이 당신의 의견을 재미있게 들었으리라 확신합니다. 감사합니다. 안녕히 가십시오.

Mr. Smith : 즐거웠읍니다.

✱ 새로 나온 단어와 어귀 ✱

interviewer「회견하는 사람」 morning newspaper「조간신문」 latest「최신」 news「뉴우스, 소식」 interesting「재미있는」 excellent「우수한, 탁월한」 music「음악」 modern「현대의」 symphonies「교향악」symphony의 복수 audience「청중, 시청자」 enjoy「즐기다」

EXERCISES

1. Begin each of the following questions with the phrase in parentheses. Follow the example. Use contractions wherever possible.

   Example: Will you go to school tonight? (*do you think*)
   Do you think you'll go to school tonight?

   a. Is it going to rain tomorrow? (*do you think*)
   b. Are you mistaken about that? (*don't you think*)
   c. Was Mr. Cooper tired because he worked hard all day? (*do you suppose*)

   d. Will I enjoy the movie? (*do you believe*)
   e. Can you give me your honest opinion? (*do you feel*)
   f. Is Mr. Cooper angry because he didn't have lunch today? (*don't you feel*)

   g. Is Mr. Cooper happy because today is his birthday? (*don't you believe*)

   h. Does Mr. Cooper prefer warm weather? (*don't you suppose*)
   i. Does she love winter weather? (*do you think*)
   j. Did he work hard all day? (*do you believe*)

2. Answer the following questions using the expression "I don't know whether . . . or not" as shown in the examples. Use contractions wherever possible.

   Examples: Are you going to school tonight?
   I don't know whether I'm going to school tonight or not.

   Does John enjoy school?
   I don't know whether John enjoys school or not.

   a. Will it rain tomorrow?
   b. Will John enjoy the movie?
   c. Will John give you his honest opinion?
   d. Will you see Mr. Cooper next Sunday?
   e. Is she mistaken about that?
   f. Does Mr. Cooper prefer warm weather?
   g. Will you finish working early today?
   h. Did she have lunch yet?
   i. Does John always eat good food?

3. Complete the following sentences with the correct word from the list below.

like   judgment   correct
wonderful   wrong   naturally

 a. Give me your opinion. I really want to know your _____.

 b. We prefer sunshine. We _____ hot weather best.

 c. I think finishing work early before a holiday is an excellent idea. In my opinion, that will be _____.

 d. I think John is mistaken about that. Do you also believe he is _____?

 e. Your conclusion is absolutely right about that. I know you are _____.

 f. Of course I will give you my frank opinion. _____, I will be honest with you.

4. Answer the following questions with "yes" and "no."

Example: Do you understand the lesson? *Yes, I do. No, I don't.*

 a. Is Mr. Cooper tired?
 b. Do you like my pet dog?
 c. Do you want to know what I think?
 d. Does she like music?
 e. Am I sad?
 f. Are we happy?
 g. Was he working yesterday?
 h. Were we at home?
 i. Did you enjoy the winter?
 j. Did you think a lot of Mr. Cooper?
 k. Does he like my accent?
 l. Is Mary always so happy?
 m. Am I mistaken?
 n. Is Mr. Cooper working late tonight?

WORD LIST

angry	honest	pet
art	idea	poem
attractive	incorrect	recommendation
certainly	judgment	religion
conclusion	literature	so
excellent	marvelous	story
excited	mathematics	summertime
food	medical	sunshine
frank	medicine	whether
garden	music	why
good, better, best	naturally	wonderful
holiday	personally	wrong

Verb Forms

enjoy, enjoyed (*p. and p. part.*)
love, loved (*p. and p. part.*)
prefer, preferred (*p. and p. part.*)
suppose, supposed (*p. and p. part.*)

Expressions

be mistaken
get a letter
give an opinion
of course

Supplementary Word List

(Conversation and Reading Practice)

animals	nature
baseball	plants
expert	realized
game	respected
interviewer	symphonies
job	traveled
modern	

REVIEW TWO

1. Verbs: Future action with BE GOING TO and WILL

Change these sentences to future form with "tomorrow."

a. This morning I got up at 7 o'clock. (*tomorrow*)

b. Yesterday I had breakfast at 9 o'clock.

c. Last night I went to the movies with a friend of mine.

d. We had dinner at home last night.

e. This morning I got dressed quickly.

f. I had toast and coffee for breakfast this morning.

g. My brother got up later than I did this morning.

h. Yesterday I finished working at 5:30 in the afternoon.

i. My sister went to sleep immediately last night.

j. My parents left the house at 10 o'clock yesterday morning.

k. It rained all day yesterday.

l. There was a cool breeze last night.

m. Last week it snowed.

n. I don't feel well today.

o. My little brother took a bath before he went to bed last night.

p. Last night we were tired when we came home from work.

q. Did it rain yesterday?

r. Was he sick yesterday?

s. The weather was very nice yesterday.

t. She went out for lunch at 12 noon yesterday.

u. Did you have dinner at home last night?

v. When I got sleepy last night, I went to bed.

w. After breakfast this morning I got ready to go to work.

x. Mrs. Cooper went to sleep at about 11:30 last night.

y. My brother wakes up at 7 o'clock.

z. She got dressed at 6:30 yesterday morning.

2. Verbs: Negative future action

Change these sentences to future form (negative) with "tomorrow.'

a. I didn't get up at 6 o'clock this morning. (*tomorrow*)

b. My birthday was yesterday.

c. We didn't have dinner at home last night.

d. I eat dinner every day at 8 p.m.

e. I watch television for an hour every evening.

f. Last year we used to work from 9 a.m. until 5:30 p.m.

g. This morning I measured the windows to see how wide they are.

h. I was able to go to sleep immediately last night.

i. They bought the house on the corner.

j. My cousin got married yesterday.

3. Practice with questions

Write the proper question for each answer.

a. _____? Yes, I got up at 6 o'clock.

b. _____? No, I'm still single.

c. _____? They've been married for quite a few years.

d. _____? No, they don't know when the wedding will be.

e. _____? The weather is nice today.

f. _____? No, it's not raining now.

g. _____? It's about 70° this afternoon.

4. Conversation Practice

a. Talking about the weather.

You and your friend, Fred, are talking about the weather. You ask Fred how the weather is, and he tells you. Then, you ask about how the weather was yesterday, and what the weather will be tomorrow.

You:

Fred:

_ _ _ _ _ _⁄_ _ _ _ _

b. Talking about sickness and health.

You meet Mr. Cooper. Mr. Cooper doesn't feel well. Mr. Cooper's brother doesn't feel well, either. His brother has a pain in his back. Mr. Cooper sees your hand. Your hand is swollen. Mr. Cooper recommends you see a doctor.

You:

Mr. Cooper:

_ _ _ _ _ _ _ _ _ _ _

5. Answer the questions

a. What time are you going to get up tomorrow morning?

b. What are you going to have for breakfast tomorrow morning?

c. What do you do when you get sleepy at night?

d. What time will you be able to go to sleep tomorrow night?

e. How many brothers and sisters do you have?

f. Where do your brothers and sisters live?

g. Do you like hot weather or cold weather?

h. Do you think it will rain tomorrow?

i. Do you comb your hair several times a day?

j. How many days a week do you work?

k. Do you know why Mr. Cooper is so tired?

6. Sentence Review

Study and review Base Sentences 376 to 450.

WORD INDEX

TO BOOK 3

The following is a listing of words introduced in Book Three. Each word in the listing is accompanied by the sentence in which the word was introduced in the text. The number shown in parentheses indicates the unit in which the sentence appeared.

A

able to	If you are able to, will you call me tomorrow?	(2)
aches	I don't feel very well. My arm aches.	(8)
across	The restaurant is across the street from the hotel.	(3)
advise	Would you please advise him that I'm here?	(2)
again	After eating breakfast, I go back upstairs again.	(9)
ahead	It's two blocks straight ahead.	(3)
airport	Can you tell me where the airport is?	(3)
angry	Why is Mr. Cooper so angry?	(10)
ankle	How did you break your ankle?	(8)
anniversary	When is your grandparents' wedding anniversary?	(4)
apartment	What size apartment do you own?	(1)
approximately	Approximately how long have they been married?	(4)
argue	Please don't argue with me now. I'm very busy.	(2)
arms	Which of your arms is sore?	(8)
around	The school is just around the corner.	(3)
art	I like geography, but I prefer art.	(10)
as . . . as	This window is just as wide as that one.	(1)
attractive	I think you have very attractive children.	(10)
awful	The weather was awful last week.	(7)
awfully	It's not awfully heavy, but I don't know the exact weight.	(1)

B

baby	They had a baby last month.	(4)
bachelor	My cousin is a bachelor.	(4)
back	I've got a pain in my back.	(8)
backache	My brother has a bad backache.	(8)
bad	My brother has a bad headache.	(8)
bank	Which direction is it to the bank?	(3)
basement	The restaurant is in the basement.	(3)
bath	My little brother takes a bath before he goes to bed at night.	(9)
bathes	John goes into the bathroom and bathes.	(9)
bathroom	After getting up, I go into the bathroom and take a shower.	(9)
beautiful	What beautiful trees those are!	(5)
because	He can't dress himself yet because he's too young.	(9)

bedtime	At bedtime, I take off my clothes and put on my pajamas.	(9)
beg	I beg your pardon.	(3)
behind	He always forgets to wash behind his ears.	(9)
best	I like hot weather best.	(10)
better	It's bleeding. You'd better go see a doctor about that cut.	(8)
better	I was sick yesterday, but I'm better today.	(8)
bigger	This pencil is bigger than that one.	(1)
bleeding	It's bleeding.	(8)
bother	Please don't bother me now. I'm very busy.	(2)
bought	Who bought that new house down the street from you?	(5)
box	Would you help me lift this heavy box?	(2)
break	How did you break your leg?	(8)
breeze	There's a cool breeze this evening.	(7)
bright	My book has a bright red cover.	(1)
bring	Please bring me those magazines.	(2)
broke	I slipped on the stairs and fell down. I broke my leg.	(8)
brush	Then, I shave, brush my teeth and comb my hair.	(9)
building	They're building a new building up the street from me.	(5)
building	They're building a new house up the street from me.	(5)
built	All of those houses have been built in the last ten years.	(5)
button	He tries to button his own shirt, but he can't do it.	(9)
buy	If you buy that home, will you spend the rest of your life there?	(5)

C

camera	What color is your camera?	(1)
captain	Excuse me, Captain.	(3)
carry	Would you help me carry this heavy box?	(2)
centigrade	The temperature is about zero degrees centigrade.	(7)
certainly	Certainly. You're absolutely right about that.	(10)
changes	There have been a lot of changes here in the last 20 years.	(5)
chest	My fever is gone, but I still have pains in my chest.	(8)
childhood	My friend spent his childhood in California.	(5)
chilly	It's been chilly all morning.	(7)
church	Which direction is it to the church?	(3)
clear up	It'll probably clear up this afternoon.	(7)
closet	Hang up my coat in the closet, will you please?	(2)
clothes	After brushing my teeth, I put on my clothes.	(9)
cloudy	It's been cloudy all morning.	(7)
cold	My fever is gone, but I still have a bad cold.	(8)
colonel	Excuse me, Colonel.	(3)
color	What color is your book?	(1)
comb	Then, I shave, brush my teeth and comb my hair.	(9)
conclusion	Of course I want to know what your conclusion is.	(10)
cool	There's a cool breeze this evening.	(7)
corner	Turn right at the next corner.	(3)

fever	My fever is gone, but I still have a cough.	(8)
finger	Your finger is swollen.	(8)
fix	He can't fix his own breakfast yet because he's too young.	(9)
flowers	What beautiful flowers those are!	(5)
foggy	It's foggy today.	(7)
food	I don't know why. Maybe it's because he always eats good food.	(10)
foot	Which foot hurts?	(8)
forks	Please pick up those knives and forks, will you?	(2)
frank	Please give me your frank opinion.	(10)
freezing	It's freezing today.	(7)
friendly	Are your neighbors very friendly?	(5)

G

garden	What do you think of my garden?	(10)
get	Get me a hammer from the kitchen, will you?	(2)
go back	After eating breakfast, I go back upstairs again.	(9)
got	I've got a pain in my back.	(8)
got	I don't know why. Maybe it's because he got a letter from his friend.	(10)
grandchild	Our grandchild wants to get married in June.	(4)
grandchildren	Their grandchildren are grown up now.	(4)
granddaughter	My granddaughter got married in 1945.	(4)
grandfather	My grandfather got married in 1931.	(4)
grandmother	My grandmother got married in 1945.	(4)
grandparents'	When is your grandparents' wedding anniversary?	(4)
grandson	My grandson got married in 1945.	(4)
grew up	I grew up right here in this neighborhood.	(5)
grocery	There used to be a grocery store on the corner.	(5)
grown up	Their grandchildren are grown up now.	(4)
grow up	Where did you grow up?	(5)
gusty	There's a gusty wind this evening, isn't there?	(7)

H

hail	It's going to hail tomorrow.	(7)
hair	Then, I shave, brush my teeth and comb my hair.	(9)
hammer	Get me a hammer from the kitchen, will you?	(2)
hand	Your right hand is swollen.	(8)
hand	Please hand me those magazines.	(2)
hang up	Hang up my coat in the closet, will you please?	(2)
happen to	Do you happen to know Mr. Cooper's telephone number?	(3)
hard	This material feels hard.	(1)
head	I'm not feeling very well today. My head aches.	(8)
headache	My brother has a bad headache.	(8)
healthy	My brother is healthy.	(8)
heavy	It's not too heavy, but I don't know the exact weight.	(1)

height	Do you happen to know Mr. Cooper's height and weight?	(3)
help	Would you help me lift this heavy box?	(2)
herself	She can't dress herself yet because she's too young.	(9)
high	Will you please measure this window to see how high it is?	(1)
himself	He can't dress himself yet because he's too young.	(9)
holiday	Mr. Cooper is happy because today is a holiday.	(10)
honest	Please give me your honest opinion.	(10)
hungry	I'm always hungry when I come home from work.	(9)
hurts	My right arm hurts.	(8)

I

idea	In my opinion, that's an excellent idea.	(10)
ill	I was ill yesterday, but I'm better today.	(8)
improvements	There have been a lot of improvements here in the last 20 years.	(5)
inches	The walls are three inches thick.	(1)
incorrect	What do you think? Is that incorrect?	(10)
information	Excuse me, sir. Can you give me some information?	(3)
interrupt	Please don't interrupt me now—I'm very busy.	(2)
into	Please pour this milk into that glass.	(2)

J

jacket	He tries to button his own jacket, but he can't do it.	(9)
judgment	Of course I want to know what your judgment is.	(10)
jump	I jump out of bed at about 7 o'clock every morning.	(9)

K

kind	Are your neighbors very kind?	(5)
kitchen	Get me a hammer from the kitchen, will you?	(2)
knee	I've got a pain in my knee.	(8)
knives	Please pick up those knives and forks, will you?	(2)
know	We all know each other pretty well.	(5)

L

ladies' room	Could you tell me where the nearest ladies' room is?	(3)
large	One of my suitcases is large, and the other one is medium size.	(1)
leave	Leave your books on the table, will you please?	(2)
leg	How did you break your leg?	(8)
length	That street is only two miles in length.	(1)
let . . . know	Would you please let him know that I'm here?	(2)
library	Take these books to the library with you tonight.	(2)
lift	Would you help me lift this heavy box?	(2)
light	My book has a light blue cover.	(1)
lighter	This pencil is lighter than that one.	(1)
lights	Please ask John to turn on the lights.	(2)

like	What was the weather like yesterday?	(7)
literature	I like geography, but I prefer literature.	(10)
living room	John goes downstairs to the living room.	(9)
long	How long is Jones Boulevard?	(1)
love	Personally, I love winter weather.	(10)

M

mailing	Would you mind mailing this letter for me?	(2)
married	Are you married?	(4)
marry	Who did George marry?	(4)
marvelous	In my opinion, that's a marvelous idea.	(10)
material	This material feels soft.	(1)
mathematics	I like geography, but I prefer mathematics.	(10)
matter	What's the matter with you?	(8)
measure	Will you please measure this window to see how wide it is?	(1)
medical	Please give me your medical opinion.	(10)
medicine	I like geography, but I prefer medicine.	(10)
medium	One of my suitcases is small, and the other one is medium size.	(1)
men's room	Could you tell me where the nearest men's room is?	(3)
miles	That street is only two miles long.	(1)
miserable	The weather was miserable last week.	(7)
miss	You can't miss it.	(3)
miss	Excuse me, miss.	(3)
mistaken	I think you're mistaken about that.	(10)
move	Would you help me move this heavy box?	(2)
moved in	A young married couple moved in next door to us.	(5)
music	I like geography, but I prefer music.	(10)
myself	I can't dress myself yet because I'm too young.	(9)

N

nail	Get me a nail from the kitchen, will you?	(2)
narrow	This narrow table weighs about forty-five pounds.	(1)
naturally	Naturally.	(10)
neck	I've got a pain in my neck.	(8)
nephew	I'm single, and my nephew is still single.	(4)
new	They're building a new house the street from me.	(5)
nice	The weather is nice today.	(7)
niece	Your niece is engaged, isn't she?	(4)
noisy	Are your neighbors very noisy?	(5)
number	Do you happen to know Mr. Cooper's telephone number?	(3)

O

occupied	I beg your pardon. Is this seat occupied?	(3)
of course	Of course I want to know what your opinion is!	(10)
off	I get into bed at about 11:30, and go right off to sleep.	(9)

sunny	What was the weather like yesterday? Was it sunny?	(7)
sunshine	I like sunshine best.	(10)
suppose	Do you suppose it's going to rain tomorrow?	(10)
supposed to	They don't know when the wedding is supposed to be.	(4)
sweater	He tries to button his own sweater, but he can't do it.	(9)
swollen	Your right hand is swollen.	(8)

T

take	Take these books home with you tonight.	(2)
take back	Would you please ask John to take back these books?	(2)
taken	I beg your pardon. Is this seat taken?	(3)
take off	At bedtime, I take off my clothes and put on my pajamas.	(9)
take place	They don't know when the wedding will take place.	(4)
teeth	Then, I shave, brush my teeth and comb my hair.	(9)
temperature	What's the temperature today?	(7)
terrible	The weather was terrible last week.	(7)
that	Would you please tell Mr. Cooper that I'm here?	(2)
themselves	They can't dress themselves yet because they're too young.	(9)
the rest of	If you buy that home, will you spend the rest of your life there?	(5)
thick	The walls are three inches thick.	(1)
throat	My fever is gone, but I still have a sore throat.	(8)
throw	Please throw me those magazines.	(2)
thumb	Your thumb is swollen.	(8)
tired	I'm always tired when I come home from work.	(9)
toe	Your toe is swollen.	(8)
too	It's not too heavy, but I don't know the exact weight.	(1)
toothache	My brother has a bad toothache.	(8)
trees	What beautiful trees those are!	(5)
tries	He tries to button his own shirt, but he can't do it.	(9)
turn	Turn right at the next corner.	(3)
turn off	Please ask John to turn off the lights.	(2)
turn on	Please ask John to turn on the lights.	(2)
typewriter	How much does that typewriter weigh?	(1)

U

until	He lived in California until he was seventeen.	(5)
up	The restaurant is up those stairs.	(3)
upstairs	After eating breakfast, I go back upstairs again.	(9)

W

walk	It's a short walk from here to the university.	(3)
warm	It's been warm all morning.	(7)
wash	I wash his face and hands, and then I dress him.	(9)
way	It's a long way from here.	(3)
wedding	When is your grandparents' wedding anniversary?	(4)
weekend	Do you think you'll go to the movies next weekend?	(6)

weigh	How much does that typewriter weigh?	(1)
weight	It's not too heavy, but I don't know the exact weight.	(1)
wet	This material feels wet.	(1)
whether	I don't know whether it will rain or not.	(10)
which of	Which of your arms is sore?	(8)
why	Why is Mr. Cooper so tired?	(10)
wide	Will you please measure this window to see how wide it is?	(1)
widow	She's a widow. Her husband died last year.	(4)
width	This window is two feet wide. What's the width of that window?	(1)
wind	There's a strong wind this evening, isn't there?	(7)
windy	It's windy today.	(7)
winter	Today is the first day of winter.	(7)
wonderful	In my opinion, that's a wonderful idea.	(10)
wrap	Would you help me wrap this heavy box?	(2)
wrist	How did you break your wrist?	(8)
wrong	What do you think? Is that wrong?	(10)

Y

yards	That street is only 300 yards long.	(1)
yardstick	Get me a yardstick from the kitchen, will you?	(2)
yourself	You can't dress yourself yet because you're too young.	(9)

Z

zero	The temperature is about zero degrees centigrade.	(7)

KEY

UNIT 1

Page 9

1. *a.* 25 lbs., *b.* heavier, *c.* lighter, *d.* 36 feet, *e.* wider, *f.* width, *g.* narrower, *h.* thick

2. *a.* color, *b.* shape, *c.* weight, *d.* length, *e.* size , *f.* height, *g.* width, *h.* material

3. *a.* light, *b.* large, *c.* hard, *d.* narrow, *e.* dry, *f.* thin, *g.* short, *h.* thick, *i.* wide, *j.* heavy, *k.* soft, *l.* wet, *m.* long

4. *a.* What is the weight; *b.* How wide; *c.* How long; *d.* How thick; *e.* What is the width; *f.* How much heavier; *g.* What color; *h.* What sizes; *i.* What shape; *j.* What is the length; *k.* how tall

5. *a.* weigh, *b.* weigh, *c.* weighs, *d.* measure, *e.* measures, *f.* am, *g.* are, *h.* are, *i.* weigh, *j.* measuring, *k.* weighing, *l.* is , *m.* measuring, *n.* is, *o.* measure

UNIT 2

Page 20

1. *a.* turn . . . on; *b.* Put . . . down; *c.* Hang . . . up; *d.* wait for; *e.* doing . . . for; *f.* pick up; *g.* taking . . . back; *h.* turn . . . off

2. *a.* Would you please get me a hammer?
   b. Would you please count the chairs in this room?
   c. Would you please pour this milk into that glass?
   d. Would you please help me lift this heavy box?
   e. Would you please take these books home?
   f. Would you please turn the lights off?
   g. Would you please bring me those magazines?

3. *a.* help, *b.* helping, *c.* help, *d.* help, *e.* mail, *f.* mailing, *g.* mail, *h.* mail, *i.* hang, *j.* hanging, *k.* hang, *l.* hang

4. *a.* Don't wait for me at five o'clock.
   b. She won't have time to do me a favor.
   c. He didn't get me a glass of milk yesterday.
   d. Aren't you going to help me wrap this box?
   e. Don't bring me a yardstick.
   f. These nails don't weigh too much.
   g. I didn't turn off the radio.
   h. I'm not very busy.
   i. Don't pour me a cup of coffee.
   j. He didn't help me lift the heavy box.
   k. Don't count all the chairs in this room.
   l. He isn't bothering me.
   m. Isn't he talking to you?
   n. Don't take these magazines back to the library.
   o. Don't leave your books on the table.

UNIT 3

Page 30

1. *a.* way,   *b.* straight ahead,   *c.* far,   *d.* miss,   *e.* across,
   f. long drive,   *g.* miles,   *h.* taken,   *i.* right,   *j.* corner

2. *a.* Peach Street is two miles straight ahead.
   b. The bank is five miles from here.
   c. The nearest restaurant is across the street.
   d. You should go to the right at the next corner to get to the post office.
   e. The nearest telephone is in the men's room or the ladies' room.
   f. The school is in the middle of the next block.
   g. The railroad station is around the corner.
   h. The National Theater is right on the corner of Washington Street.
   i. It is a long drive from here to the airport.
   j. The university is about two miles to the left.

3. *a.* How far is the church from here?
   b. Where is the bank?
   c. Who is this seat reserved for?
   d. Whose address don't I know?
   e. Which way should we turn at the next corner?
   f. What is a short walk from the

g. What is around the corner?

h. Who gave me some information?

i. Which way is the National Theater?

j. Where is the telephone?

k. What time will the post office open?

l. How old is Mr. Cooper?

m. How far is the airport from the town?

n. When am I going to school?

o. How often is this table reserved for Mr. Cooper?

p. Whose telephone number is this?

q. Which seat is occupied?

UNIT 4

Page 40

1. *a.* grandparents, *b.* aunt, *c.* uncle, *d.* cousin, *e.* niece,
   f. nephew, *g.* grandchildren, *h.* brother, *i.* sister
   j. grandmother, *k.* grandfather, *l.* husband

2. *a.* Our, *b.* My, *c.* your, *d.* Their, *e.* His, *f.* Her

3. *a.* She's a widow. Her husband died last year.
   b. He's engaged to be married.
   c. They're going to have a baby.
   d. You're still single.
   e. They don't know when the wedding will be.
   f. She didn't get married last year.
   g. Mr. and Mrs. Cooper don't have any children but they'd like to.
   h. George isn't a bachelor; he's been married for a long time.
   i. I'm a bachelor, but I'd like to get married.
   j. They've been married for approximately three years.
   k. I'm going to get married in exactly three days.
   l. My sister's been engaged for two months.
   m. Today's my parents' anniversary.

4. *a.* Your nephew is engaged, isn't he?
   b. Your granddaughter got married in 1945, didn't she?
   c. You're still a bachelor, aren't you?
   d. They had a child last month, didn't they?
   e. Yesterday was your anniversary, wasn't it?
   f. They've been married for many years, haven't they?

g. She's been a widow since last year, hasn't she?

h. Mr. and Mrs. Cooper have several children, don't they? (haven't they?)

i. Your wedding will take place in June, won't it?

j. You're engaged now, aren't you?

k. Your niece is married, isn't she?

l. You got married last year, didn't you?

UNIT 5

Page 50

1. *a.* grow up, *b.* grew up, *c.* grow up, *d.* grew up, *e.* grow up, *f.* grows up

2. *a.* woke up, *b.* wake up, *c.* wakes up, *d.* woke up, *e.* woke up

3. *a.* spent, *b.* spend, *c.* spend, *d.* spent, *e.* spent

4. *a.* of, *b.* up, *c.* on, *d.* in, *e.* from, *f.* until, *g.* from, *h.* on, *i.* in, *j.* up

5. *a.* What a large building that is!

   b. What beautiful flowers those are!

   c. What quiet neighbors you have!

   d. What a happy childhood he had!

   e. What a noisy neighborhood this is!

   f. What a friendly couple that is!

6. *a.* he did, *b.* I did, *c.* she has, *d.* I don't, *e.* I am, *f.* he hasn't, *g.* she won't, *h.* she did, *i.* there have, *j.* they are

REVIEW ONE

Page 54

2. *a.* weigh, *b.* weighed, *c.* liked, *d.* feels, *e.* owned, *f.* have, *g.* measured, *h.* weighs, *i.* asked, *j.* bothering, *k.* hung up, *l.* wrapping, *m.* pouring, *n.* building, *o.* moved in, *p.* spent, *q.* buys, *r.* used to, *s.* grew up, *t.* bought, *u.* are, *v.* telling, *w.* is, *x.* got married, *y.* died, *z.* wants to

3.

No Key answers can be given for these exercises.

4.

UNIT 6

Page 64

1. *a.* left, *b.* leave, *c.* will leave, *d.* went, *e.* am going (go),
   f. will go, *g.* was, *h.* will be, *i.* woke up, *j.* will wake up,
   k. watched, *l.* will watch

2. *a.* John'll probably wake up soon.
   b. He'll have breakfast after he wakes up.
   c. Then he'll get ready to go to work.
   d. After that, he'll leave the house.
   e. He'll read the newspaper on the way to work.
   f. John won't wake up in the middle of the night.
   g. He won't go out for breakfast.
   h. He won't leave the house before breakfast.
   i. He won't finish working until 5:30.
   j. He won't get home by 6:30.
   k. He'll get home at 7:00.
   l. He'll be able to eat dinner with us.
   m. Next, he'll probably watch television.
   n. After that, he'll go to sleep.

3. *a.* Do you think you'll finish reading the newspaper at 5:30?
   b. Do you think he got home by 6:00 yesterday?
   c. Do you think John'll go to the movies with us?
   d. Do you think she'll be able to go out for lunch?
   e. Do you think they woke up early yesterday morning?
   f. Do you think he used to leave the house at 8 o'clock?
   g. Do you think you'll be able to make some phone calls after breakfast?
   h. Do you think they wrote some letters after breakfast?
   i. Do you think we'll finish working at 5:30?
   j. Do you think I'll be able to get home by 6 o'clock?
   k. Do you think your friend went to sleep right away?
   l. Do you think John made some phone calls early this morning?
   m. Do you think she'll be ready to go to work right away?
   n. Do you think Mr. Cooper'll be able to eat dinner with us a week from today?

UNIT 7

Page 74

1. *a.* it did, *b.* it isn't, *c.* it is, *d.* it hasn't, *e.* it has, *f.* it isn't, *g.* it is, *h.* it wasn't, *i.* it doesn't, *j.* there is, *k.* they are

2. *a.* hailed, *b.* snowing, *c.* hotter, *d.* raining, *e.* nice, *f.* drizzling, *g.* wind, *h.* cloudy, *i.* cleared up, *j.* terrible

Student A	Student B
3. *a.* It's cold today, isn't it?	Yes, it is.
b. Today is the first day of spring, isn't it?	Yes, it is.
c. There's a strong wind this evening, isn't there?	Yes, there is.
d. The temperature will be about 70 degrees today, won't it?	Yes, it will.
e. It'll probably clear up this afternoon, won't it?	Yes, it will.
f. It's been cloudy all morning, hasn't it?	Yes, it has.
g. The weather was miserable last week, wasn't it?	Yes, it was.
h. It snowed all day yesterday, didn't it?	Yes, it did.
i. It's been cold all winter, hasn't it?	Yes, it has.
j. There was a terrible storm in New York, wasn't there?	Yes, there was.

4. *a.* It, *b.* You, *c.* There, *d.* She, *e.* We, *f.* He, *g.* they, *h.* I

UNIT 8

Page 84

1. *a.* don't, *b.* is, *c.* has, *d.* hurts, *e.* break, *f.* slipped, *g.* slips, *h.* hopes, *i.* is, *j.* broken, *k.* hope to, *l.* got, *m.* better, *n.* swollen

2. *a.* sick, *b.* coughing, sore throat, *c.* had to, *d.* matter, *e.* ached, *f.* better, *g.* pains

3. *a.* fell, *b.* swollen, bleeding, *c.* ought to, *d.* hurts, *e.* break, *f.* pain

4. *a.* I've got a terrible toothache.
   b. He's got a broken leg.
   c. You'd better see a doctor about that.
   d. She doesn't feel well this morning.
   e. He shouldn't go to work with a bad cold.
   f. I don't feel better today.
   g. My fever's gone.
   h. My arm's broken.

5. *a.* John doesn't have a fever.
   b. I haven't got a headache.
   c. I didn't hurt my leg when I fell down.
   d. Haven't you ever had a sore throat?
   e. Didn't you have a toothache yesterday?
   f. Aren't you feeling sick today?
   g. Shouldn't you see a doctor about that?
   h. Didn't she feel better this morning?

UNIT 9

Page 95

1. *a.* I get out of bed every morning about 7 o'clock.
   b. I brush my teeth after taking a shower.
   c. I go downstairs after I put on my clothes.
   d. I eat breakfast downstairs in the kitchen.
   e. My brother can't dress himself yet because he is too young.
   f. I feel tired and hungry when I come home from work.
   g. I put on my pajamas at bedtime.
   h. I get into bed about 11:30.

2. *a.* get out, *b.* getting up, *c.* put on, *d.* wake up, *e.* go into, *f.* take off, *g.* get into, *h.* go . . . off

3. *a.* My little brother still can't dress himself.
   b. My little brother can't bathe himself yet.
   c. I always get up at 7:00 every morning.
   d. He usually brushes his teeth after he shaves.
   e. He still hasn't combed his hair.
   f. He hasn't washed his face and hands yet.
   g. I'm always hungry when I wake up.
   h. I'm usually tired when I come home from work.

4. *a*. my,   *b*. his,   *c*. himself,   *d*. her,   *e*. herself,   *f*. them-
selves,   *g*. yourself,   *h*. their,   *i*. your,   *j*. they,   *k*. he,
l. we,   *m*. I (we),   *n*. she,   *o*. you

5. *a*. brush,   *b*. comb,   *c*. fix,   *d*. button,   *e*. shave,   *f*. wash,
g. take,   *h*. jump,   *i*. put,   *j*. take

UNIT 10

Page 107

1. *a*. Do you think it's going to rain tomorrow?
    b. Don't you think you're mistaken about that?
    c. Do you suppose Mr. Cooper was tired because he worked hard all day?
    d. Do you believe I'll enjoy the movie?
    e. Do you feel you can give me your honest opinion?
    f. Don't you feel Mr. Cooper is angry because he didn't have lunch today?
    g. Don't you believe Mr. Cooper is happy because today is his birthday?
    h. Don't you suppose Mr. Cooper prefers warm weather?
    i. Do you think she loves winter weather?
    j. Do you believe he worked hard all day?

2. *a*. I don't know whether it'll rain tomorrow or not.
    b. I don't know whether John will enjoy the movie or not.
    c. I don't know whether John will give you his honest opinion or not.
    d. I don't know whether I'll see Mr. Cooper next Sunday or not.
    e. I don't know whether she's mistaken about that or not.
    f. I don't know whether Mr. Cooper prefers warm weather or not.
    g. I don't know whether I'll finish working early today or not.
    h. I don't know whether she had lunch yet or not.
    i. I don't know whether John always eats good food or not.

3. *a*. judgment,   *b*. like,   *c*. wonderful,   *d*. wrong,   *e*. correct,
    f. Naturally

4. *a*. Yes, he is. No, he isn't.
    b. Yes, I do. No, I don't.
    c. Yes, I do. No, I don't.

d. Yes, she does. No, she doesn't.
e. Yes, you are. No, you aren't.
f. Yes, we are. No, we aren't.
g. Yes, he was. No, he wasn't.
h. Yes, we were. No, we weren't.
i. Yes, I did. No, I didn't.
j. Yes, I did. No, I didn't.
k. Yes, he does. No, he doesn't.
l. Yes, she is. No, she isn't.
m. Yes, you are. No, you aren't.
n. Yes, he is. No, he isn't.

REVIEW TWO

Page 110

1. a. I will (am going to) get up at 7 o'clock tomorrow.
   b. I will (am going to) have breakfast at 9 o'clock tomorrow.
   c. I will (am going to) go to the movies with a friend of mine tomorrow.
   d. We will (are going to) have dinner at home tomorrow.
   e. I will (am going to) get dressed quickly tomorrow.
   f. I will (am going to) have toast and coffee for breakfast tomorrow.
   g. My brother will (is going to) get up later than I will tomorrow.
   h. I will (am going to) finish working at 5:30 in the afternoon tomorrow.
   i. My sister will (is going to) go to sleep immediately tomorrow.
   j. My parents will (are going to) leave the house at 10 o'clock tomorrow.
   k. It will (is going to) rain all day tomorrow.
   l. There will (is going to) be a cool breeze tomorrow.
   m. It will (is going to) snow tomorrow.
   n. I won't (am not going to) feel well tomorrow.
   o. My little brother will (is going to) take a bath before he goes to bed tomorrow.
   p. We will (are going to) be tired when we come home from work tomorrow.
   q. Will it (Is it going to) rain tomorrow?
   r. Will he (Is he going to) be sick tomorrow?
   s. The weather will (is going to) be very nice tomorrow.

t. She will (is going to) go out for lunch at 12 noon tomorrow.

u. Will you (Are you going to) have dinner at home tomorrow?

v. When I get sleepy tomorrow, I will (am going to) go to bed.

w. After breakfast tomorrow, I will (am going to) get ready to go to work.

x. Mrs. Cooper will (is going to) go to sleep at about 11:30 tomorrow.

y. My brother will (is going to) wake up at 7 o'clock tomorrow.

z. She will (is going to) get dressed at 6:30 tomorrow.

2. *a.* I won't get up at 6 o'clock tomorrow.

   b. My birthday will not be tomorrow.

   c. We won't have dinner at home tomorrow.

   d. I will not eat dinner at 8 p.m. tomorrow.

   e. I will not watch television for an hour tomorrow.

   f. We will not work from 9 a.m. until 5:30 p.m. tomorrow.

   g. Tomorrow I will not measure the windows to see how wide they are.

   h. I will not be able to go to sleep immediately tomorrow.

   i. They will not buy the house on the corner tomorrow.

   j. My cousin will not get married tomorrow.

3. *a.* Did you get up at 6 o'clock?

   b. Are you married yet?

   c. How long have they been married?

   d. Do they know when the wedding will be?

   e. Is the weather nice today?

   f. Is it raining now?

   g. What is the temperature this afternoon?

4.

No Key answers can be given for these exercises.

5.

ENGLISH

900

WORKBOOK THREE

prepared by
ENGLISH LANGUAGE SERVICES, INC.
Washington, D.C.

The Macmillan Company
Collier-Macmillan Limited, London
Collier-Macmillan Canada, Ltd.

INTRODUCTION

is workbook is one of a series of six prepared
r students of English as a second language. The
workbooks contain drill and review material
vering all the basic patterns of English.

ne workbooks are self-teaching. The student
ows immediately whether his answer to each
estion is right or wrong. He works by himself,
th little or no outside assistance, and he can
oceed rapidly through material he knows and
ore slowly through material which is difficult for
m. The material in each book is divided into ten
nits.

hese workbooks have been designed to be used
dependently by students of English, but they can
lso be used as supplements to the six textbooks in
he same series, or with any other series of textbooks.

DIRECTIONS

Read item 1 below. Write in your answer. If you
elect "am", you are directed to item 6, as the arrow
below shows. Here you are told that your answer to
tem 1 is right. So you go ahead and try item 6.
From item 6 go to the number that appears next to
he answer you have selected, and so on.

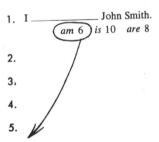

1. I _____ John Smith.
    am 6   is 10   are 8

2.

3.

4.

5.

6. Right! Go to next question.

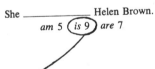

   She _____ Helen Brown.
       am 5   is 9   are 7

7.

8.

9. Right! Go to next question.

Read item 1 again. If you select "is" as the answer,
you are directed to item 10 (see below). Now see
what happens. Here you are told that your answer
is wrong. Item 10 contains some study sentences to
help you correct your mistake, and another question.
Read item 10 and write in your answer to this question. Go to the number that appears next to the
answer you have selected. Again you will be told
whether your answer is right or wrong.

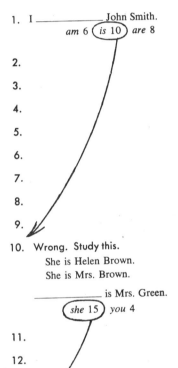

1. I _____ John Smith.
       am 6   is 10   are 8

2.

3.

4.

5.

6.

7.

8.

9.

10. Wrong. Study this.
    She is Helen Brown.
    She is Mrs. Brown.

    _____ is Mrs. Green.
       she 15   you 4

11.

12.

13.

14.

15. Right! Go to next question.

Now go ahead and begin the first question in Unit
One.

머 리 말

본 workbook은 영어를 제2 외국어로하는 학도를 위해서 만들어진 것으로 전부 6권으로 되어 있다. 6권의 workbook에는 각각 영어의 기본 문형에 관한 연습문제(drill)와 복습문제(review)가 들어 있다.

본 workbook은 자습용으로서, 독자는 자신의 해답이 정답인지 오답인지 곧 알 수 있도록 되어 있으며, 선생의 도움이 없어도, 잘 아는 문제라면 빠르게, 좀 힘든 문제라면 천천히라도 할 수는 있을 것이다. 각권은 각기 10개의 Unit로 나누어져 있다.

본 workbook은 독립적으로 이용되도록 만들어진 것이지만, 같은 자매서인 English 900 나 또 다른 textbook와 같이 사용해도 무방할 것이다.

본 workbook 이용 방법

아래의 1번을 보고 답을 맞춰보라. 만일 "am"을 골랐으면 아래의 화살표가 가리키듯이 몇개의 항을 건너 뛰어 6번을 보게 되어 있다. 그러면 6번에는, 1번에 대한 너의 답이 정답(Right!)이라 쓰여있다. 그러면 이번에는 6번의 답을 맞추어 보자. 6번에서도 역시 네가 선택한 답의 옆에 쓰어 있는 숫자를 따라 가서 너의 답이 옳았는지 틀렸는지 알아보게 되어있다.

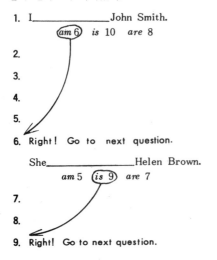

1. I_____John Smith.
   am 6   is 10   are 8

2.
3.
4.
5.
6. Right! Go to next question.
   She_____Helen Brown.
      am 5   is 9   are 7
7.
8.
9. Right! Go to next question.

1번을 다시 보자. 만일 "is"를 골랐다면 "is"옆의 숫자 10을 따라 10번을 보아야 한다. 자 어떻게 되었을까? 10번에는 너의답이 틀렸다(Wrong)고 쓰여 있다. 뿐만 아니라 10번에는 역시 너의 잘못을 정정해 주는 예문과 또 다른 Sentence가 또 쓰여 있을 것이다. 그러면 이번에는 10번을 읽고 답을 맞춰보자. 그리고 네가 선택한 답 옆의 숫자를 따라가 보면, 또다시 네가 옳았는지 틀렸는지 여부를 알수 있게 되어 있다.

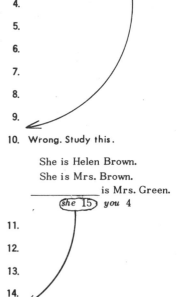

1. I_____John Smith.
      am 6   is 10   are 8

2.
3.
4.
5.
6.
7.
8.
9.
10. Wrong. Study this.

    She is Helen Brown.
    She is Mrs. Brown.
    _____ is Mrs. Green.
         she 15   you 4

11.
12.
13.
14.
15. Right! Go to next question.

   자 그러면 Unit One의 제일 첫문제 부터 풀어보자.

UNIT *1* DESCRIBING OBJECTS

Write your answers.

1. Begin here.

   This book is not _____ heavy.
        two 13   *too* 8   *to* 22

2. Wrong. Study this:
   This table is heavy.
   That chair is dark blue.
   We want to see that car.
   Come to my house this evening.

   Return to 8.

3. Wrong. Study this:
   John has a car.
   We have a nice house.

   Jane has _____ hair.
       long 20   *longs* 15

4. Wrong. Study this:
   I like these men.
   She likes her house.
   Jack feels better today.
   I don't feel well now.

   Return to 27.

5. Wrong. Study this:
   These books are heavy.
   John is tall.

   Bill is Mrs. _____ boy.
       Brown 9   *Brown's* 6

6. Right! Go to the next question.

   John and Mary _____ coming here.
       are 27   *am* 9

7. Right! Go to the next question.

   They work _____ fast for me.
       too 8   *to* 19

8. Right! Go to the next question.

   John is _____ man over there.
       this 14   *that* 21

9. **Wrong. Study this:**
She is Jane's aunt.
They are here.
I am going to the bank.

Return to 11.

10. **Wrong. Study this:**
I can measure the window.
He feels the material.

Jack _____ a car.
owns 18   *own* 4

11. **Right! Go to the next question.**

What color _____ your book?
are 5   *is* 27   *am* 12

12. **Wrong. Study this:**
We are going to the bank.
This room is dark.

Jack's _____ is big.
houses 9   *house* 6

13. **Wrong. Study this:**
That car is too heavy.
I like to write.

We have too much _____.
works 19   *work* 7

14. **Wrong. Study this:**
That is Bill's pen over there.
This is my pen here.

That is _____ hat on the table.
Bill 2   *Bill's* 23

15. **Wrong. Study this:**
We have a car.
This book has a cover.
Mrs. Brown has a family.
They have two pencils.

Return to 21.

16. **Right! Go to the next question.**

She _____ a cold yesterday.
has 24   *had* 31

17. **Right! Go to the next question.**

Mr. Jones _____ to go yesterday.
has 26   *had* 31

18. **Right! Go to the next question.**

Mary wants to _____ the material.
feel 17   *feels* 4

19. **Wrong. Study this:**
Bill is too heavy.
Your hair is too long.
We want to eat.
This book is too heavy.

Return to 1.

20. **Right! Go to the next question.**

The man _____ a watch.
have 15   *has* 11

21. **Right! Go to the next question.**

You _____ to leave.
has 3   *have* 11

22. **Wrong. Study this:**
    I have to go.
    She has two boys.

    It's too _____.
    long 7   *longer* 19

23. **Right! Go to the next question.**

    John's car is _____ one over there.
    this 2   *that* 21

24. **Wrong. Study this:**
    Our house has large rooms.
    We had a party last night.
    It has a blue cover.
    Jack has to see the doctor.

    Return to 17.

25. **Wrong. Study this:**
    Tom has a small car.
    The length of that street is four miles.
    This window is twenty-six inches wide.

    This map _____ thirty inches wide
    are 28   *is* 34

26. **Wrong. Study this:**
    We had a car last year.
    Jack has four books now.

    We had our lessons _____.
    yesterday 16   *tomorrow* 24

27. **Right! Go to the next question.**

    I will _____ the typewriter.
    weighs 10   *weigh* 17

28. **Wrong. Study this:**
    This is a small car.
    The car has a length of ten feet.
    This city has wide streets.
    This small house is only twenty feet wide.

    Return to 31.

29. **Right! Go to the next question.**

    I'm _____ that window now.
    measured 38   *measuring* 39

30. **Wrong. Study this:**
    Jack has a house forty feet in length.
    This small car is easy to drive.
    He has a wide house.

    Mr. Ames _____ a small house.
    owns 34   *own* 28

31. **Right! Go to the next question.**

    This road is twenty feet _____.
    wide 29   *small* 25   *length* 30

32. **Right! Go to the next question.**

    This book _____ two pounds.
    weight 45   *weighs* 41   *weigh* 35

33. **Wrong. Study this:**
    I measured the table an hour ago.
    Jack is measuring the table.
    Are you measuring it now?
    We measured it yesterday.

    Return to 29.

34. **Right! Go to the next question.**

    This road is twenty miles in _____ .
    small 28   *length* 29

35. **Wrong. Study this:**
    We will weigh our suitcases.
    What is the weight of your car?

    Will _____ please weigh your
    suitcase?
    your 42   *you* 44

36. **Wrong. Study this:**
    This car is long.
    My house is longer than his house.

    This street is longer than that _____ .
    streets 37   *street* 43

37. **Wrong. Study this:**
    My pencil is longer than yours.
    Our street is a long street.
    This table is longer than that one.
    Today has been a long day.

    Return to 39.

38. **Wrong. Study this:**
    He measured the table yesterday.
    He is measuring the table now.

    Has _____ measured the table?
    him 33   *he* 40

39. **Right! Go to the next question.**

    This pencil is _____ than that pencil.
    longer 32   *long* 36

40. **Right! Go to the next question.**

    Are you sure you _____ it?
    measuring 33   *measured* 39

41. **Right! End of Unit 1.**

    Now go to Unit 2.

42. **Wrong. Study this:**
    Our suitcases weigh forty-five pounds.
    We will weigh our briefcases.
    The weight of that dog is twenty pounds.
    Their cat doesn't weigh much.

    Return to 32.

43. **Right! Go to the next question.**

    Is this pen _____ than that pen?
    longer 32   *long* 37

44. **Right! Go to the next question.**

    This pencil _____ two ounces.
    weigh 42   *weighs* 41

45. **Wrong. Study this:**
    I can't weigh that book.
    The weight of this pencil is two ounces.

    _____ suitcase weighs twenty
    pounds.
    These 42   *This* 44

UNIT 2 ASKING PEOPLE TO DO THINGS

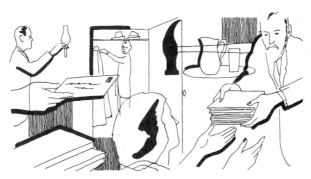

Begin here.

Would you _____ going over there?
    mind 24   *bothers* 25

Wrong. Study this:
  She told me it was here.
  Please tell her tomorrow.

Jack told _____ yesterday.
    he 10   *him* 19

Wrong. Study this:
  Please take Jane's book to her.
  You can get a book at the school.

Please get my book for _____.
    I 11   *me* 30

Right! Go to the next question.

It's dark today. Please _____ the light.
    turn off 12   *turn on* 16

---

5. Wrong. Study this:
  Jack bothers his brother.
  Don't bother me now.

_____ is bothering his mother.
    Him 27   *He* 15

---

6. Right! Go to the next question.

It's dark in here. Please _____ the light.
    turn off 9   *turn on* 16

---

7. Right! Go to the next question.

He _____ my coat in the closet.
    hung down 18   *hung up* 29

---

8. Right! Go to the next question.

Don't _____ me now. I'm busy.
    bother 24   *bothers* 23

222

9. Wrong. Study this:
   We have too much light. Turn off the
   lights.
   John already turned on the lights.

   Will you please _____ off the lights?
        turns 12   turn 4

0. Wrong. Study this:
   I told him yesterday.
   She tells him at night.
   I haven't told Mother yet.
   Jack told me that.

   Return to 24.

11. Wrong. Study this:
    Get the book for me, please.
    He took it to John yesterday.
    Where did he get his dog?
    He brought it to me from New York.

    Return to 31.

12. Wrong. Study this:
    John already turned on the lights.
    Please ask John to turn the lights on.
    It's dark now. Please turn on the lights.
    We don't need the light. Please turn it off.

    Return to 6.

13. Right! Go to the next question.

    Do I _____ you?
        bothers 5   bother 34

14. Wrong. Study this:
    I already put my coat in the closet.
    He picks up his books at about 7 o'clock.

    Will you please pick _____ your
    book?
        up 17   down 21

15. Right! Go to the next question.

    Does that man _____ you?
        bothers 27   bother 34

16. Right! Go to the next question.

    Please _____ those cups and take
    them to the kitchen.
        pick up 7   put 14

17. Right! Go to the next question.

    Will you please _____ your coat i
    the closet?
        pick 21   put 7

18. Wrong. Study this:
    Please put it down.
    Hang it up in the closet.

    Why don't you hang it _____ ?
        up 22   down 26

19. Right! Go to the next question.

    Tom _____ Jack he was coming.
        tell 10   told 6

20. Wrong. Study this:
    Bring your friend to my house.
    I brought my book with me.

    Please bring _____ sister over here
        you 11   your 30

21. Wrong. Study this:
    I already put my books down.
    She picks up the cups and saucers every
    time.
    Please put that cup there.
    Please pick up that chair.

    Return to 16.

22. Right! Go to the next question.

   She _____ her book _____
   on the table.
         put . . . down 29   *hung . . . up* 26

23. Wrong. Study this:
   He doesn't bother me now.
   Tom is bothering Mary.
   I don't mind doing it.
   She doesn't mind reading.

   Return to 1.

24. Right! Go to the next question.

   Please _____ Mr. Jones we are here.
         told 2   *tell* 6

25. Wrong. Study this:
   I don't want to bother you.
   He doesn't mind doing it.

   Jane bothers _____ little brother.
         she 23   *her* 8

26. Wrong. Study this:
   I already put my books down.
   Will you please hang my coat up?
   I already hung it up.
   Please put your pencil down.

   Return to 7.

27. Wrong. Study this:
   My brother bothers me.
   Jack and Jim bother their sister.
   She bothers me.
   Please don't bother her.

   Return to 13.

28. Wrong. Study this:
   I will ask him where it is.
   She will tell me if she knows.

   John will tell _____.
         her 32   *she* 33

29. Right! Go to the next question.

   Please _____ John we're going.
         ask 28   *tell* 31

30. Right! Go to the next question.

   He _____ it at the store.
         take 11   *got* 13

31. Right! Go to the next question.

   Will you _____ it to his house?
         take 13   *brings* 3   *got* 20

32. Right! Go to the next question.

   I _____ her to go with me.
         asked 31   *tells* 33

33. Wrong. Study this:
   Please tell her for me.
   He asked her for it.
   Ask her for a pencil.
   Jack told her where to go.

   Return to 29.

34. Right! End of Unit 2.

   Go to Unit 3.

UNIT **3** GETTING INFORMATION
AND DIRECTIONS

1. **Begin here.**

   Mother _____ me from the table last
   night.

   excuses 18   *excused* 7

2. **Right! Go to the next question.**

   I don't _____ to know John.
   happen 37   *happens* 9

3. **Right! Go to the next question.**

   We are going in the right _____.
   directions 15   *direction* 27

4. **Wrong. Study this:**
   I will excuse you, Tom.
   She excuses someone every day.
   I excused her from class.
   Excuse me, sir.

   Return to 1.

5. **Right! Go to the next question.**

   The church is in that _____.
   direction 27   *directions* 35

6. **Right! Go to the next question.**

   How _____ is it to the bank?
   for 26   *far* 20

7. **Right! Go to the next question.**

   Can you _____ me some
   information?
   take 30   *give* 3   *gave* 11

8. **Right! Go to the next question.**

   Which _____ is it to the church
   way 12   *weigh* 39

9. **Wrong. Study this:**
   Mr. Cooper's telephone happens to be busy
   Do you happen to know his age?
   She happens to have his address.
   His street happens to be the same as mine.

   Return to 38.

10. **Wrong. Study this:**
   It is straight ahead.
   You can turn to the right here.

   Turn to the right ＿＿＿＿＿＿＿.
   mile 36   *here* 13

11. **Wrong. Study this:**
   Jack gave you that yesterday.
   Mary takes her book every day.

   ＿＿＿＿＿＿＿ gives it to him.
   Her 21   *She* 29

12. **Right! Go to the next question.**

   Should I ＿＿＿＿＿＿＿ this way?
   go 38   *went* 23   *gone* 28

13. **Right! Go to the next question.**

   Can I turn ＿＿＿＿＿＿＿ at the next corner?
   straight 36   *right* 34

14. **Wrong. Study this:**
   The typewriter weighs a lot.
   There are many ways to go there.

   ＿＿＿＿＿＿＿ the church this way?
   Are 39   *Is* 8

15. **Wrong. Study this:**
   The theater is in that direction.
   Here are the directions.

   This direction ＿＿＿＿＿＿＿ wrong.
   am 35   *is* 5

16. **Wrong. Study this:**
   John went for his book.
   She had to go far.

   ＿＿＿＿＿＿＿ not too far from it.
   Your 26   *You're* 6

17. **Wrong. Study this:**
   He begs to go along.
   We beg to stay.

   ＿＿＿＿＿＿＿ begs his pardon.
   Her 19   *She* 40

18. **Wrong. Study this:**
   Excuse me, I need some information.
   I was excused yesterday.

   Please excuse ＿＿＿＿＿＿＿.
   me 33   *I* 4

19. **Wrong. Study this:**
   John begs for many things.
   He begs to be excused every day.
   Why do you beg so much?
   He begs for a car.

   Return to 37.

20. **Right! Go to the next question.**

   It's a long ＿＿＿＿＿＿＿ to school.
   weigh 14   *way* 12   *went* 32

21. Wrong. Study this:
    Take her that pencil.
    Jack gave it to her yesterday.
    John gives her a book.
    What did she take to him?

    Return to 7.

22. **Right! Go to the next question.**

    I _____ this way yesterday.
    go 25   *went* 38

23. Wrong. Study this:
    He goes to his house.
    I have gone to my school.

    _____ to your room.
    Goes 25   *Go* 22

24. Wrong. Study this:
    Jack happens to know it.
    I happen to have it.

    _____ happened to know it.
    You 2   *Your* 9

25. Wrong. Study this:
    Go this way for two miles.
    John has gone to the house.
    Mary went yesterday.
    Can we go tomorrow?

    Return to 12.

26. Wrong. Study this:
    John went very far.
    How far am I from it?
    My house is far away.
    What did he go for?

    Return to 34.

27. **Right! Go to the next question.**

    Turn _____ at the next corner.
    straight 10   *right* 34

28. Wrong. Study this:
    Jack went yesterday.
    I want to go home.

    Does she _____ to go?
    have 22   *has* 25

29. **Right! Go to the next question.**

    John will _____ me that information.
    give 3   *take* 21

30. Wrong. Study this:
    I can give you directions.
    She can take her car.

    I will take it with _____.
    me 29   *I* 21

31. **Right! End of Unit 3.**

    Go to Unit 4.

32. Wrong. Study this:
    I weigh 120 pounds.
    The church is that way.

    _____ went that way to school.
    Her 39   *She* 8

33. **Right! Go to the next question.**

    We left when we were _____.
    excuses 4   *excused* 7

34. Right! Go to the next question.

It is not _____ to the school.
    far 20   *for* 16

37. Right! Go to the next question.

I _____ your pardon.
    beg 31   *begs* 17

38. Right! Go to the next question.

Do you _____ to know his number?
    happens 24   *happen* 37

35. Wrong. Study this:
    Which direction is it to the bank?
    It is in this direction.
    Who can give me directions?
    You have to go in this direction.

Return to 3.

39. Wrong. Study this:
    We don't know the way to the church.
    Please tell us the way.
    Is it a long way to the church?
    This table weighs a lot.

Return to 20.

36. Wrong. Study this:
    Turn left at the next corner.
    You can only turn right.
    We must go straight ahead.
    Go to the left at the next road.

Return to 27.

40. Right! Go to the next question.

I _____ to go, too.
    beg 31   *begs* 19

UNIT 4 TALKING ABOUT FAMILY AND RELATIVES

1. **Begin here.**

   Are you _____?

   marry 9   *married* 8

2. **Wrong. Study this:**
   My grandfather got married in 1931.
   My sister wants to get married.

   Jack got _____ in June.

   marry 4   *married* 13

3. **Right! Go to the next question.**

   That couple is _____.

   marry 6   *married* 8

4. **Wrong. Study this:**
   Jack wanted to get married.
   She will never get married.
   John and Betty got married last year.
   We got married in June.

   Return to 8.

5. **Wrong. Study this:**
   Jack and Mary have been engaged for two months.
   She has been engaged to Jack for a long time.

   Has she _____ engaged for a long time?

   be 17   *been* 23

6. **Wrong. Study this:**
   Jack was married last year.
   I am now married.
   My mother married young.
   Jack is not married.

   Return to 1.

7. **Right! Go to the next question.**

   He _____ to go home.

   want 12   *wants* 18

Right! Go to the next question.

She wants to _____ married.
    got 2   *get* 11

Wrong. Study this:
  John is married.
  Jim will marry Jane.

_____ not married.
    I'm 3   *He am* 6

Wrong. Study this:
  My mother died last year.
  Did his cousin die in June?
  His uncle died in California.
  My old dog may die soon.

Return to 39.

Right! Go to the next question.

My sister _____ engaged for a year.
    have been 5   *has been* 7

. Wrong. Study this:
  Jack wants a new car.
  Do you want to see him?

I want to _____ it now.
    had 14   *have* 19

3. Right! Go to the next question.

Mr. and Mrs. Green _____ married
in 1940.
    get 4   *got* 11

14. Wrong. Study this:
  Does she want to get married?
  I think she wants to get married.
  They want to go home.
  She wants a new coat.

Return to 7.

15. Wrong. Study this:
  He doesn't have a car.
  I don't have one, either.

She doesn't have to _____.
    went 16   *go* 24

16. Wrong. Study this:
  Who doesn't have a book?
  We don't have any children.
  My grandfather doesn't have any friends.
  They don't have enough time.

Return to 18.

17. Wrong. Study this:
  We have been engaged too long.
  You have been engaged for a long time.
  Have you been engaged long?
  They've been engaged for quite a long time.

Return to 11.

18. Right! Go to the next question.

They _____ know when they can
come.
    doesn't 15   *don't* 25

19. Right! Go to the next question.

Paul _____ to see the house.
    wants 18   *want* 14

20. Wrong. Study this:
    Jane has a baby.
    This neighborhood has many babies.

    When _____ they have a baby?
    did 29   *does* 21

21. Wrong. Study this:
    We have had four babies.
    When we have another baby, we will have
    to move.
    She has a small baby.
    They have a new baby.

    Return to 25.

22. Right! Go to the next question.

    My _____ church is near here.
    parents' 37   *parents* 30

23. Right! Go to the next question.

    John has been _____ for a long time.
    engage 17   *engaged* 7

24. Right! Go to the next question.

    Jane and Tom _____ have children.
    doesn't 16   *don't* 25

25. Right! Go to the next question.

    They _____ a baby last month.
    had 28   *have* 27   *has* 20

26. Wrong. Study this:
    My parents are nice people.
    Your parents' garden is pretty.

    I would _____ you to meet my
    parents.
    likes 30   *like* 22

27. Wrong. Study this:
    Bob and Betty had a baby last month.
    When they have a baby, their house will I
    too small.

    _____ parents had four babies.
    My 29   *Mine* 21

28. Right! Go to the next question.

    When is your _____ anniversary?
    parents' 37   *parent* 33   *parents* 26

29. Right! Go to the next question.

    Many people _____ babies at home
    has 21   *have* 28

30. Wrong. Study this:
    My mother and father are my parents.
    His father's friend is nice.
    His parent's grandfather died.
    Our parents' friends came over.

    Return to 28.

31. Right! Go to the next question.

    Jane is going to be _____ next week
    marry 32   *married* 39

32. Wrong. Study this:
    It is going to be hard to do.
    The wedding is going to be in May.
    I am going to the bank.
    Jack has gone to church.

    Return to 37.

Wrong. Study this:
My parents' house is old.
His other parent's aunt died.

Who _____ your parents' friends?
      are 22   *is* 30

Right! End of Unit 4.

Go to Unit 5.

Right! Go to the next question.

Your flowers may _____ if you don't
water them.
      die 34   *died* 10

Wrong. Study this:
We will all die some day.
My grandfather died many years ago.

I'm afraid to _____.
      die 35   *died* 10

37. Right! Go to the next question.

The wedding is _____ to be in June.
      gone 38   *going* 39

38. Wrong. Study this:
They have gone away.
They are going away.

They are _____ to go away.
      gone 32   *going* 31

39. Right! Go to the next question.

One of his friends _____ last night.
      die 36   *died* 34

UNIT 5 TALKING ABOUT NEIGHBORS AND FRIENDS

1. Begin here.

Our children are _____ now.
    grow up 12   *grown up* 3
    grew up 9

2. Right! Go to the next question.

John _____ a little building.
    built 11   *building* 13

3. Right! Go to the next question.

I _____ my childhood on a farm.
    spends 8   *spent* 10

4. Wrong. Study this:
    We spent our childhood there.
    They will spend their childhood here.
    My early years were spent in school.
    My father spent his childhood in America

Return to 3.

5. Right! Go to the next question.

Did you _____ your childhood in America?
    spent 4   *spend* 10

6. Wrong. Study this:
    He built a beautiful house.
    Building a house is not easy.

_____ you building a new house?
    Am 13   *Are* 2

7. Right! Go to the next question.

My children are _____ now.
    grown up 3   *grew up* 17

8. Wrong. Study this:
    Where did you spend your time?
    I spent my time at home.

She spent _____ time cooking.
    she 4   *her* 5

9. Wrong. Study this:
    They grew up very fast.
    They have grown up now.

    _____ you think they have grown
    up?
        Does 17   *Do* 7

10. Right! Go to the next question.

    Mr. Green has _____ a new home
        built 11   *building* 6

11. Right! Go to the next question.

    We're going to _____ a house.
        build 16   *building* 30   *built* 22

12. Wrong. Study this:
    When I grow up, I will be tall.
    They have grown up now.

    She will grow up to be a _____.
        woman 7   *man* 17

13. Wrong. Study this:
    We are building a home next year.
    When will you build another one?
    He built it last year.
    He's trying to build it quickly.

    Return to 10.

14. Wrong. Study this:
    There have been many people here.
    There has been a change in John.

    There _____ been many changes in
    cars.
        has 20   *have* 23

15. Right! Go to the next question.

    John is going to build a _____.
        building 16   *build* 19

16. Right! Go to the next question.

    They're _____ in now.
        move 27   *moving* 18   *moves* 25

17. Wrong. Study this:
    She was grown up when she married.
    Children grow up very fast.
    When we grew up, we were married.
    Grandmother grew up in Virginia.

    Return to 1.

18. Right! Go to the next question.

    We _____ this house last month.
        buy 35   *bought* 31

19. Wrong. Study this:
    A house is a building.
    They built a house last year.
    We are going to build a building.
    We built a building last year.

    Return to 11.

20. Wrong. Study this:
    See if there have been any changes.
    There has been a change in this book.
    There have been many changes in this city.
    There has been a big change in Mary.

    Return to 41.

234

21. **Wrong. Study this:**
    There has been a change in John.
    We have made changes in the book.

    He has made some _____ in his plans.

    changes 36   *change* 26

22. **Wrong. Study this:**
    John built a house.
    A building was built.

    They _____ a building last year

    build 19   *built* 15

23. **Right! Go to the next question.**

    You will see where there _____ been changes in the book.

    has 20   *have* 28

24. **Right! Go to the next question.**

    When do we start _____?

    moving 18   *moved* 29

25. **Wrong. Study this:**
    We moved last year.
    We're moving in tomorrow.

    _____ moved last week.

    They 24   *Them* 29

26. **Wrong. Study this:**
    There have been many changes in these books.
    We will have a change in the weather tomorrow.
    I have had to change my plans.
    You will see many changes in this neighborhood.

    Return to 28.

27. **Wrong. Study this:**
    I want to move soon.
    Moving is not easy.

    When _____ move, I want to go too.

    them 29   *they* 24

28. **Right! Go to the next question.**

    There have been many _____ in this neighborhood.

    change 33   *changes* 37
    changed 21

29. **Wrong. Study this:**
    Paul moved the table over there.
    Please help me move this.
    Moving this table takes two men.
    Moving day is coming soon.

    Return to 16.

30. **Wrong. Study this:**
    Jane and Bob have built a house.
    They have to build a building.

    You _____ a new building last year.

    build 19   *built* 15

31. **Right! Go to the next question.**

    Did you _____ him pretty well?

    knew 42   *know* 41

32. **Right! Go to the next question.**

    I _____ her before he did.

    know 38   *knew* 41

33. **Wrong. Study this:**
    I see only one change in this building.
    Changes have been made in this building.

    We've seen a _____ in this town.
    changes 26   *change* 36

34. **Right!** Go to the next question.

    I _____ this house yesterday.
    buy 40   *bought* 31

35. **Wrong. Study this:**
    If you buy it, will you live there?
    Who bought this house?

    We bought it from _____father.
    he's 40   *his* 34

36. **Right!** Go to the next question.

    Will we have a _____ in the
    weather?
    changes 26   *change* 37

37. **Right!** Go to the next question.

    Mr. Brown _____ rented the big
    house.
    is 39   *has* 43

38. **Wrong. Study this:**
    We knew each other in California.
    They already knew each other.
    I would know him if I saw him.
    I didn't know him very well.

    Return to 31.

39. **Wrong. Study this:**
    She is renting her farm.
    John has rented a car.

    When is _____ renting the building?
    he 46   *him* 49

40. **Wrong. Study this:**
    When are you going to buy it?
    We have already bought it.
    I am sorry we bought it.
    I am sorry we did not buy it.

    Return to 18.

41. **Right!** Go to the next question.

    There_____ been many
    changes in this city.
    has 14   *have* 28

42. **Wrong. Study this:**
    Jack knew Mary for a long time.
    I want to know who he is.

    I knew they _____married.
    was 38   *were* 32

43. **Right!** Go to the next question.

    Mr. Jones _____ his home.
    rent 52   *rents* 50

44. **Right!** Go to the next question.

    I _____my house to him.
    rent 50   *rents* 48

45. Wrong. Study this:
    We go across the street to the store every·
    day.
    John went around the corner to buy some
    flowers.

    Why did you _____ around the
    block?
        goes 53   go 51

46. Right! Go to the next question.

    They _____ rented it for two years.
        were 49   have 43

47. Right! End of Unit 5.

    Go to Unit 6.

48. Wrong. Study this:
    You rent your house to me.
    He rents his house from me.
    We rent our house to them.

    Return to 43.

49. Wrong. Study this:
    They are going to rent my home.
    Has he rented it yet?
    No, he is renting it soon.
    She has rented a little house.

    Return to 37.

50. Right! Go to the next question.

    We like that house _____ the stree
        across 47   around 45

51. Right! Go to the next question.

    Why should we go _____ the street
        across 47   around 53

52. Wrong. Study this:
    We want to rent a new home.
    He rents houses.

    She _____ her house to me.
        rent 48   rents 44

53. Wrong. Study this:
    We rented the house across the street.
    We took a walk around the block.
    Does she live across the street from you?
    Did she move around the corner from you?

    Return to 50.

T 6 TALKING ABOUT FUTURE ACTIVITIES

Begin here.

What time are you going to _____?
  got up 2   *get* 9   *get up* 10

Wrong. Study the following:
  He will get up early.
  She got up late this morning.

They are going to get _____ late.
  of 4   *up* 11

. Right! Go to the next question.

You _____ probably get sleepy.
  'll 6   *are* 18

. Wrong. Study the following:
  They get up at seven o'clock.
  We have to get up early.
  I didn't get up very early this morning.
  I got up early yesterday.

Return to 1.

5. Right! Go to the next question.

What are you going to do _____?
  than 8   *then* 3

6. Right! Go to the next question.

I think he will _____ able to get up
early.
  be 19   *been* 17

7. Right! Go to the next question.

If I get up too early, I _____
probably get sleepy.
  'll 6   *are* 12

8. Wrong. Study the following:
  We will go to the bank tomorrow. We will
  get some money then.
  This pencil is longer than that one.
  Let's eat at six o'clock; we can talk then.
  If we get up then, we will still be sleepy.

Return to 10.

9. **Wrong. Study the following:**
   I am going to get up early.
   When will you get up?

   I _____ going to get up late.
   am 11   *is* 4

16. **Right! Go to the next question.**

   After I _____ dressed, I'll have
   breakfast.
   got 25   *get* 22   *gets* 30

10. **Right! Go to the next question.**

   What will you do _____?
   than 15   *then* 3

17. **Wrong. Study this:**
   I am able to get up early.
   I will be able to get up tomorrow.

   I _____ been able to get up early
   many mornings.
   having 13   *have* 24

11. **Right! Go to the next question.**

   When are they going to _____?
   got up 4   *get up* 10

18. **Wrong. Study this:**
   I am going to get up early.
   I am going to stay late.

   _____ you going to get up early?
   Are 7   *Will* 12

12. **Wrong. Study the following:**
   You'll have to get up at seven.
   When we get up, I'll get dressed.
   I am going to go after I eat.
   Are you going to get up at seven?

   Return to 3.

13. **Wrong. Study this:**
   Jane was sick yesterday, but she is able to
   work today.
   I have been able to eat every day.
   He has been able to go to work every day.

   Return to 6.

19. **Right! Go to the next question.**

   Are you able to go _____?
   yesterday 28   *now* 16

20. **Right! Go to the next question.**

   When will she _____ home?
   got 29   *get* 22

14. **Right! Go to the next question.**

   John will probably be ready _____
   than 27   *then* 16

15. **Wrong. Study this:**

   I like this table better than that one.
   She will then go to the bank.

   Can _____ leave then?
   she 5   *her* 8

21. **Wrong. Study this:**
   Jack left early this morning.
   Jane leaves home late every morning.
   I leave the house at seven o'clock every
   day.
   When will she leave for work?

   Return to 22.

2. Right! Go to the next question.

When will you _____ to go to the movies?
    leaves 23   *left* 34   *leave* 26

23. Wrong. Study this:
He leaves the house early every day.
Jack leaves his office at 5:00.

Mr. Rice will _____ his car at home.
    leaves 21   *leave* 31

24. Right! Go to the next question.

Will you _____ able to get up fo breakfast?
    been 13   *be* 19

25. Wrong. Study this:
I'll have to get up early.
She got up late this morning.

_____ gets up early every day.
    Her 29   *She* 20

26. Right! Go to the next question.

What will she _____ then?
    does 38   *do* 35

27. Wrong. Study the following:
First, we will eat; then we'll go to work.
I want to watch television now.
The cat wants to eat now.
I'll probably go to lunch then.

Return to 19.

28. Wrong. Study this:
What will you do then?
I am ready to go now.

Can we _____ now?
    eating 27   *eat* 14

29. Wrong. Study this:
He gets dressed at 7 o'clock.
They got ready to go.
I get ready before 6 o'clock.
They get ready very early.

Return to 16.

30. Wrong. Study this:
Paul gets up early every day.
They got ready for bed when they got sleepy.

Why don't _____ get ready for bed?
    your 29   *you* 20

31. Right! Go to the next question.

After he _____, let's eat dinner.
    leaves 26   *leave* 21

32. Right! Go to the next question.

When _____ I have to go to work?
    do 35   *does* 41

33. Right! Go to the next question.

Jack _____ to his home early.
    left 40   *went* 36

34. Wrong. Study this:
I left yesterday.
He left for work late.

When _____ he leave for school?
    do 21   *does* 31

35. Right! Go to the next question.

Mr. Brown _____ home for the office.
    left 36   *went* 45

36. Right! Go to the next question.

I'll probably _____ at 7 o'clock.
    woke up 44   *wakes up* 37
    wake up 43

37. Wrong. Study this:
I woke up early this morning.
We wake up at 7 o'clock each morning.

He _____ not wake up very early.
    does 42   *do* 39

38. Wrong. Study this:
They do the same thing every day.
I'll do that work tonight.

Do you _____ to go?
    has 41   *have* 32

39. Wrong. Study this:
She'll probably wake up early tomorrow.
We woke up early.
He wakes up when he has slept a long time.
When do we have to wake up?

Return to 36.

40. Wrong. Study this:
Mrs. Jones left the store at 8 o'clock.
She went to the bank.
We went to the theater after we left the restaurant.
I left the house after dinner.

Return to 35.

41. Wrong. Study this:
He does the same work every day.
We do our work before we watch television.
She does the same thing every day.

Return to 26.

42. Right! Go to the next question.

They _____ up early yesterday.
    wake 39   *woke* 43

43. Right! End of Unit 6.

Go to Unit 7.

44. Wrong. Study this:
We woke up early.
Paul wakes up early every morning.

John and _____ wake up about the same time.
    him 39   *he* 42

45. Wrong. Study this:
I left work early.
I went to my home early.

When I left home, I went to

_____ office.
    my 33   *me* 40

UNIT 7 TALKING ABOUT THE WEATHER

1. **Begin here.**

   The weather will _____ tomorrow.
      clears up 10   *cleared up* 3
      clear up 9

2. **Wrong. Study this:**
   It clears up nearly every day before noon.
   I think it will clear up tonight.
   It cleared up this morning.
   When do you think it will clear up?

   Return to 1.

3. **Wrong. Study this:**
   It will clear up tonight.
   It cleared up yesterday.

   _____ it cleared up yet?
      Have 2   *Has* 12

4. **Right! Go to the next question.**

   Do you think it will _____ than it is now?
      gets hotter 17   *get hotter* 8

5. **Right! Go to the next question.**

   It has been _____ cold lately.
      quiet 18   *quite* 14

6. **Wrong. Study this:**
   It has rained quite hard.
   It is quiet when it snows.
   Has it ever been quite so cold?
   He is a quiet man.

   Return to 5.

7. **Wrong. Study this:**
   The days will get hotter in July.
   The days get hot by noon.

   The weather _____ gets hotter every year.
      hear 17   *here* 4

8. **Right! Go to the next question.**

   I _____ very well, thank you.
      has been 16   *have been* 5

9   Right! Go to the next question.

The weather here _____ every year.
    get hot 7   *gets hotter* 8
    get hotter 13

10. Wrong. Study this:
     It clears up every afternoon.
     I think it will probably clear up.

Maybe it _____ clear.
    'll 12   *has* 2

11. Right! Go to the next question.

It _____ cloudy all day.
    has been 5   *have been* 20

12. Right! Go to the next question.

It _____ at about 3 o'clock yesterday afternoon.
    clears up 2   *cleared up* 9

13. Wrong. Study this:
     The days get hotter every year.
     It gets hotter later in the day.

When _____ it get hotter than it is now?
    do 17   *does* 4

14. Right! Go to the next question.

What will the weather _____ tomorrow?
    be like 21   *like* 22

15. Right! Go to the next question.

I hope tomorrow will _____ today.
    like 30   *be like* 21

16. Wrong. Study this:
     It has been warm today.
     The days have been warm.

Have the _____ been warm?
    day 20   *days* 11

17. Wrong. Study this:
     Each day gets hotter than the day before.
     I like it when the days get hot.
     When do you think it will get hotter?

Return to 9.

18. Wrong. Study this:
     Are your neighbors quiet?
     I think it's quite cold.

He _____ he is quite hot.
    says 23   *say* 6

19. Wrong. Study this:
     It is colder than it was last winter.
     I'm very cold in this weather.
     Yesterday was colder than the day before
     This weather isn't as cold as it was.

Return to 44.

20. Wrong. Study this:
     Has it been cloudy all morning?
     I have been very well.
     Have you ever been to Florida?
     It has been snowing all day.

Return to 8.

21. Right! Go to the next question.

It's going to _____ tomorrow.
    snowed 29   *snow* 31   *snowing* 24

2. Wrong. Study this:
I think tomorrow will be like today.
I like to go to church.

Tomorrow _____ be like today.
wasn't 30   won't 15

23. Right! Go to the next question.

It is _____ at night.
quite 6   quiet 14

24. Wrong. Study this:
Has it started snowing yet?
I don't think it will snow today.

I think it _____ snow tomorrow.
is 27   will 36

25. Wrong. Study this:
It has been raining for a week.
They have come in to the warm house.
When has it snowed so hard?

Return to 31.

26. Wrong. Study this:
It rained last night.
Do you think it will rain today?

How hard _____ it rain last night?
do 42   did 35

27. Wrong. Study this:
It usually snows in January and in March.
It hasn't started snowing yet.
I don't believe it snowed one day last month.
When it starts snowing we will go to the house.

Return to 21.

28. Right! Go to the next question.

It _____ hard last night.
rains 26   rain 39   rained 32

29. Wrong. Study this:
It snowed a lot last winter.
I think it will snow.

I think it _____ going to snow soon.
am 27   is 36

30. Wrong. Study this:
I hope this summer will be like last summer.
I like to live here.
Wouldn't it be nice if the weather would be like this?

Return to 14.

31. Right! Go to the next question.

It _____ been cold this winter.
has 28   have 40

32. Right! Go to the next question.

What _____ the temperature today?
's 44   are 45

33. Right! Go to the next question.

What _____ the weather like today?
are 38   's 44

34. Wrong. Study this:
It is colder today than it was yesterday.
It is not so cold today.

The days _____ getting colder.
is 19   are 41

35. Right! Go to the next question.

It's going to _____ tomorrow.
rains 42   *rain* 32

36. Right! Go to the next question.

It _____ all day yesterday.
snowed 31   *snow* 27

37. Right! Go to the next question.

It _____ been warm today.
has 28   *have* 25

38. Wrong. Study this:
How's the weather?
It's cool today.
There's a cool breeze this evening.
The days are getting longer.

Return to 32.

39. Wrong. Study this:
It usually rains hard here.
I don't believe it will rain today.

We can't _____ if it rains.
went 42   *go* 35

40. Wrong. Study this:
It has been raining.
They have gone to the house.

It has been _____ all day.
raining 37   *rain* 25

41. Right! Go to the next question.

Do you think it will be _____ today
than it was yesterday?
colder 43   *cold* 19

42. Wrong. Study this:
If it rains tonight, it won't rain tomorrow.
When can we expect it to rain?
It rained very hard yesterday.
It gets colder when it rains.

Return to 28.

43. Right! This is the end of Unit 7.

Go to Unit 8.

44. Right! Go to the next question.

The days aren't as _____ as they
were.
cold 43   *colder* 34

45. Wrong. Study this:
The temperature is about freezing.
The days are getting shorter.

_____ the nights getting longer?
Is 38   *Are* 33

UNIT 8 TALKING ABOUT SICKNESS AND HEALTH

1. **Begin here.**

   How did you _____ your leg?

         break 16   *broke* 12   *breaks* 5

2. **Right! Go to the next question.**

   How did Jane _____ her leg?

         break 16   *broke* 10

3. **Wrong. Study this:**
   My arm hurts now.
   My arm hurt more yesterday.

   My arm _____ hurting any more.

         is not 6   *am not* 11

4. **Right! Go to the next question.**

   I slipped on the stairs and _____ down.

         fall 13   *fell* 17

5. **Wrong. Study this:**
   He breaks his arm every year.
   He broke it last year.

   How will he break _____ arm?

         his 2   *he's* 10

6. **Right! Go to the next question.**

   My arm was _____ more yesterday.

         hurting 4   *hurts* 11

7. **Wrong. Study this:**
   I break my arm every time I fall down.
   Mary was hurt when she fell down.
   Mr. Jones slipped and fell down.
   Mrs. Cooper is very old; I hope she doesn't fall down.

   Return to 4.

8. Wrong. Study this:
   He hopes she will be better.
   I hope I can go tomorrow.

   Mary and John hope their mother

   will _____.
   go 23   *went* 9

9. Wrong. Study this:
   He hopes the movie will be good.
   They hoped to go to church today.

   Return to 17.

10. Wrong. Study this:
   He will break his leg again.
   Mrs. Brown broke her arm.
   Jack breaks his leg again and again.

   Return to 1.

11. Wrong. Study this:
   Is it hurting as much as it did?
   John's arm hurts.
   I am sorry that it hurts.
   I will be glad when it stops hurting.

   Return to 16.

12. Wrong. Study this:
   I broke my leg last week.
   She will break her leg doing that.

   It _____ when I broke my arm.
   hurts 10   *hurt* 2

13. Wrong. Study this:
   I fell down yesterday.
   You might fall down.

   I hope I _____ fall down.
   doesn't 7   *don't* 20

14. Wrong. Study this:
   He hoped to go with us today.
   They hope to come with us.

   I hoped _____ would feel better.
   her 9   *she* 23

15. Right! Go to the next question.

   I don't _____ very well today.
   feel 21   *feeling* 25

16. Right! Go to the next question.

   Yesterday my arm was _____.
   hurts 3   *hurting* 4

17. Right! Go to the next question.

   I _____ you'll soon be well.
   hopes 8   *hope* 15   *hoped* 14

18. Wrong. Study this:
   Your hand is bleeding.
   My hand was bleeding last night.

   Mary's hand was bleeding _____.
   tomorrow 22   *yesterday* 27

19. Right! Go to the next question.

   She doesn't _____ well tonight.
   feeling 30   *feel* 21

20. Right! Go to the next question.

   Jack _____ down yesterday.
   fall 7   *fell* 17

1. Right! Go to the next question.

   My nose _____ bleeding now.
         isn't 32   *weren't* 18

22. Wrong. Study this:
   Your arm is bleeding.
   She was bleeding a lot at the time.
   Is he still bleeding?
   It isn't bleeding.

   Return to 21.

23. Right! Go to the next question.

   I _____ you'll feel like eating.
         hope 15   *hoped* 9

24. Wrong. Study this:
   I slip on my stairs often.
   He slipped on the street yesterday.

   He broke _____ arm when he
   slipped.
         he's 38   *his* 29

25. Wrong. Study this:
   I am feeling better today.
   I'm not going if I don't feel well.

   How _____ you feel?
         does 30   *do* 19

26. Right! Go to the next question.

   My brother is _____ since he took
   that medicine.
         good 31   *well* 33

27. Right! Go to the next question.

   Why _____ your hand bleeding any
   more now?
         weren't 22   *isn't* 32

28. Wrong. Study this:
   It was a good television show.
   My mother is not well since she slipped and
   fell.
   My head aches; I don't feel very well.
   Her sick mother is not well enough to go.

   Return to 26.

29. Right! Go to the next question.

   Did you _____ on the stairs this
   morning?
         slip 26   *slips* 38

30. Wrong. Study this:
   He doesn't feel well.
   I haven't been feeling well for some time.
   Hasn't he been feeling well?
   She will feel better after seeing the doctor.

   Return to 15.

31. Wrong. Study this:
   It was a good dinner.
   I don't feel well.

   That is _____ medicine.
         good 40   *well* 28

32. Right! Go to the next question.

   I _____ on the stairs this morning.
         slip 24   *slipped* 26   *slips* 35

33. Right! Go to the next question.

My fever is gone, _____ I still have
a cough.
     and 36   *but* 37

37. Right! End of Unit 8.

Go to Unit 9.

34. Wrong. Study this:
I slipped on the stairs, but it didn't hurt me.
I hurt my leg, and I hurt my arm.
His hand isn't bleeding, but it still hurts.
Doctor Jones saw me, and he gave me some
medicine.

Return to 33.

38. Wrong. Study this:
I slipped and fell this morning.
She slips on these stairs every day.
When I slip I usually don't fall.
We slipped when we went down the street
yesterday.

Return to 32.

35. Wrong. Study this:
He slips very often.
Mrs. Johnson slipped yesterday.

He _____ hurt himself when he
slipped and fell.
     doesn't 38   *didn't* 29

39. Right! Go to the next question.

My arm is swollen, _____ it
still hurts.
     but 34   *and* 37

36. Wrong. Study this:
I was sick yesterday, but I feel better today.
I had a fever and a cough yesterday.

He has a broken arm _____ a
swollen hand.
     but 34   *and* 39

40. Right! Go to the next question.

My brother got _____.
     well 33   *good* 28

UNIT 9 TALKING ABOUT DAILY HABITS

1. **Begin here.**

   After getting up, I _____ into the bathroom.

   go 10   goes 13

2. **Wrong. Study this:**
   John goes downstairs to the kitchen every morning.
   I go back upstairs every morning after breakfast.
   They go into the dining room.
   Mary goes to the kitchen.

   Return to 1.

3. **Right! Go to the next question.**

   Did you _____ this morning?
   shaves 6   shaved 19   shave 7

4. **Right! Go to the next question.**

   After they _____ their showers they will go to work.
   take 3   take off 9

5. **Right! Go to the next question.**

   She _____ to the store every day.
   go 2   goes 10

6. **Wrong. Study this:**
   He shaves every morning before breakfast.
   A man usually shaves once each day.

   When may _____ shave?
   I 11   them 16

7. **Right! Go to the next question.**

   She _____ before breakfast.
   dress 20   dresses 18

8. **Wrong. Study this:**
   I would go if I had time to dress.
   Can we dress after we shave?
   She dresses before breakfast.
   He dresses in his best suit.

   Return to 7.

9. **Wrong. Study this:**
   Please take off your coat.
   I must take a bath first.
   She takes a shower before she eats breakfast.
   I take off my coat when I come home.

   Return to 10.

10. **Right! Go to the next question.**

    I want to _____ a shower before breakfast.
    take 3   *take off* 15

11. **Right! Go to the next question.**

    Did he _____ this morning?
    shaved 16   *shave* 7

12. **Right! Go to the next question.**

    Will he _____ early enough?
    dresses 8   *dress* 18

13. **Wrong. Study this:**
    He goes into the bathroom.
    I go into the bathroom at 7 o'clock.

    John goes into the bathroom and

    _____ a shower.
    take 2   *takes* 5

14. **Wrong. Study this:**
    She usually combs it before breakfast.
    She combed it before breakfast.

    He never combs _____ hair.
    him 21   *his* 30

15. **Wrong. Study this:**
    I take off my clothes before I go to bed.
    She takes a shower every morning.

    Do you have to take a shower

    _____?
    now 4   *new* 9

16. **Wrong. Study this:**
    I usually brush my hair after I shave.
    He won't eat breakfast until he shaves.
    I shaved two times today.
    They shaved before they went to class.

    Return to 3.

17. **Right! Go to the next question.**

    After I _____ up, I go into the bathroom.
    getting 31   *get* 23   *got* 22

18. **Right! Go to the next question.**

    I _____ my hair three times yesterday.
    comb 24   *combed* 17   *combs* 14

19. **Wrong. Study this:**
    John shaved before 7 o'clock.
    I have to shave every day.

    Who has time _____ shave?
    to 11   *too* 16

20. **Wrong. Study this:**
    After he takes his shower, he dresses.
    They dress after breakfast.

    They dress when they _____ up.
    got 8   *get* 12

21. **Wrong. Study this:**
I want to comb my hair now.
I've combed my hair this way for a long
time.
She combs her hair in a different way.
Why does she comb her hair so often?

Return to 18.

22. **Wrong. Study this:**
We got up at 8 o'clock this morning.
They usually get up early.

I got out of bed at 7 o'clock _____
morning.
tomorrow 27   *yesterday* 36

23. **Right! Go to the next question.**

He always _____ to wash behind his
ears.
forgets 26   *forgotten* 33   *forget* 25

24. **Wrong. Study this:**
Please comb your hair.
I combed my hair after I brushed my teeth.

Will I have time to comb _____
hair?
mine 21   *my* 30

25. **Wrong. Study this:**
John forgets to brush his teeth each
morning.
Mary forgets to dress her little sister.

Will you forget to comb _____ hair?
you 32   *your* 37

26. **Right! Go to the next question.**
At bedtime I take off my clothes

and _____ my pajamas.
take off 29   *put on* 34

27. **Wrong. Study this:**
I get up before he gets up.
I get out of bed by 8 o'clock.
My brother got out of bed at about
8 o'clock.
After getting up, he dressed.

Return to 17.

28. **Wrong. Study this:**
Yesterday I took off my pajamas and put
on my clothes.
Will you take off that shirt, please?
Please put on this coat.
Don't forget to take off your clothes before
taking a shower.

Return to 26.

29. **Wrong. Study this:**
I take off my clothes before putting on my
pajamas.
He takes off his clothes before he takes a
shower.

After brushing _____ teeth, he puts
on his clothes.
he 28   *his* 35

30. **Right! Go to the next question.**

She usually _____ her hair three
times each day.
comb 21   *combs* 17

31. Wrong. Study this:
    After getting up, I shave.
    He gets up at 6 o'clock.

    Why can't _____ get up that early?
        you 36   *your* 27

32. Wrong. Study this:
    I forgot to call Mr. Cooper last night.
    John always forgets to eat.
    I can't forget that girl.
    John will forget to get the newspaper.

    Return to 23.

33. Wrong. Study this:
    I forgot to ask her yesterday.
    I always forget her name.

    Did you forget to _____ her?
        asks 32   *ask* 37

34. **Right! End of Unit 9.**

    Go to Unit 10.

35. Right! Go to the next question.

    Take off your pajamas and _____
    your clothes.
        take off 28   *put on* 34

36. Right! Go to the next question.

    After _____ up, I go into the
    bathroom.
        got 27   *getting* 23

37. Right! Go to the next question.

    Why does he always _____ to write
    his mother a letter?
        forgot 32   *forget* 26

T 10 GETTING OTHER PEOPLE'S OPINIONS AND IDEAS

Begin here.

I think you're _____ about that.
      mistake 12   *mistaken* 2

Right! Go to the next question.

He _____ hard all day yesterday.
      work 13   *worked* 14   *working* 6

Right! Go to the next question.

My friends _____ hard every day.
      work 14   *working* 11

Right! Go to the next question.

We thought you were _____ about that.
      mistake 8   *mistaken* 2

5. **Wrong. Study this:**
    I think a lot of my father.
    Jack thought a lot of his wife.

    What _____ you think of my baby?
        does 10   *do* 18

6. **Wrong. Study this:**
    They work hard every day.
    I've worked in New York for a long time.

    She worked at home _____.
        yesterday 3   *tomorrow* 11

7. **Wrong. Study this:**
    Personally, I prefer winter weather.
    They like the movies, but they prefer
    television.
    Which do you think he prefers?
    I like to drive, but I prefer to walk.

    Return to 15.

254

8. **Wrong. Study this:**
   He's mistaken about that.
   John thinks you're mistaken about that.
   In my opinion, they are mistaken.

   Return to 1.

9. **Wrong. Study this:**
   You are correct; it is right.
   She made a mistake and is incorrect.

   If you _____ get it right. you are
   incorrect
        aoesn't 19   *don't* 24

10. **Wrong. Study this:**
    She thought a lot of her cat; she loved it.
    I think a lot of my children; I love them.
    We thought a lot of her; we miss her very much.
    I think a lot of your book; it's excellent.

    Return to 14.

11. **Wrong. Study this:**
    When we work, we work hard.
    I can't get him to work.
    I couldn't go because I was working.
    We worked hard last night.

    Return to 2.

12. **Wrong. Study this:**
    I made a mistake.
    I'm mistaken about that.

    Isn't he mistaken about _____?
        that 4   *than* 8

13. **Wrong. Study this:**
    I work hard too.
    He was working in California last year.

    Has she always worked _____ New York?
        in 3   *to* 11

14. **Right! Go to the next question.**

    You __ _____ a lot of Mr. Cooper, didn't you?
        think 5   *thought* 15

15. **Right! Go to the next question.**

    I like geography, but I _____ musi
        like to 22   *prefer* 17

16. **Right! Go to the next question.**

    He _____ swim best, but she prefers to work.
        likes to 17   *prefers* 7

17. **Right! Go to the next question.**

    You aren't _____ about that; you a wrong.
        incorrect 9   *correct* 27

18. **Right! Go to the next question.**

    What does she _____ of my new ca
        think 15   *thought* 10

Wrong. Study this:
  If you are wrong, you are incorrect.
  If you are right, you are correct.
  You aren't incorrect about that; you are
  absolutely right.
  Perhaps it is incorrect, but I think it's right.

Return to 17.

Wrong. Study this:
  I thought you were mistaken about that.
  We often make mistakes.

It _____ really a mistake.
      aren't 23   *isn't* 30

Right! Go to the next question.

I _____ to like the blue one better.
      happens 34   *happen* 28

Wrong. Study this:
  We prefer to go now instead of later.
  I like to study religion.

I like to _____ in my garden, but I
prefer to read.
      works 7   *work* 16

Wrong. Study this:
  Isn't he mistaken about that?
  I don't make as many mistakes as I once
  did.
  We make a lot of mistakes in our class.
  You must be mistaken about that.

Return to 27.

4. Right! Go to the next question.

  We will be pleased if our work is

  _____; we want it to be absolutely
  right.
      correct 27   *incorrect* 19

25. Right! Go to the next question.

  It is my _____ that we should go
  now.
      ideas 31   *opinion* 21

26. Right! Go to the next question.

  He _____ to like summer weathe
      happens 28   *happen* 38

27. Right! Go to the next question.

  Sometimes I make a lot of _____.
      mistaken 20   *mistakes* 29

28. Right! Go to the next question.

  I _____ that we're making a mistake.
      feel 36   *feels* 33

29. Right! Go to the next question.

  In my _____, you are wrong.
      ideas 35   *opinion* 21

30. Right! Go to the next question.

  She doesn't make many _____
      mistaken 23   *mistakes* 29

31. Wrong. Study this:
  Our opinion is that we should not go.
  I think it's an excellent idea to go to the
  movies.
  Your opinion is no better than mine.

Return to 29.

256

32. **Wrong. Study this:**
This is the way I feel about that.
I feel that we should leave soon.
I think that we should leave soon.
How do you feel about going now?

Return to 28.

33. **Wrong. Study this:**
She feels that she would like to say
something.
He feels the time has come to do something.

How do you feel about _____?
than 32   *that* 37

34. **Wrong. Study this:**
He happens to like swimming.
They happen to like our ideas.

How did you happen to _____ _____ of
that?
thinks 38   *think* 26

35. **Wrong. Study this:**
Your idea is a good one.
In my opinion, we should eat first.

What _____ your opinion ab
that?
is 25   *am* 31

36. **Right! End of Workbook III.**

Go on to Workbook IV.

37. **Right! Go to the next question.**

I _____ that it's going to slee
tonight.
feel 36   *feels* 32

38. **Wrong. Study this:**
We happen to like John.
John happens to like coffee better.
He happens to prefer coffee.
I happen to like to swim.

Return to 21.

ENGLISH 900 합본
(원본＋주해서＋WORKBOOK) 값 9,000원

편저자　정헌진 · 이동호
발행인　김계덕
발행처　계원출판사(자매사 도서출판 문장)
　　　　서울특별시 중구 을지로 6가 45-4
　　　　전화: 02) 929-9495
　　　　팩스: 02) 929-9496
　　　　등록번호: 2-204
인　쇄　청림정판
제　책　평범사
공　급　한국출판협동조합
　　　　중판발행